MW00897041

# THE SAUCE SOURCE

# The Sauce Source

Compiled
and
Edited
By

# Edward A. Meany

Copyright © 2004 by Edward A. Meany.
ISBN: 1-4134-4056-8

All rights reserved. No portion of this book may be performed, nor set to music,
nor reproduced nor transmitted in any form or by any means, electronic or
mechanical, including photocopying, recording, or by any information storage and
retrieval system, without permission in writing from the author.

This book was printed in the United States of America.

SAUCE (sos) n. [ME. < ofr. sauce, saulse < L. Salsa,
salted food < pl. of salsus, pp of salire, to salt
< sakm sakt] 1. A liquid or soft dressing
served with food as a relish.
(Webster's New World Dictionary, 2nd College Edition )

In the ancient world there were no refrigeration or cooling systems to keep food fresh for long periods of time. To preserve foods for later use they had to be salted down ; soaked in strong brines, buried in salt, had salt rubbed into the meat, fish. poultry. To eat this heavily salted food required soaking it in fresh water to remove as much of the salt as possible. Thus it was difficult to keep meats, fish, fowl for any length of time before cooking without having the stuff get, shall we say, a bit aromatic.

Somewhere, at some time, someone discovered that herbs and spices, mixed with some liquids, such as wine, could cover the smell of the deteriorating foodstuffs and make them palatable. This probably came about when there was such unpalatable food at hand because the hunting had been too poor to provide fresh meat for the table and the pangs of hunger needed to be quieted.

Sauces were thus born. And they have ever after titillated the palates of mankind.

How many times have you looked for a recipe for a sauce to try a new dish? To make a dessert something special? How many times have you had to search a number of cookbooks to locate just the sauce you want?

What we have attempted here is to compile sauces from many sources. This has meant a lot of duplications—though you will notice that there are slight variations in each—in some of the more common categories. We have provided a list of such categories for which to use these sauces : Eggs, Fish, Game, Ham, Lamb, Meats, Pasta, Poultry, Vegetables, Desserts. The recipes are in alphabetical order with page references and a notation as to what food the sauce will enhance. A Category Section follows the alphabetical and, under each category are listed the sauces, with page numbers where they may be found. The Index, too, should assist you in quickly locating a sauce.

Here, then, a SAUCE SOURCE, all in one, neat, no frills, easy to use volume. A Treasury of taste to help the professional chef, the weekend gourmet, the everyday cook trying hard to make the family meals a joyous occasion.

# Sauces

AIOLI — Garlic mayonnaise sauce used for fish, beef or vegetables ( Pages 27-28 )

ALLEMANDE — Rich chicken flavored white sauce used for poultry ( Page 28)

AMANDINE — Almond flavored sauce for fish or eggs ( Page 29 )

A L'AMERICAINE — Tomato-garlic sauce cooked in wine with fish ( Page 29 )

ANCHOVY — Sauce made with anchovies and served over shellfish, fish or pasta ( Pages 30 )

APPLE — Fresh cooked apples often seasoned with spices and used for ham, pork, fish or eggs ( Page 31 )

AROMATIC — A fragrant sauce made of fish stock and herbs and served with fish ( Page 31 )

AURORE — Rich cream sauce flavored with tomato served with eggs or poultry ( Page 32 )

AVGOLEMONO — Sauce made with eggs and stock flavored with lemon and served over vegetables ( Page 33 )

AVOCADO — Avocado pulp mixed with oil, vinegar, lemon and seasonings, used for fish ( Page 33 )

BARBEQUE — Highly seasoned vinegar sauce used to baste beef, pork, chicken, fish. Can be served on the side ( Pages 34-37 )

BEARNAISE — Sauce of egg yolk, butter, lemon juice or vinegar and herbs, used over grilled beef,

|  | poultry, fish, eggs ( poached ) and vegetables ( Pages 42-46•) |
|---|---|
| BECHAMEL | White sauce made with milk, butter, flour, flavored with herbs. Used with fish, shellfish, veal, poultry, eggs, vegetables ( Pages 47-50 ) |
| BERCY | Made with wine and shallots, served with fish ( Page 50-51 ) |
| BORDELAISE | Sauce thickened with roux and flavored with Red Bordeaux wine and shallots. Served with beef ( Page 51-53 ) |
| BOURGUINONNE | Sauce prepared with fish stock and red wine. Served with fish. ( Page 53 ) |
| BREAD | Seasoned milk sauce thickened with bread crumbs. Served with wild game, fish, poultry, beef or vegetables ( Page 54 ) |
| BRETONNE | White sauce mixed with fish or meat stock, cooked with celery, leeks, onions and mushrooms. Serve with beef or fish ( Page 55 ) |
| BROWN | Sauce made from meat stock, flavored with herbs or tomato. Served with fish, poultry, veal, tongue ( Pages 55-60 ) |
| BUTTER | Sauce made from butter flavored with wine or seasonings. Served with fish, vegetables, pasta or shellfish. ( Pages 61-64) |
| CALYPSO | Sweet-sour sauce flavored with rum and spices. Served with shrimp, pork, chicken ( Page 64 ) |
| CAMBRIDGE | An oil based sauce made with anchovies, egg yolks, spices. Served with cold duck ( Page 64 ) |
| CAPER | A butter-flour sauce seasoned with capers. Served with lamb, mutton or fish ( Pages 65-66 ) |
| CARDINAL | Cream sauce made with fish stock and truffles. Served with Lobster ( Page 67 ) |
| CASANOVA | Mayonnaise sauce flavored with eggs, truffle, shallots. Served with lamb ( Pages 67 ) |

| | |
|---|---|
| CELERY | A cream sauce made with celery and chicken stock. Served with fish or game birds ( Pages 67-68 ) |
| CHASSEUR | Beginning with Brown sauce base to which is added white wine, shallots, mushrooms and tomatoes. Served with any meat, wild game or poultry ( Page 68-70 ) |
| CHEESE | Seasoned cream sauce made with various cheeses. Served with fish, lamb, beef, pasta ( Pages 70-72 ) |
| CHERRY | Brandy flavored sauce made using black cherries, Served with wild duck or ham ( Pages 72 ) |
| CHEVREUIL | Wine sauce with added butter and sugar. Served with wild game or marinated meats ( Page 73 ) |
| CHEVREUSE | Wine sauce flavored with tomato, horseradish, truffles. Served with game birds ( Page 73 ) |
| CHIFFON | Cream sauce with vinegar, stiffened egg whites. Served with cold fish ( Page 73 ) |
| CHINESE OMELET | Chicken stock seasoned with soy sauce. Served with seafood omelet ( Page 73 ) |
| CHIVRY | Cream sauce with wine, herbs and spinach. Served with eggs and poultry dishes ( Page 74 ) |
| CHORON | Bearnaise sauce with tomato sauce added. Served with eggs ( Page 74 ) |
| CHUTNEY | Sweet sauce with chutney and lemon juice. Served with ham ( Page 74 ) |
| CIDER | Sauce made with cider, apple jelly, flour, butter and water. Served with wild game dishes ( Page 74 ) |
| CLAIR DE LUNE | Egg sauce made with mayonnaise, herbs and capers. Served with cold fish ( Page 75 ) |
| CLAM | Sauce made from clams, shallots, spices. Served with pasta( Page 75 ) |
| COCHER DE FIACRE | Tomato-mayonnaise sauce flavored with herbs and gherkins. Served with boiled beef or cold meats ( Page 76 ) |

| COCKTAIL | Highly seasoned sauce made from chili sauce, Served with fish, shellfish ( Pages 77-78 ) |
| CRABMEAT | Cream sauce flavored with sherry wine, spices, crabmeat. Served with fish ( Page 79) |
| CRANBERRY | Sauce made from boiled cranberries, sugar, water. Served with poultry, roast pork, ham, tongue ( Pages 79-80 ) |
| CREAM | Cream sauce made with milk, cream and flour with seasonings. Served with vegetables, poultry, game birds ( Pages 80-83 ) |
| CREOLE | Sauce made with tomato, onion, green pepper. Served with fish ( Pages 84-85 ) |
| CRESSON | Mayonnaise-chili sauce with watercress. Served with fish, shellfish ( Page 85 ) |
| CUCUMBER | Cream sauce made with cucumber and seasonings. Served with fish, vegetables, cold meats ( Pages 85-89 ) |
| CUMBERLAND | A mustard-currant sauce. Served with ham, wild game, cold meats, venison, poultry ( Pages 89-90 ) |
| CURRY | Curry flavored sauce with a variety of flavors. Served with fish, poultry, hot meats ( Pages 90-93 ) |
| DAIKON | Radish sauce. Served with fish, chicken ( Page 93 ) |
| DEVIL | Highly seasoned tomato-butter sauce. Served with fish ( Page 93 ) |
| DIABLE | Wine sauce made with peppercorns and seasonings. Served with broiled chicken, meats ( Page 94 ) |
| DIANE | Poivrade sauce base with eggs, truffles, whipped cream. Served with wild game ( Page 94 ) |
| DUVAL | Seasoned egg sauce with chili and tartar sauce. Served with boiled beef ( Page 94 ) |

| EGG | Served with fish, egg dishes. ( Page 95 ) |
|---|---|
| ESPAGNOLE | Brown sauce made with stock, bacon, vegetables. Use to glaze beef ( Page 95) |
| EXTINGUISHER | Seasoned yogurt-cucumber sauce. Served with fish.( Page 96) |
| FLEMISH | Seasoned butter sauce. Served with duck, fish ( Page 96 ) |
| FLORENTINE | Bread sauce with seasonings and spinach ( Page 97 ) |
| FRENCH QUARTER | Anchovy sauce with oil, vinegar. Served with chilled shrimp ( Page 97 ) |
| GARLIC | Garlic oil sauce. Served with pasta ( Page 98 ) |
| GENEVOISE | Herb-wine sauce, stock base. Served with fish ( Page 98 ) |
| GRAND VENEUR | Poivrade sauce with truffles and rabbit blood. Served with wild game meats ( Page 98 ) |
| GRAPE | Egg sauce with chicken stock or fish stock and seedless grapes. Served with poultry, fish ( Page 98 ) |
| GREEN GODDESS | Mayonnaise-sour cream sauce with seasonings. Served with fish ( Page 99) |
| GRIBICHE | Egg sauce seasoned. Served with fish, cold meats ( Page 99 ) |
| HERB | Served with fish, game, poultry, pasta, vegetables, meats ( Pages 100-102 ) |
| HOLLANDAISE | Sauce of butter, egg yolk, lemon juice or vinegar. Served with vegetables, fish (Pages 102-109 ) |
| HONGRIS | Bordelaise sauce made from chicken broth with paprika, Served over eggs ( Page 110 ) |
| HORSERADISH | Cream sauce with horseradish. Served with baked ham, corned beef, fish, beef, lamb, pork ( Pages 110-113 ) |
| HUNGARIAN | Cream sauce made with chicken stock, white wine. Served with poultry ( Page 113 ) |
| IABBLE VERTE AU BEURRE | Seasoned butter sauce. Served with kidneys ( Page 114 ) |

| | |
|---|---|
| IMPERIALE | Mayonnaise-tomato sauce with brandy. Served with ham ( Page 114 ) |
| INDIAN | Coconut flavored curry sauce. Served over rice ( Page 114 ) |
| L'INDIENNE | Curry sauce. Served with vegetables, fish ( Page 115 ) |
| IRISH | Cream sauce with eggs and whipped cream. Served with fish ( Page 115 ) |
| ITALIAN SAUSAGE | Tomato sauce with sausage. Served with pasta ( Page 116 ) |
| ITALIENNE | Tomato-herb sauce. Served with meat, fish, poultry ( Page 116 ) |
| IVORY | Bechamel sauce to which is added meat extract. Served with fish, eggs ( Page 117 ) |
| LAMB | Sweet-sour sauce. ( Page 117 ) |
| LEMON | Served with vegetables, wild game dishes ( Pages 117 ) |
| LOBSTER | Cream sauce. Served with Lobster, fish ( Page 118 ) |
| LOUIS | Mayonnaise-olive sauce. Served with seafoods ( Page 118) |
| LYONNAISE | Wine-onion sauce. Served with vegetables, meats ( Page 119 ) |
| MAITRE D'HOTEL | Veloute sauce with herbs, lemon. Served with vegetables ( Page 119 ) |
| MARINARA | Tomato sauce with herbs, olive oil. Served with Pasta ( Page 120 ) |
| MARINIERE | Veloute sauce seasoned with shallots, cream. Served with fish ( Pages 121 ) |
| MATELOTE | Red wine-mushroom sauce. Served with fish ( Page 121 ) |
| MAYONNAISE | Oil, egg yolks, spices. Served with vegetables, shellfish, fish ( Pages 122-123 ) |
| MEAT | See ( Page 123-124 ) |
| MENAGERE | Cream sauce with egg yolk, paprika, gherkins added. Served with vegetables, eggs ( Page 127 ) |
| MEUNIERE | Lemon flavored butter sauce. Served with fish ( Page 127 ) |

| | |
|---|---|
| MILANAISE | Butter sauce with mushrooms, ham, cheese, tomato puree. Served with pasta ( Page 127 ) |
| MINT | Served with Lamb ( Pages 127-128 ) |
| MORNAY | Bechamel sauce with added cheese. Served with vegetables, fish, poultry, eggs, seafood ( Pages 130-131 ) |
| MUSCOVITE | Juniper berry sauce with nuts, raisins, grapes. Served with wild game ( Page 132 ) |
| MOUSSELINE | Mayonnaise sauce with anchovy, sour cream, greens. Served with vegetables, fish ( Page 132 ) |
| MUSHROOM | Served with beef, poultry, vegetables ( Pages 133-135 ) |
| MOREL | Served with meats, poultry, fish ( Page 135-137 ) |
| MUSSEL | Wine sauce with mussels, shrimp, butter. Served with fish, shellfish, pasta ( Page 137 ) |
| MUSTARD | Bechamel sauce with mustard, seasonings. Served with fish, cold meats, ham, poultry, vegetables ( Pages 137-140 ) |
| NANTUA | Bechamel sauce with cream, crayfish, butter. Served with fish, shellfish ( Page 141 ) |
| NEWBERG | Creamy butter sauce, egg yolks, clam juice. Served with seafoods ( Page 141 ) |
| NICOISE | Mayonnaise sauce seasoned with tomato, peppers, herbs. Served with shellfish, cold fish ( Page 142 ) |
| NORMANDE | Egg sauce, mushrooms, cream, fish stock. Served with fish ( Page 142 ) |
| NUT | Served with Chicken. ( Pages 142 ) |
| ORANGE | Served with duck, goose ( Pages 145-148 ) |
| ORIENTAL | Served with pork, meat, poultry ( Page 148 ) |
| OYSTER | Bechamel sauce with fish stock. Served with oysters ( Page 149 ) |
| PAPRIKA | Bechamel sauce flavored with paprika. Served with lamb, veal, poultry, eggs ( Page 149 ) |
| PEPPER | ( Page 149 ) |
| PERIGUEUX | Espagnole sauce with Madeira wine. Served with roast meats, chicken ( Page 149-150 ) |

| | |
|---|---|
| PICANTE | Served for dips ( Page 150 ) |
| PINEAPPLE | With curry. Served with ham ( Page 151 ) |
| PIQUANT | Onion sauce. Served with liver ( Page 151 ) |
| PLUM | Seasoned plum sauce. Served with pheasant, duck ( Page 151) |
| POIVRADE | Red wine with peppercorn. Served with venison, wild game ( Pages 151-152 ) |
| POULETTE | White sauce with egg yolks. Served with fish, poultry ( Pages 152-153 ) |
| PROVENCALE | Tomato-oil sauce. Served with pasta ( Pages 153-154 ) |
| PRUNIER | Mayonnaise with lobster. Served with shellfish ( Page 154 ) |
| RADZIWILL | Spicy Mayonnaise sauce. Served with smoked meats, game ( Page 154 ) |
| RAISIN | Sweet sauce made with raisins, spices. Served with smoked meats, pork, ham, Cornish hens ( Pages 154-155 ) |
| RAREBIT | Creamy cheese sauce. Served with broiled tomatoes, rice ( Page 156 ) |
| RAVIGOTE | Oil and vinegar sauce with herbs. Served with boiled meats, chicken, fish ( Page 157 ) |
| RED | Tomato sauce. Served with fish, meat, poultry ( Page 158 ) |
| REMOULADE | Mayonnaise with herbs, chopped capers, gherkins. Served with cold shellfish, egg dishes ( Pages 158-160 ) |
| ROBERT | A pickle-mayonnaise sauce. Served with vegetables, shellfish, game, turkey ( Pages 160-161 ) |
| ROMANA | Romano cheese, butter, herbs. Served with pasta ( Page 161) |
| ROUENNAISE | Red wine, peppery. Served with duck ( Page 162 ) |
| SALMI | Wine sauce seasoned. Served with wild game ( Page 162 ) |
| SHALLOT | Cream sauce with shallots. Served with game birds, fish ( Page 163 ) |

| | |
|---|---|
| SHRIMP | Served with fish, vegetables ( Pages 163-164 ) |
| SOUBISE | White sauce with pureed onions. Served with sweet breads, fish, lamb, veal, poultry ( Pages 164-165 ) |
| SOUR CREAM | Served with vegetables ( Pages 166-168 ) |
| SPADOIS | Wine sauce with cloves. Served with duck, smoked turkey ( Page 168 ) |
| SPAGHETTI | ( Pages 169-170 ) |
| SPANISH | Tomato sauce seasoned. Served with omelets, steaks, liver, pasta ( Pages 170-172 ) |
| STRATFORDSHIRE | Wine with mushrooms. Served with venison ( Page 173 ) |
| SUPREME | White sauce with veal or chicken stock, cream, egg yolk. Served with eggs poultry, vegetables ( Pages 173-174 ) |
| SWEET-SOUR | Served with fish, pork ( Pages 174-177 ) |
| TARTAR | Mayonnaise with cream, chives, gherkins. Served with fish ( Pages 177-180 ) |
| TERIAKI | Sweet soy sauce. Served with pork, shrimp, chicken ( Page 180 ) |
| TOMATO | Served with vegetables, chicken, fish, pasta, rice. ( Pages 181-189 ) |
| TOULONNAISE | Spiced Wine sauce, capers, gherkins. Served with fish ( Page 189 ) |
| TRUFFLE | Wine sauce with truffles. Served with beef ( Page 189 ) |
| VATEL | Spicy tomato sauce. Served with cold duck ( Page 190 ) |
| VELOUTE | White sauce with veal, chicken or fish stock, cream, egg yolk. Served with fish, vegetables, veal, poultry ( Pages 191-192 ) |
| VERTE | Spiced mayonnaise. Served with cold fish, shellfish( Page 193 ) |
| VILLEROI | Veloute sauce with additional egg yolk. Used to coat chicken, lamb, sweetbreads, vegetables ( Page 193 ) |
| VINAIGRETTE | Served with salads, sliced cold meats, fish ( Pages 193-196) |

WHITE SAUCE          Butter, flour, stock, seasoned. Served
                     with rice, pasta, vegetables, eggs,
                     seafoods ( pages 197-200 )

WINE                 ( Pages 200-207 )

# USE OF SAUCES

EGGS        Amandine (29), Apple-Curry (31), Aurora (32), Bearnaise (42-46), Bechamel (47-50), Chinese Omelet (73), Chivry (74), Choron (74), Egg (95), Ivory (117), Menagere (127), Mornay (130-131), Paprika (149), Spanish (170-172), White (197-200).

FISH        Aioli (27-28), Amandine (29), A L'Americaine (29), Anchovy (30), Apple (31), Aromatic (31), Avocado (33), Barbecue (34-37), Bearnaise (42-46), Bechamel (47-50), Bercy (50-51), Bourguignonne, (53), Bread (54), Bretonne (55), Brown (56-60), Butter (61-64), Caper (65-66), Cardinal (67), Celery (67-68), Cheese (70-72) Chiffon (73), Clare de Lune (75), Cocktail (77-78), Crabmeat (79), Creole (84-85), au Cresson (85), Cucumber (85-89), Curry (90-93), Daikon (93), Devil (93), Egg (95), Extinguisher (96), Flemish (96) French Quarter (97), Genevoise (98), Grape (98), Green Goddess (99), Gribiche (99), Herb (100-102), Hollandaise (102-109), Horseradish (110-113), Indienne (115), Irish (115), Italienne (116), Ivory (117), Lobster (118), Louis (118), Mariniere (121), Matelote (121), Mayonnaise (121-123), Meuniere (127), Mornay (130-131), Mousseline (132), Mussel (99) Mustard (99-102), Nantua (102), Newburg (103), Nicoise (142), Normande (142), Oyster (149), Paulette (152-153), Prunier (154), Ravigote (157), Remoulade (158-160), Shallot (163), Shrimp (163-164), Soubis (164-165 ), Sweet-Sour (166-168), Tartar (177-180), Tomato (181-189), Toulonnaise (189), Veloute (191-192), Verte (193), Vinaigrette (193-196),White (197-200), Wine (200-207).

GAME        Bread (54), Brown (55-60, Cambridge (64), Celery (67-68), Chasseur (68-70), Cherry (72), Chevreuil (73), Chevreuse (73),

Cider (74), Cream (80-83), Cumberland (89-90), Diane (94), Flemish (96), Grand Veneur (98), Herb (100-102), Lemon (117), Moscovite (132), Orange (145-148), Plum (151), Poivrade (151-152), Radzwill (154), Robert (160-161), Rouennaise (162), Salmi (162), Shallot (163), Spadois (168) Stratfordshire (173), Vatel (190), Wine (200-207).

HAM      Apple (31), Cherry (72), Chutney (74), Cranberry (79-80), Cucumber (85-89), Cumberland (89-90), Horseradish (110-113), Imperial (114), Mustard (137-140), Pineapple (151), Raisin (154-155), Wine (200-207).

LAMB      Caper (65-66), Casanova (67), Cheese (70-72), Horseradish (110-113), Mint (127-128), Paprika (149), Soubise (164-165), Villeroi (193), Wine (200-207).

MEATS      Aioli (27-28), Barbecue (34-37), Bearnaise (42-46), Bordelaise (51-52), Bread (54), Brown (55-60), Chasseur (68-70), Chevreuil (73), Cocher (76), Cucumber (85-89), Curry (90-93), Diable (94), Duval (94), Herb (100-102), Horseradish (110-113), Italienne (116), Lyonnaise (119), Meat (123-124), Mushroom (133-135), Morel (135-137), Mustard (137-140), Oriental (148), Pepper, (149), Perigueux (149-150), Piquant (151), Radziwill (154), Raisin (154-155), Ravigote (157), Spanish (170-172), Truffle (189), Viniagrette (193-196), Wine (200-207).

COLD MEATS      Aioli (27-28), Cocher (76), Cucumber (85-89), Cumberland (89-90), Gribiche (99), Horseradish (110-113), Mustard (137-140), Viniagrette (193-196).

PASTA      Anchovy (30), Butter (61-64), Cheese (70-72), Clam (75), Garlic (98), Herb (100-102), Italienne (116), Marinara (120), Meat (123-124), Milanaise (127), Mushroom (133-135), Romana (161), Spaghetti (169-170), Spanish (170-172), Tomato (181-189), White (197-200), Wine (200-207).

PORK      Apple (31), Barbecue (34-37), Calypso (64), Cranberry (79-80), Horseradish (110-113), Oriental (148), Raisin (154-155), Sweet-Sour (174-177).

POULTRY          Allemande (28), Aurore (32), Barbecue (34-37),
Bearnaise (42-46), Bechamel (47-50), Bread (54), Brown (55-60),
Calypso (64), Chasseur (68-70), Chivry (74), Cranberry (79-80),
Cream (80-83), Cumberland (89-90), Daikon (93), Diable (94), Grape
(98), Herb (100-102), Hungarian (113), Italienne (116), Mornay (130-
131), Mushroom (133-135), Morel (135-137), Mustard (137-140), Nut
(142), Oriental (148), Paprika (149), Ravigote (157), Soubise (164-165),
Supreme (173-174), Teriyaki (180), Tomato (181-189, Veloute (191-192),
Villeroi (193), Wine (200-207).

## WHAT WAS SAUCE FOR THE GOOSE WAS
## SAUCE FOR THE GANDER
R. Head and F. Kirkman
English Rouge, II, 120 ( 1671 )

SHELLFISH          Anchovy (30), Barbecue (34-37), Bechamel (47-
50), Butter (61-64), Calypso (64), Cardinal (67), Cocktail (77-78), au
Cress (85), French Quarter (97), Louis (118), Mayonnaise (122-123),
Mussel (137), Nantua (141), Newburg (141), Nicoise (142), Oyster
(149), Remoulade (158-160), Teriyaki (180), Verte (193).

TONGUE          Brown (55-60), Cranberry (79-80), Cucumber (85-
89), Horseradish (110-113), Meat (123-124), Mustard (137-140), Raisin
(154-155), Wine (200-207).

VEAL          Bechamel (47-50), Brown (55-60), Chasseur (68-70),
Paprika (149), Soubise (164-165), Veloute (191-192), Wine (200-207).

VEGETABLES          Aioli (27-28), Avgolemono (33), Bechamel (47-
50), Bread (54), Butter (61-64), Cream (80-83), Cucumber (85-89),
Espagnole (95), Herb (100-102), Hollandaise (102-109), Indienne (115),
Lemon (117), Lyonnaise (119), Mayonnaise (122-123), Menagere (127),
Mornay (130-131), Mushroom (133-135), Mustard (137-140), Shrimp
(163-164), Sour Cream (166-168), Tomato (181-189), Villeroi (193),
White (197-200).

# Spices and Herbs

ALLSPICE ( Pimenta Officinalis )
A Flavoring made from the berry of a West Indies tree of the myrtle family.

ANGELICA ( Angelicus )
Belonging to the parsley family. The fruit is used for flavoring.

ANISE ( Pimpinella Anisum )
A plant of the parsley family. The seeds are used as a flavoring.

BASIL ( Ocimum Basilicum )
Of the mint family. The leaves are used for flavoring.

BAY LEAVES
These are the laurel family of plants. The dried leaves are used as a spice flavoring

CARAWAY ( Carum Carvil )
A biennial plant of the parsley family. Its strong smelling, spicy seeds are used as a flavoring,

CELERY ( Apium Graveolens )
A biennial plant of the parsley family. The crushed seeds combined with salt are used for seasoning.

CHIVES ( Allium Schoenoprasum )
Of the lily family. Used as flavoring

CINNAMON(Cinnamomum)
>    This yellowish-brown spice is derived from the dried, inner bark
>    of several trees and shrubs of the laurel family that are native
>    to the East Indies and Southeast Asia. It is used as a flavoring.

CLOVE ( Eugenia Aromatica )
>    This tropical evergreen tree is of the myrtle family. Its dried
>    flower buds provide a fragrant, pungent spice.

CORIANDER ( Coriandrum Sativum )
>    A European herb of the parsley family. An annual. The strong
>    smelling, seed-like fruit is used in flavoring.

CUMIN ( Cuminum Cyminum)
>    A small plant of the parsley family. It's aromatic fruits are
>    used as flavoring.

CURRY POWDER
>    Made from turmeric, spices and herbs. It is used in seasoning.

DILL ( Anethum Graveolens )
>    A plant of the parsley family. The seeds and aromatic leaves
>    are used in flavoring.

FENNEL ( Foeniculum Vulgare)
>    A tall herb plant of the parsley family. Its aromatic seeds are
>    used for seasoning.

GINGER ( Zingiber Officinale )
>    An Asiatic plant of the ginger family. The aromatic root is
>    used as a spice.

HORSERADISH ( Armorcia Lapathifolia )
>    A mustard family plant used as a seasoning.

MACE
>    A spice made from the dried outer covering of nutmeg.
>    Usually in ground form.

MARJORAM ( Marjorana Hortensis)
A perennial plant of the mint family. Its aromatic leaves are used as a seasoning.

MINT ( Mentha )
The leaves of this plant are used both as a flavoring and as a garnish.

MUSTARD ( Brassica )
From the mustard family of plants. Used as a seasoning

NUTMEG ( Myristica Fragrans)
An East India tree. The seeds are aromatic and, when ground or grated, are used as a spice.

OREGANO ( Origanum Vulgare )
A plant of the mint family. Its fragrant dried leaves are used as seasoning.

PAPRIKA
From the pepper family, a condiment. Has little flavoring value. More decorative.

PARSELY ( Petroselinum Hortense )
A cultivated plant whose leaves are used as flavoring and as a garnish.

PEPPER ( Piper Nigrum )
A pungent condiment from the fruit of the pepper plant. Black pepper comes from grinding the entire fruit, including the fleshy covering; white pepper comes from using the internal flesh of the fruit only.

PEPPERMINT ( Mentha Piperita )
A plant of the mint family. Its oil is used as a flavoring.

RED PEPPER ( Capsicum Frutescens )
A plant of the night shade family. There are many varieties such as sweet pepper, cayenne pepper, etc.

ROSEMARY ( Rosmarinus Officinalis )
Of the mint family. The fragrant essential oil is used for flavoring.

SAGE ( Salvia ) : Scarlet Sage ( Salvia Splendens ) : Garden Sage ( Salvia Officinalis)
These plants are of the mint family. Their aromatic leaves, dried, are used as seasoning.

SASSAFRAS ( Sassafras Albidum )
Of the laurel family. The dried roots are used as flavoring.

SAVORY ( Satureia ):
Summer Savory ( Satureia Hortensis)
Winter Savory ( Satureia Montana )
Calamint ( Satureia Calamintha )
Aromatic mints used for flavoring

SPEARMINT ( Mentha Spicata )
A perennial plant of the mint family. Used as flavoring.

TARRAGON ( Artemisia Dracunculus )
A wormwood plant whose leaves are used as a seasoning.

THYME ( Thymus )
An herb of the mint family. Its leaves are used for flavoring.

TURMERIC ( Curcuma Longa )
A plant of the ginger family of the East Indies used as a seasoning in powder form.

VANILLA ( Vanilla )
An extract of vanilla pod beans used as flavoring.

WATERCRESS ( Nasturtium Officinale )
A water plant of the mustard family used as a garnish and in cooking.

## AIOLI SAUCE

Crush 8 garlic cloves very thoroughly and pound in 1/4 tsp. salt. Put the mixture in a bowl with two (2) egg yolks. Mix thoroughly. Add a few drops of olive oil and beat vigorously. Continue adding olive oil, a little at a time, until two (2) Tbls. have been added, then, in a thin stream, until one (1) cup had been added, beat constantly. If the mixture seems too thick, add 1/2 tsp. or more of water. Add the juice of 1/2 lemon.

## AIOLI SAUCE

Mash 3-5 garlic cloves with one (1) egg yolk, 1/2 tsp. salt, 1/4 tsp. pepper until very smooth. Add 3/4 cup good olive oil, one (1) Tbls. at a time, beating well until the mixture is thick like mayonnaise. Add One (1) Tbls. lemon juice. Beat again.

## IF YOU CAN'T TAKE THE HEAT, GET OUT OF THE KITCHEN

Unknown

## AIOLI SAUCE

12 cloves garlic
3 cups plus 3 Tbls. olive oil
4 egg yolks
salt
lemon juice

To prepare in a blender : blend the garlic in the container with one (1) egg yolk and three (3) Tbls. olive oil. Combine this paste with a very heavy mayonnaise, made with three (3) egg yolks and three

(3) cups of olive oil ( depending on the size of the eggs ). Season with salt and lemon juice to taste.

To prepare in a food processor : combine 6-8 garlic cloves, one (1) whole egg, two (2) Tbls. lemon juice, salt, and fresh ground black pepper in the beaker. With the chopping blade in place, process, gradually adding 1 1/2 cups olive oil.

To prepare in a mortar : pound the garlic cloves in the mortar. Gradually add the egg yolks, finally pound in the olive oil, a Tbls. at a time ( approximately 3 1/2 cups ) until a thick mayonnaise consistency is attained. Season with salt and lemon juice to taste.


## AIOLI SAUCE

1 egg
1/2 tsp. dry mustard
1/2 tsp. salt
2 Tbls. lemon juice
1 cup olive oil
3 cloves garlic, split

Break the egg into the blender. Add the mustard, salt, lemon juice and 1/4 cup of olive oil. Turn blender on low speed. Add the remaining oil in a steady stream. When the mixture is ready, add the garlic and blend for ten (10) seconds.


## ALLEMANDE SAUCE

2/3 cup concentrated chicken broth
2 cups Veloute Sauce ( see pages 191 )
3 egg yolks
1 Tsp. lemon juice

The chicken broth is made with one (1) bouillon cube dissolved in 1/3rd less water than required for broth. Simmer Veloute Sauce in a double boiler and slowly beat in the egg yolks until smooth and creamy. Stir the warm stock into the sauce and simmer with frequent stirring until the sauce becomes very thick and creamy. Remove from the heat, stir in lemon juice until it is well blended and the sauce is smooth

## ALLEMANDE SAUCE

Using two (2) cups of Supreme Sauce ( see pages 126 ), mix two (2) lightly beaten egg yolks, with a little cream, into the sauce. Stirring constantly, cook the sauce until it comes to a boil. Finish with two (2) Tbls. heavy cream.

## AMANDINE SAUCE

2 Tbls. clarified butter
2 Tbls. slivered, blanched almonds
2 Tbls. fresh lemon juice
Salt and pepper to taste

Heat butter in a small skillet over medium-low heat. Add almonds. Saute and stir until golden. Almonds will continue to brown a little after removing from the heat. Remove the almonds from the butter and sprinkle over fish or vegetables. Stir lemon juice into butter, increase heat and boil until syrupy. Pour over prepared dish. You may season with salt and pepper to taste

## A L'AMERICAINE SAUCE

3 Tbls. butter
1 small chopped onion

6 chopped shallots or green onion
5 ripe tomatoes, peeled, seeded, chopped
1 clove garlic, chopped
3 Tbls. tomato paste

3 Tbls. parsley, chopped
1 Tbls. fresh tarragon chopped ( or
1 tsp. dried tarragon)
1 1/2 tsp. thyme
fresh ground black pepper

Melt the butter and saute the onion for few minutes. Add the shallots, tomatoes, garlic, herbs and simmer for one (1) hour. Season to taste and continue cooking down, blend thoroughly. Add the tomato paste at the last, blend with 1 1/2 cups of white wine or fish stock that has been used to cook the shellfish. Pour over the prepared dish.

## ANCHOVY SAUCE

Saute One (1) clove garlic, chopped fine, in 1/4 cup olive oil over low heat until it begins to color. Add 12 anchovy fillets, cut in pieces. When they are heated stir in 2/3 cup of tomato puree. Season to taste with salt, fresh ground pepper and sweet basil.

## ANCHOVY SAUCE

1/4 cup olive oil
1 small clove garlic, halved
2 ounces anchovy fillets, drained, chopped
2 Tbls. minced parsely
2 Tbls. Parmesan cheese, grated
1 tsp. lemon juice

In saucepan over medium heat, brown garlic in olive oil. Remove from heat, discard garlic, stir in the remaining ingredients until well mixed

## ANCHOVY EGG SAUCE

To one (1) cup thin Cream Sauce, ( see pages 80-81 ), add anchovy paste—about the size of a large pea. Boil the mixture, stirring constantly for about 3 minutes. Remove from the heat and add two (2) hard cooked eggs, that have been finely minced

## ANCHOVY GREEN SAUCE

In food chopper add one (1) Tbls. each chervil, parsley, green pepper, onion, green celery leaves, chives, 1 tsp. each chopped sweet-sour gherkins, chopped green olives, three (3) anchovy fillets that have been washed in tepid water and dried, one (1) slice of garlic. Chop. To the mixture add one (1) cup sweet cream. Season to taste with salt, cayenne, nutmeg. Put two (2) ice cubes in the mixture and stir until the mixture puffs to half again its original volume. Add one (1) tsp. prepared mustard. Chill the sauce. Stir the sauce just before serving until it is well puffed.


SPANISH ANCHOVY SAUCE

Dissolve two (2) tsp. anchovy paste in 3/4 cup melted butter. Gradually stir in 1/4 cup sherry wine. Bring the mixture to a boil, reduce heat and simmer very gently for ten (10) minutes. Season to taste with salt and pepper. Stir in two (2) Tbls. washed capers, chopped, and one (1) tsp. each lemon juice, finely chopped chervil.


**VEGETARIANISM IS HARMLESS ENOUGH,
ALTHOUGH IT IS APT TO FILL A MAN WITH WIND
AND SELF-RIGHTEOUSNESS**
Dr. Robert Hutchinson

APPLE AND CURRY SAUCE

In a double boiler cook one (1) cup green cooking apples, cubed, and 1/2 cup finely chopped onions, in three (3) Tbls. butter until apples are tender and the onions transparent. Stir frequently without bruising the apples. Remove from the heat and sprinkle in two (2) Tbls. sifted flour, two (2) Tbls. curry powder, 1/2 tsp. salt, a dash of nutmeg and a dash of cayenne. Blend well and gradually add one and one-half (1 1/2) cups of milk that has been scalded, a thin slice of garlic, one (1) small bay leaf, four (4) sprigs of fresh parsley, six (6) thin slices of onion. Bring the sauce to a boil, stirring constantly, until it thickens and bubbles. Set the pan over hot water and simmer for five (5) or six (6) minutes, stirring occasionally. Taste for seasoning.


AROMATIC SAUCE

To one (1) cup of fish stock, add a pinch of powdered thyme, a pinch each of basil, savory, marjoram, sage. Bring to a boil. Remove from the heat and add a tsp. each of finely chopped chives, shallots, a few grains of nutmeg, three (3) coarsely ground peppercorns. Season with salt. Cover pan and let mixture stand for fifteen (15) minutes. Blend together one (1) tsp. each butter and flour over medium heat. Add the stock mixture, ( strained ), and bring to a boil for five (5) minutes. Add one (1) Tbls. each lemon juice, finely chopped parsley, tarragon.

## AURORE SAUCE

Add three (3) Tbls. tomato puree, ( or well reduced tomato sauce ), to two (2) cups of Bechamel Sauce, ( see pages 47-49 ), or Mornay Sauce, ( see pages 93-94 ). Add one (1) Tbls. butter. Stir well.

## AURORE SAUCE

2 Tbls. tomato sauce
3/4 cup Veloute Sauce ( see pages 191 )
4 Tbls. butter

In a double boiler stir the tomato sauce into the Veloute Sauce, stir in butter a spoonful at a time until mixture is a smooth blend.

## AURORE SAUCE

1 cup Veloute Sauce ( see pages 191 )
1/2 cup tomato paste
1/2 cup cream
2 egg yolks

Combine Veloute Sauce with tomato paste. Mix the egg yolks and cream thoroughly and gradually add to the sauce. Stir until thickened and smooth but do not let the mixture boil. Taste for seasoning.

## AVGOLEMONO SAUCE

2 Tbls. lemon juice
2 Tbls. flour
1/4 tsp. salt
1/8 tsp. white pepper
2 cups vegetable water or broth
2 eggs, well beaten

Mix the lemon juice, flour, salt, pepper and enough water/broth to thin mixture. Bring the rest of the water/broth to a boil and add the lemon mixture. Bring up to a boil again, stirring until the sauce is slightly thickened. Stir this hot broth slowly into the egg yolks. Return to the heat and cook, stirring, over low heat until thickened

## AVOCADO SAUCE

Force One (1) large avocado through a sieve. Combine avocado pulp, 1/4 cup olive oil, two (2) Tbls. strained lemon juice, one (1) Tbls. tarragon vinegar, salt and white pepper to taste, a few grains of cayenne. Beat together. Chill. Add one (1) egg yolk and beat the mixture just before serving.

## BACON-KETCHUP SAUCE

| | |
|---|---|
| 3/4 cup chopped onion | 1 3/4 cup milk |
| 1 Tbls. butter | 1 Tbls. ketchup |
| 8 bacon slices, cut up | 1/4 tsp. salt |
| 2 Tbls. flour | dash Worcestershire sauce |

Saute the onions in butter until soft. Add bacon pieces and cook until crisp. Sprinkle flour over mixture in skillet. Gradually stir in milk, cook, stirring until smooth. Season with the ketchup, salt and Worcestershire sauce.

## BARBECUE SAUCE

| | |
|---|---|
| 1/4 cup ketchup | 2 Tbls. water |
| 3 Tbls. vinegar | 2 tsp. Worcestershire sauce |
| 1 1/2 Tbls. salad oil | 1/4 tsp. salt |

Combine ketchup, vinegar, salad oil, water, Worcestershire sauce and salt. Bring to a boil, stirring occasionally. Cook three (3) minutes.

## BARBECUE SAUCE

| | |
|---|---|
| 2 medium onions, finely chopped | 1/2 cup steak sauce |
| 1/4 cup olive oil | 1/4 cup Worcestershire sauce |
| 1 cup tomato sauce | 1 tsp. dry mustard |
| 1 tsp. salt | 1/2 cup strained honey |
| 1 tsp. basil | 1/2 cup red wine |

Saute onions in olive oil until lightly browned. Add tomato sauce, salt, basil, steak sauce, Worcestershire sauce, mustard and honey. Simmer five (5) minutes, stirring constantly. Add wine and allow sauce to come to the boiling point. Remove from heat. Taste for seasoning. Strain through a fine sieve.

## HE HATH EATEN ME OUT OF HOUSE AND HOME
II Henry IV, II, i, 80

## BARBECUE SAUCE

| | |
|---|---|
| 1/2 cup soy sauce | 1 tsp. finely powdered oregano |
| 2 garlic cloves, chopped | 1/2 cup orange juice |
| 4 Tbls. tomato sauce | 1 tsp. fresh ground black pepper |
| 2 Tbls. lemon juice | |
| 1/4 cup chopped parsley | |

Mix all ingredients thoroughly. Baste meat or fish with mixture

## BARBECUE SAUCE

| | |
|---|---|
| 1/2 cup butter | 1 tsp. salt |
| 1 large onion, grated | 1/2 tsp. pepper |
| 1/2 cup water | 2 tsp. paprika |
| 1 Tbls. Worcestershire sauce | 1/2 tsp. dry mustard |
| 3 Tbls. lemon juice | 1 Tbls. brown sugar |
| 2 Tbls. tomato paste | |

Melt butter, add onion and cook until wilted. Add remaining ingredients, simmer ten (10) minutes.

## BARBECUE SAUCE

Saute 1 medium minced onion in one (1) Tbls. butter until tender. Add 1/2 cup ketchup, two (2) Tbls. Worcestershire sauce, 1/2 tsp. chili powder, 1/4 tsp. salt, dash of Tabasco, 1/2 cup water. Bring to a boil. Remove from heat.

## BARBECUE SAUCE

| | |
|---|---|
| 1 Tbls. vegetable oil | 2 Tbls. brown sugar |
| 1 small onion, chopped | 2 Tbls. Worcestershire sauce |
| 1 cup ketchup | 1 tsp. Tabasco |
| 1/2 cup water | 1 tsp. ground black pepper |
| 1/4 cup white vinegar | 1/2 tsp. salt |

In medium saucepan, over medium heat, saute onion in hot oil until tender. Add ketchup and remaining ingredients. Over high heat bring to boil. Reduce heat to low, cover and simmer twenty (20) minutes. Stir occasionally

## BARBECUE SAUCE

3 Tbls. butter, melted
1 medium onion, chopped
1 tsp. salt
1/2 tsp. garlic salt
1/4 tsp. paprika
1/4 tsp. hot pepper sauce
1/4 tsp. Marjoram

1/4 cup dry mustard
1/4 cup ketchup
3 Tbls. Worcestershire sauce
3 Tbls. cider vinegar
1 Tbls. celery flakes
1/8 tsp Thyme

Mix all ingredients except celery flakes, marjoram, thyme. Heat and stir well. Simmer ten (10) minutes. After applying sauce to meat then sprinkle celery flakes, marjoram, thyme over meat too.

## BARBECUE SAUCE

1/4 cup ketchup
1 Tbls. vinegar
1 Tbls. brown sugar

1 tsp. Worcestershire sauce
dash Tabasco
1 garlic clove, minced

Blend all ingredients and apply to meat.

## BARBECUE SAUCE

2 Tbls butter
1/4 cup onions, chopped
1/4 cup garlic, chopped
3 cups ketchup
1 cup chili
1 Tbls. mustard

1 Tbls. soy sauce
1 Tbls. Worcestershire sauce
2 Tbls. lemon juice
1/2 tsp. cayenne
2 Tbls. maple sugar
1/2 cup orange juice

In a skillet heat the butter. Saute onion and garlic. Add remaining ingredients. Cook until mixture reaches a boil. Stir constantly. Remove from heat.

## BARBECUE SAUCE

1 cup sesame seed oil
1/4 cup soy sauce
1/2 cup sherry wine

Combine the ingredients and baste chicken, shrimp or other fish dishes.

## VARIETY'S THE VERY SPICE OF LIFE
Cowper

## BRAZILIAN BARBECUE SAUCE

Saute two (2) cups coarsely chopped spanish onions in 1/4 cup butter until they are transparent. Add one (1) finely chopped garlic clove, 1/2 tsp. oregano, the juice of one (1) lime and salt and pepper to taste. Cook the mixture over low heat three (3) to four (4) minutes. Add two (2) cups red wine and bring the sauce to a boil. Reduce heat and simmer gently for about five (5) minutes. Just before serving add 1/2 cup each butter, parsley ( chopped)

## CALIFORNIA BARBECUE SAUCE

Combine 1-1/2 cups olive oil, one (1) cup red wine, 1/4 cup vinegar, one (1) tsp. chopped parsley, one (1) Tbls. salt, two (2) garlic cloves, chopped, 1/4 tsp fresh ground black pepper.

## CAJUN BARBECUE SAUCE

Heat two (2) Tbls. butter over low heat until foams. Saute one (1) green pepper, one (1) small onion, 1/2 small clove garlic—all finely chopped—until golden brown. Stir in one (1) Tbls. flour and blend. Stir in two (2) cups tomato puree. Cook mixture until thickens, stirring constantly. Add 1/4 cup chopped celery tops, three (3) Tbls. Worcestershire sauce, one (1) Tbls. each finely chopped parsley, chives, two (2) tsp. chili powder, 1/2 tsp salt. Simmer gently over very low heat until vegetables are tender. If sauce seems too thick add a little water.

## CHINESE BARBECUE SAUCE

Mix six (6) tsp. dry mustard with enough white wine to make a thick paste. Add six (6) preserved kumquats—finely chopped— and one (1) Tbsl. of the kumquat syrup. Add two (2) to three (3) Tbls. soy sauce. Blend thoroughly.

## CHINESE GINGER BARBECUE SAUCE

Mix together one (1) cup soy sauce, two (2) garlic cloves crushed/ chopped, one (1) Tbls. grated fresh ginger, 1/2 cup each sherry wine and ketchup. Use this sauce as a marinade for spareribs or pork cuts.

## COOKED BARBECUE SAUCE

In a saucepan saute five (5) garlic cloves, chopped, in 1/3 cup olive oil until garlic is golden. Add 1/4 cup A-1 Sauce, two (2) Tbls. brown sugar, one (1) tsp. each salt, pepper, mustard, oregano, one (1) cup brown stock, 1/2 cup tomato paste. Simmer over low heat fifteen (15 ) minutes. Correct seasoning to taste with dash Tabasco and lemon juice.

## UNCOOKED BARBECUE SAUCE

Mix 1 1/2 cups ketchup, one (1) dry chili pepper soaked in water until soft, then finely chopped, 1/4 cup lemon juice, 1 tsp. each prepared mustard, freshly ground black pepper, one (1) Tbls Worcestershire sauce. Add one (1) garlic clove, split, one (1) onion, halved, one (1) bay leaf.

## CREOLE BARBECUE SAUCE

In a saucepan melt 1/2 cup butter, saute one (1) onion, two (2) garlic cloves, one (1) green pepper (seeded), one (1) stalk celery—all coarsely chopped. Add two (2) cups fresh tomatoes, 1/2 cup tomato puree, 1/2 cup water, 1/2 cup brown sugar, two (2) Tbls. vinegar, one (1) tsp. each salt, pepper and a dash of Tabasco. Bring to a boil then simmer gently for thirty (30) minutes. Correct seasoning to taste.

## FISH BARBECUE SAUCE

Saute 1/2 cup finely chopped onions in 1/4 cup olive oil until golden brown. Add one (1) cup tomato paste, two (2) Tbls. Worcestershire sauce, 1/2 cup honey, one (1) tsp. each basil, salt. Simmer for five (5) minutes, stirring constantly. Add 1/2 cup red wine. Strain through a fine sieve before using as a basting sauce.

## FISH BARBECUE SAUCE

| | |
|---|---|
| 2 medium onions, chopped | 1 tsp. basil |
| 1/4 cup olive oil | 1/2 cup steak sauce |
| 1 cup tomato paste | 1/4 cup Worcestershire sauce |
| 1 tsp. salt | 1 tsp. dry mustard |
| 1/2 cup red wine | 1/2 cup honey |

Saute onions in oil until lightly browned. Add all other ingredients except wine. Simmer five (5) minutes while stirring constantly. Add wine, bring to a boil. Remove from heat and strain.

## LEMON BUTTER BARBECUE SAUCE

In saucepan combine one (1) cup butter with 1/4 cup each lemon juice and sherry wine, one (1) tsp. Worcestershire sauce, one (1) garlic clove, one (1) tsp. chopped parsely, 1/2 tsp. salt. Bring to boiling and remove immediately from heat.

## MARYLAND BARBECUE SAUCE

In saucepan combine one (1) cup ketchup, 1/2 cup butter, one (1) Tbls. Worcestershire sauce, one (1) tsp. salt, juice of one (1) lemon. Simmer for ten (10) minutes.

## MEXICAN BARBECUE SAUCE

Combine one (1) cup olive oil, 1/2 cup vinegar, three (3) Tbls. each finely chopped shallots and green pepper, one (1) cup tomato juice, one (1) tsp. oregano, one (1) Tbls. chili powder, four (4) crushed garlic cloves, one (1) Tbls. salt. Simmer for ten (10) minutes. Strain before using.

## ORANGE BARBECUE SAUCE

Saute four (4) crushed garlic cloves, 3/4 cup chopped onions in one (1) cup olive oil until golden. Add one (1) cup each ripe olives, tomatoes—chopped—one (1) cup red wine, two (2) Tbls. Worcestershire sauce, 1/2 cup each orange juice, brown sugar, the juice of one (1) lemon, one (1) grated orange rind, one (1) tsp. rosemary, three (3) Tbls. chopped green pepper, 1/4 cup chopped fresh parsley. Bring to a boil then simmer gently for ten (10) minutes. Strain.

## SEAFOOD BARBECUE

| | |
|---|---|
| 2 small onions, sliced | 1 tsp. salt |
| 1/2 cup ketchup | 2 tsp. Worcestershire sauce |
| 1/3 cup olive oil | 2 tsp. lemon juice |
| 2 Tbls. celery, diced | 1/4 tsp. pepper |

Simmer all ingredients over medium heat for ten (10) minutes, stirring frequently until onions and celery are tender.

## A GOOD DINNER SHARPENS WIT
## WHILE IT SOFTENS THE HEART.
Doran

## SPICY BARBECUE SAUCE

2 Tbls. olive oil                   1 Tbls. Worcestershire sauce
1 medium onion, chopped             4 tsp. chili pepper
8 ounce can tomato sauce            2 tsp. salt
1/2 cup brown sugar                 1/4 tsp. dry mustard
1/4 cup white vinegar

In a saucepan, over medium heat, cook onion in olive oil until tender, stirring occasionally. Add remaining ingredients, bring to a boil, stir constantly. Can be used both to baste and put on meats when served

## SWEET-SOUR BARBECUE SAUCE

Mix, in a saucepan, one (1) cup each red wine vinegar, water, brown sugar. Add three (3) Tbls. ketchup, soy sauce, one (1) tsp. dry mustard, one (1) cup pineapple chunks, one (1) green pepper—seeded and cut into strips—two (2) tomatoes—peeled and cut into wedges. Bring the mixture to a boil, then simmer for ten (10) minutes. Add 1 1/2 Tbls. cornstarch which has been mixed to a smooth paste with 1/4 cup water, continue cooking, stirring constantly, until sauce is clear and thickened.

## FOOD IMPROPERLY TAKEN, NOT ONLY PRODUCES DISEASES, BUT AFFORDS THOSE THAT ARE ALREADY ENDANGERED IN BOTH MATTER AND SUSTENANCE; SO THAT, LET THE FATHER OF DISEASE BE WHAT IT MAY, INTEMPERANCE IS ITS MOTHER
Burton

## TEXAS BARBECUE SAUCE

Heat three (3) Tbls. bacon drippings, stir in 1/4 cup grated onion, one (1) mashed garlic clove. Cook over medium heat two (2) minutes, stir constantly. In a separate bowl mix one (1) cup ketchup, 1/4 cup each cider vinegar, Worcestershire sauce, one (1) Tbls. prepared mustard, two (2) tsp. paprika, one (1) tsp. each Tabasco, chili powder, 1/2 tsp. salt. Add this to the saucepan and cook all stirring constantly over low heat until thickened. Then simmer gently for Ten (10) minutes. Should be used very hot in basting.

## BEARNAISE SAUCE

Boil 3/4 cup dry white wine, 1/4 cup tarragon vinegar, one (1) Tbls. finely chopped shallots, one (1) tsp. chopped fresh parsley, 1/4 tsp. tarragon, 1/4 tsp. thyme, 1/8 tsp. black pepper. Boil until reduced to half the volume. Strain. Beat in three (3) egg yolks, one at a time, alternating with as much melted butter as needed to keep sauce the consistency of mayonnaise.

**IT IS NOT THE QUANTITY OF THE MEAT,
BUT THE CHEERFULNESS OF THE GUESTS,
WHICH MAKES THE FEAST**
Clarendon

## BEARNAISE SAUCE

Combine one (1) cup white wine, one (1) Tbls. tarragon vinegar, one (1) Tbls. chopped shallots, one (1) small sprig of fresh parsley, two (2) small stalks of tarragon herb—chopped—two (2) bruised peppercorns, Cook over hot heat until reduced to 2/3 original volume. Cool slightly. Add three (3) egg yolks gradually, constantly vigorously stirring and alternating with 1/2 pound of melted butter—or as much more as sauce can retain until the sauce is the consistency of heavy cream. Blend thoroughly over low heat. Strain. Add dash of cayenne, one (1) tsp. each finely chopped tarragon leaves, chervil.

## BEARNAISE SAUCE

| | |
|---|---|
| 1 tsp. shallots, chopped | 1/4 cup tarragon vinegar |
| 1 small sprig fresh tarragon, chopped | 5 egg yolks |
| 1 small sprig fresh chervil, chopped | 3/4 cup melted butter |
| 2 peppercorns | pinch cayenne pepper |
| pinch salt | |

Simmer shallots, tarragon, chervil, peppercorns and salt in vinegar over low heat until vinegar is almost all evaporated. Cool to lukewarm. Add egg yolks and beat biskly with whisk. Return to low heat and gradually add butter whisking until sauce thickens. Strain. Season to taste with cayenne and some minced tarragon and chervil.

## BEARNAISE SAUCE

Divide one (1) cup butter at room temperature into three (3) parts. Combine three (3) sprigs tarragon, three (3) sprigs chervil, two (2) shallots—all finely chopped—four (4) crushed peppercorns, with 1/4 cup each tarragon vinegar, white wine in top of a double boiler. Cook over direct heat until reduced to a thick paste. Cool slightly. Place pan over hot water, add three (3) egg yolks and one (1) Tbls. water, whisk briskly until mixture is light and fluffy. Add first portion of butter, stirring constantly until mixture is smooth and thick. Add second and third parts of butter, stirring vigorously after adding each part. Season to taste with salt and a pinch of cayenne. Strain through a fine sieve. Add three (3) sprigs of finely chopped tarragon and chervil.

## BEARNAISE SAUCE

Combine one (1) cup white wine with one (1) Tbls. each tarragon vinegar, finely chopped shallots, two (2) small stalks of tarragon—chopped—one (1) small sprig each parsely, chervil—chopped—and two (2) bruised peppercorns. Cook over high heat until reduced by 1/3rd. Strain. Cool slightly. Constantly stirring add three (3) egg yolks—lightly beaten—alternately with one (1) cup melted butter,

or enough butter to make sauce the consistency of heavy cream.
Blend thoroughly over low heat. Strain. Finish with dash of
cayenne, one (1) tsp. each finely chopped tarragon, chervil.


## BEARNAISE SAUCE

| | |
|---|---|
| 2 Tbls. red wine vinegar | 4 egg yolks |
| 1 1/2 tsp. green onion, chopped | 3/4 cup softened butter |
| 1 1/2 tsp. tarragon | 1 Tbls. chopped fresh parsely |
| 1/8 tsp. cracked | black pepper |

In a double boiler, combine red wine vinegar, green onion, tarragon,
black pepper. Over high heat, bring to boil and continue boiling
until vinegar is reduced to about one (1) Tbls.
Place top of double boiler over the bottom containing hot, not
boiling, water. Whisking constantly add egg yolks. Add butter, two
(2) Tbls. at a time, until butter is melted, constantly whisking until
mixture is thickened. Stir in parsley.


## BEARNAISE SAUCE

| | |
|---|---|
| 1 tsp. shallots, chopped | 1/4 cup tarragon vinegar |
| 1 small tarragon, chopped | 5 egg yolks |
| 1 small sprig chervil, chopped | 3/4 cup melted butter |
| 2 peppercorns | 1 pinch cayenne pepper |
| 1 pinch salt | |

Simmer shallots, tarragon, chervil, peppercorns and salt in vinegar
until vinegar is reduced by 2/3rds. Cool to lukewarm. Add egg yolks
beating briskly with whisk. Return to low heat. Add butter
gradually whisking until sauce thickens, Strain. Season with
cayenne. Stir in minced tarragon, chervil.

## BEARNAISE SAUCE

1 Tbls. white wine vinegar
1 Tbls. dry white wine
1 Tbls. minced shallots
1/2 tsp. tarragon
1 Tbls minced fresh parsley

1/4 tsp. chervil
dash salt/pepper
1 egg yolk
1/4 cup butter

In a small saucepan combine vinegar, wine, shallots, tarragon, chervil, pinch salt, pinch pepper Cover and simmer five (5) minutes. Bring to boil until liquid measures one (1) Tbls. Strain. Beat in egg yolk until well blended. With a bowl of cold water near by, cut butter into small chunks. Add two (2) chunks of butter to egg yolk mixture, whipping constantly over very low heat—do not let egg yolk get over cooked. If sauce begins to curdle, immediately immerse pan in bowl of cold water, whipping briskly all the while. When butter melts and blends into egg mixture add another chunk of butter, whipping constantly. Repeat until all butter is added and sauce is thick and smooth. Add salt to taste and minced parsley. Serve at once. If delay serving, then warm over low heat whisking constantly.

## BEARNAISE SAUCE

1 cup white wine
1/2 cup white wine vinegar
1 Tbls. shallots, chopped
2 Tbls. tarragon, chopped
2 Tbls. chervil, chopped

pinch powdered bay leaf
2 egg yolks
1/4 pound butter
dash cayenne
1 tsp. lemon juice

Heat wine. Add wine vinegar, shallots, tarragon, chervil, bay leaf. Simmer over low heat until mixture is reduced 2/3rds. Remove from heat. Beat egg yolks lightly, add a little water. Strain wine mixture into a double boiler and beat in the egg yolks until mixture is smooth and creamy. Melt butter and add slowly while beating. Add cayenne. Remove from heat, beat in lemon juice, stirring vigorously until smooth.

## BEARNAISE SAUCE

1/4 cup wine vinegar            1/4 tsp. salt
1/4 cup dry vermouth            1/8 tsp. pepper
1 Tbls. shallots, minced        3 egg yolks
1/2 tsp. tarragon               1-1/2 sticks butter

Boil the vinegar, wine, herbs, seasonings in a saucepan until liquid
is reduced to about two (2) Tbls. Cool. Then proceed as for
Hollandaise sauce ( see pages 102-107 ).

## MOCK BEARNAISE SAUCE

2 Tbls. margarine               1/8 tsp. parsley
1 Tbls. mayonnaise              1/4 tsp. dry onion flakes soaked
1 Tbls. tarragon vinegar in     3/4 cup water
Few drops imitation butter flavoring

Heat margarine in a small dish set in hot water, When it is melted, add
mayonnaise, vinegar, parsley, onion flakes, Stir vigorously. Serve at once.

## BEARNAISE TOMATO SAUCE

Use any of the above BEARNAISE sauces and add tomato paste
to taste.

## QUICK BEARNAISE

2 Tbls. white wine              1/4 tsp. black pepper
1 Tbls. tarragon vinegar        3 egg yolks
2 tsp. tarragon, chopped        2 Tbls. lemon juice
2 tsp. shallots, chopped        1/4 tsp. salt
pinch cayenne pepper

Combine wine, vinegar, tarragon, shallots, black pepper in a skillet.
Bring to a boil and cook rapidly until almost all the liquid disappears.

In a small saucepan heat the butter to bubbling, do not brown. Place the egg yolks, lemon juice, salt and cayenne in an electric blender: cover, flick on and off at high speed. Remove cover, turn on high and gradually add hot butter. Add the herb mixture and blend all for four (4) seconds

## BECHAMEL SAUCE

In a saucepan heat 1/4 cup butter, over low heat add 1/2 an onion, finely minced. Cook just a little. Stir in 1/2 cup flour. Gradually add one (1) quart milk until heated to boiling point. Cook mixture until smooth, stirring constantly. In a separate saucepan simmer 1/4 pound chopped lean veal in two (2) Tbls butter over very low heat. Season with sprig of thyme, pinch of white pepper, pinch of fresh grated nutmeg. Cook for about five (5) minutes, stirring to keep veal from browning. Add to the sauce and blend thoroughly. Add salt to taste and cook the sauce over hot water for about one (1) hour, stirring occasionally. Strain. Dot with a little butter flecks. These will melt and prevent film.)

## BASIC BECHAMEL SAUCE

| | |
|---|---|
| 4 Tbls. butter | salt |
| 3 Tbls. flour | fresh ground black pepper |
| 1/2 cup fish broth | nutmeg |
| 1 cup milk | |

Melt butter, add flour, cook until slightly colored. Add fish broth, stirring until smooth. Gradually add milk and continue stirring until thickened. Cook five (5) minutes and season to taste with salt, pepper, nutmeg

### MAN SHALL NOT LIVE BY BREAD ALONE
New Testament
Matthew, iv, 4

## BECHAMELSAUCE

| | |
|---|---|
| 1 large onion, chopped | 1 small bay leaf |
| 6 Tbls. butter | 1 sprig thyme |
| 6 Tbls. flour | 1 quart milk |
| salt/pepper | |

Chop onion fine. Heat butter. Add onion. Saute until transparent. Add flour. Cook over medium heat, stirring occasionally, for five (5) or six (6) minutes. Scald milk and when scalded pour half into the pot, whisking to prevent lumping. Add rest of milk. Stir until mixture is smooth. Bring to a boil. Add bay leaf and thyme. Reduce heat to simmer for about ten (10 ) minutes. Strain. Season to taste.

## BECHAMEL SAUCE

| | |
|---|---|
| 3 Tbls. butter | 1/2 cup clam broth |
| 3 Tbls. flour | 1/2 cup water |

Heat butter and blend in flour, stirring for two (2), three (3) minutes, until bubbly. Remove from heat. Stir in clam broth and water. Whisk to blend smoothly. Return to moderate high heat and stir until thickened and smooth ( four (4), five (5) minutes).

## BECHAMEL SAUCE

| | |
|---|---|
| 2 cups Veloute Sauce (see pages 191 ) | 1 1/2 cups heavy cream |
| 1/2 cup consomme | dash nutmeg |

Over low heat reduce Veloute sauce one-half, stirring frequently to prevent burning or sticking. Add consomme, cream and nutmeg. Reduce to 1/3rd, stirring constantly

## BECHAMEL SAUCE

| | |
|---|---|
| 1 Tbls. sliced onion | 2 Tbls. flour |
| 1 Tbls. sliced carrot | 2 Tbls. butter |

1 small bay leaf                        1/2 cup light cream
5 peppercorns                           1/2 tsp. salt
small sprig parsley                     1/4 tsp. pepper
1 cup chicken stock ( or veal stock )

Combine onion, carrot, bay leaf, peppercorns, parsley. Add stock.
Simmer twenty (20) minutes. Strain. Melt butter. Blend in flour.
Gradually add stock mixture and cream. Cook, stirring constantly,
until thick. Salt and Pepper to taste.

## BECHAMEL SAUCE

| Thin | Medium | Thick |
|---|---|---|
| 1 Tbls butter | 2 Tbls. butter | 3 Tbls butter |
| 1 Tbls flour | 2 Tbls flour | 3 Tbls flour |
| dash pepper | dash pepper | dash pepper |
| 1/2 tsp salt | 1/2 tsp salt | 1/2 tsp salt |
| 1 cup milk | lcup milk | 1 cup milk |

Melt butter in double boiler. Stir in flour, pepper, salt. Blend well.
Add milk gradually, stirring constantly until thickened. Continue
stirring for ten (10) minutes.

## BECHAMEL SAUCE

2 Tbls. butter                          freshly ground pepper
2 Tbls. flour                           nutmeg
1 cup milk                              salt

Melt butter in saucepan over moderate heat without letting it
brown. Add flour. Stir with whisk until well blended. In a separate
saucepan bring milk almost to a boil. Stirring butter/flour mixture
vigorously add milk all at once. Bring to a boil, the mixture will
thicken. Simmer for five (5) minutes. Season to taste with salt,
pepper, nutmeg.

## CURRIED BECHAMEL SAUCE

Melt one (1) tsp butter. Stir in one (1) mashed to a pulp garlic clove, one (1) tsp. each finely chopped shallots, green onions, one (1) generous tsp. curry powder and a dash each of turmeric, ground cloves, cinnamon. Stir this mixture for two (2) to three (3) minutes over low heat, stirring constantly. Stir in one cup of Bechamel Sauce and bring to a boil. Remove at once from heat.

## BECHAMEL SAUCE MAIGRE

Bring two (2) cups of milk to a boil. In a skillet, in 1/4 cup butter, saute 1/2 finely chopped small onion until soft—not browned. Stir in 1/4 cup flour. Add hot milk gradually, stirring constantly until sauce is smooth and free from lumps. Salt and Pepper to taste. Simmer for fifteen (15) minutes, stirring occasionally. Strain through a fine sieve. You may add one (1) or two (2) beaten egg yolks and heat the sauce without boiling it, to make it richer.

## BECHAMEL SAUCE MAIGRE

In a saucepan saute 1/2 an onion in 1/4 cup of butter until it is soft, not browned. Stir in 1/4 cup flour and cook slowly without letting the mixture take on color. Add gradually three (3) cups each fish stock and scalded milk, stirring vigorously with whisk. Add 1/2 tsp. salt, five (5) peppercorns (white), sprig of parsley, pinch of nutmeg. Cook slowly, stirring often, about thirty (30) minutes until liquid is reduced by 1/3rd and sauce is the consistency of heavy cream. Strain through fine sieve. Fleck with dots of butter to prevent film.

## BERCY SAUCE

Add three (3) shallots, chopped, to one (1) cup of dry white wine and simmer until the mixture is reduced by 3/4ths. Stir in 1/4 cup butter, juice of 1/2 lemon, salt and pepper to taste. When ready to serve, reheat sauce without boiling and add one (1) tsp. finely chopped parsley.

## BERCY SAUCE

Melt two (2) Tbls. butter in a saucepan and saute one (1) Tbls. chopped shallots until they are transparent. Add 1/4 cup each dry white wine, fish stock. Cook until liquid is reduced 1/2. Stir in 1/2 cup fish Veloute sauce and finish with one (1) Tbls. each butter and very finely chopped parsley.

## THE TURNPIKE ROAD TO MOST PEOPLE'S HEARTS, I FIND, LIES THROUGH THEIR MOUTHS, OR I MISTAKE MANKIND
Wolcott—Peter Pindar

## BORDELAISE SAUCE

| | |
|---|---|
| 2 Tbls. butter | 1/4 tsp. salt |
| 2 Tbls. flour | 1/8 tsp. ground black pepper |
| 1 Tbls. onion, minced | 1 can condensed beef broth |
| 1 Tbls parsley, minced | 1/4 cup dry red wine |
| 1 Bay leaf | 1/4 tsp. thyme leaves |

In a heavy saucepan, over low heat, cook the flour in butter until just lightly brown. Stir often. Stir in onion, parsley, bay leaf, thyme leaves, salt and pepper. Slowly add beef broth and red wine. Stir to blend all well. Increase to medium-high. Cook stirring constantly until mixture thickens. Discard bay leaf.

## BORDELAISE

Cook two (2) shallots, chopped, in 1/2 cup red wine until wine is reduced by 3/4. Add one (1) cup brown sauce. Simmer gently for ten (10) minutes. Just before serving add two (2) Tbls. poached beef marrow, 1/2 tsp. chopped parsley.

## BORDELAISE SAUCE

| | |
|---|---|
| 2 Tbls. butter | 2 Tbls. lemon juice |
| 2 Tbls. minced shallots | 2 Tbls. minced parsley |
| 3/4 cup dry red wine | 3/4 cup sliced mushrooms, cooked |
| 1 1/2 cup Brown sauce | salt and cayenne pepper |
| | ( see pages 55-58 ) |

Melt butter in a saucepan and cook shallots until transparent. Add wine and simmer until reduced to 1/2 volume. Add remaining ingredients and heat thoroughly.

## BORDELAISE SAUCE

| | |
|---|---|
| 1/4 cup butter | 3 Tbls. soy flour |
| 1 shallot finely chopped | 1/2 tsp. meat extract paste |
| 1 clove garlic, chopped | 1 can condensed beef bouillon |
| 2 onion slices | 1 cup burgundy wine |
| 2 carrot slices | 1/4 tsp. salt |
| 2 sprigs parsley | 1/8 tsp. pepper |
| 10 whole black peppers | 2 Tbls. chopped parsley |
| 2 whole cloves | 2 bay leaves |

In hot butter, saute shallots, garlic, onion, carrot, parsley, peppers, cloves and bay leaves until onion is golden brown. Remove from heat. Stir in flour until smooth. Stirring over very low heat about five (5) minutes until flour is light brown. Remove from heat. Add meat extract. Stir in bouillon and 3/4 cup burgundy wine. Over medium heat bring up to just boil, stir constantly. Reduce heat, simmer, ten (10) minutes. Stir occasionally. Strain. Discard vegetables and spices. Return to pan. Add salt, pepper, parsley and remaining burgundy wine. Reheat gently. Do Not Boil. Taste and add more meat extract, salt and pepper if desired.

## BORDELAISE SAUCE

| | |
|---|---|
| 1 Tbls. chopped shallots | 1 cup Espagnole Sauce |
| Pinch of thyme | ( see page 93 ) |
| 2 Tbls. butter pinch | powdered bay leaf |
| 1 cup dry red wine | dash salt |

Add shallots, thyme, bay leaf to wine. Simmer about five (5) minutes over medium high heat until volume reduced to 2/3rds. Strain this mixture into Espagnole sauce and simmer over medium heat ten (10 ) minutes. Reduce to 1/3rd. Remove from heat. Stir in butter until smooth. Salt to taste.

## BOURGUIGNONNE SAUCE

| | |
|---|---|
| 1 small onion | 6 mushrooms |
| 4 Tbls. butter | 2 cups fish stock |
| 1 cup red wine | Beurre Manie ( balls of butter |
| salt | flour kneaded together ) |
| chopped parsely | |

Chop the onion and slice mushrooms very thin. Saute these in butter until they are cooked through. Add fish stock and wine. Simmer until reduced by half. Correct seasoning and thicken with Beurre Manie. Add parsley just before serving.

## BOURGUIGNONNE SAUCE

In a skillet of two (2) Tbls. butter brown one (1) small carrot, one (1) small onion, one (1) small celery root—all chopped very fine. Add one (1) cup of red burgundy wine, 1/2 cup fish stock, a garlic clove, a pinch of thyme, a small bay leaf. Cook sauce over high heat until reduced by half. Add one (1) cup fish stock and simmer for fifteen (15) to twenty (20 ) minutes. Strain through sieve, pressing gently to push some of the pulp through, Season with salt and pepper. Stir in one (1) Tbls. sweet butter. Strain.

## BREADSAUCE

Bring to a boil two (2) cups milk in which there is one (1) onion studded with two (2) cloves, 1/2 tsp. salt, dash of cayenne pepper. Cook for five (5) minutes. Strain. Add one (1) cup fresh bread crumbs. Salt to taste. Add a little butter or heavy cream.

## BASIC BREAD SAUCE

1 slice white bread
1 cup skim milk
salt
white pepper

Put bread in blender to make crumbs. Scald milk without boiling. When tiny bubbles form around edge of pan add bread crumbs. Simmer five (5) minutes. Season to taste.

## BREAD SAUCE

| | |
|---|---|
| 1/3 cup fine, stale bread crumbs | 1/2 tsp. salt |
| 1 onion | pinch of cayenne |
| 6 cloves | 3 Tbls. butter |
| 2 cups milk | 1/2 cup coarse, stale bread crumbs |

Add fine bread crumbs, onion studded with cloves to milk in a double-boiler. Scald for thirty (30) minutes. Remove onion. Add salt, cayenne, two (2) Tbls. of butter. Brown coarse crumbs in remaining Tbls. butter. Sprinkle these on sauce.

## HORSERADISH BREAD SAUCE

In the top of a double-boiler cook 1 1/2 cups scalded milk, 1/3 cup freshly grated horseradish, three (3) Tbls. soft bread crumbs. Stir frequently for about twenty five (25) minutes. Stir in three (3) Tbls. butter. Season to taste with salt, white pepper, a little lemon juice.

## BRETONNE SAUCE

To one (1) cup of Veloute sauce ( see pages 191 ) add 1/4 cup white parts of leeks with equal parts of julienned celery, onion, mushrooms that have been cooked in butter. Add 1/4 fish or meat stock. Stir in one (1) Tbls. butter.

## BROWN SAUCE

Melt 1/2 cup beef, pork or veal drippings in a saucepan. Add one (1) small carrot, two (2) onions—coarsely chopped—and cook until onions just start to turn golden. Keep shaking the pan to ensure even cooking. Add 1/2 cup flour, stirring frequently, until flour, carrots and onions are a rich brown. Add three (3) cups hot stock, one (1) stalk celery, three (3) sprigs parsley, one (1) small bay leaf, one (1) garlic clove, a pinch of thyme—all chopped. Cook, stirring until mixture thickens. Add three (3) more cups stock. Simmer slowly over very low heat, stirring occasionally, for one and one half (1 1/2 ) hours, until mixture is reduced to about three (3) cups. During cooking skim off fat. Add 1/2 cup tomato puree, and cook for a few minutes. Strain through a fine sieve. Add two (2) more cups stock and continue cooking, slowly, for one (1) hour. Skim occasionally, until sauce is reduced to about four (4) cups. Cool, stirring occasionally. If used after a week, reheat.

## BROWN SAUCE

| | |
|---|---|
| 1 slice whole wheat bread, toasted | 2 Tbls. ketchup |
| 1 cup water | dash Worcestershire sauce |
| 1 beef bouillon cube | few drops of brown food coloring |

Cut up toast and put in blender to make crumbs. Heat water and bouillon cube in saucepan. Add bread crumbs and simmer fifteen (15) minutes. Stir in ketchup and Worcestershire sauce to taste, Simmer fifteen (15) minutes, If desired, add food coloring drops.

## BROWN SAUCE

| | |
|---|---|
| 5 pounds veal bones | 3 cloves unpeeled garlic |
| 1 large onion, quartered | 1 Tbls. salt |
| 5 small carrots, quartered | 1/2 cup flour |
| 2 stalks celery, with leaves, coarse chopped | 3 quarts water |
| 1/2 tsp. thyme | 1-1/4 cups tomato puree |
| 1 tsp. crushed peppercorns | 1/2 cup green part of leeks |
| 3 bay leaves | 3 sprigs parsley |

Preheat oven to 475 degrees F. Combine bones, onion, carrots, celery, thyme, peppercorns, bay leaves, garlic and salt in a large roasting pan. Bake for forty-five (45) minutes. Reduce heat to prevent bones from burning, if necessary. Sprinkle with flour and bake for fifteen (15) minutes more. Transfer all ingredients to a large kettle. Add two (2) cups of water to the roasting pan. Cook over moderate heat, stirring, to dissolve brown particles that cling to bottom and sides of the roasting pan. Pour this liquid into the kettle. Add balance of water, tomato puree, leeks, parsley. Bring to a rapid boil. Reduce heat and simmer for two (2) hours. Add more water if necessary. Skim often. Cool. Strain. This sauce may be frozen and used as needed. It may be stored in tight container for several weeks in refrigerator.

## BROWN SAUCE

Simmer three (3) Tbls. butter in double boiler with one (1) tsp. minced parsley, one (1) minced onion, until onion is golden brown. Proceed as for a Medium Bechamel Sauce, (see pages 47-50 ), adding flour, pepper, salt—BUT substitute bouillon for milk!

**ONE SHOULD EAT TO LIVE, NOT LIVE TO EAT**
Benjamin Franklin

## BROWN SAUCE

| | |
|---|---|
| 4 Tbls. butter | 1/2 cup dry white wine |
| 1 small veal bone with beef trimmings | 1 Tbls. tomato paste |
| 2 small onions | 1/2 bay leaf |
| 2 Tbls. flour | sprig of thyme |
| 1 1/2 quarts boiling water | 1 beef bouillon cube |

In a large saucepan, heat butter well. Brown beef trimmings and veal bone until very brown. Remove browned meats to another pan or plate. Add chopped onions to the pan and brown well. Add flour and cook with onions eight (8) to ten (10) minutes. Using whisk, add half of boiling water to pan. Whisk well. Add remainder of water. Return meat trimmings and bone to pan. Bring back to a boil and add white wine, tomato paste, bay leaf, thyme and bouillon cube. Let cook, over medium heat, forty (40) to forty-five (45) minutes or until there remains three (3) to four (4) cups of sauce. Strain.

## BROWN SAUCE

| | |
|---|---|
| 2 Tbls. butter or meat drippings | 1/2 bay leaf |
| 1 Tbls. minced onion | 2 Tbls. flour |
| 1 Tbls. minced carrot | 1 cup meat stock |
| salt | pepper |

Melt butter. Add onion, carrot and bay leaf and cook over low heat until butter is brown. Stir in flour and cook until bubbly. Add stock and cook until mixture is thick and smooth. Strain.

**SIMPLE DIET IS BEST, FOR MANY DISHES BRING MANY DISEASES, AND RICH SAUCES ARE WORSE THAN EVEN HEAPING SEVERAL MEATS UPON EACH OTHER**

Pliny

## BROWN SAUCE

| | |
|---|---|
| 4 cups beef broth | 1 tsp. orange zest |
| 1 cup tomato puree | 1/2 cup chopped leeks |
| 1/4 cup dry red wine | 2 sprigs parsley |

Combine all ingredients in a heavy bottomed saucepan. Bring to a boil. Reduce heat and simmer for one (1) hour. Strain sauce or puree it.

## I WON'T QUARREL WITH MY BREAD AND BUTTER
Swift

Polite Conversation

## BROWN SAUCE

| | |
|---|---|
| 5 pounds veal bones, cracked | 3 garlic cloves, unpeeled |
| 1 onion, quartered | 1 Tbls. salt |
| 3 stalks celery, chopped | 1/2 cup flour |
| 5 carrots, quartered | 3 quarts water |
| 3/4 tsp. thyme | 1 can tomato puree ( about 10 oz.) |
| 1 tsp. cracked black peppercorns | 3 sprigs parsley |

Preheat oven to 475 degrees F. Combine veal bones, onion, celery, carrots, thyme, pepper, garlic and salt in a large baking pan. Bake forty-five (45) minutes. If the bones start to burn reduce heat a little. When cooked, bones should be brown. Sprinkle the bones with flour and stir with fork to evenly distribute flour. Return pan to oven for fifteen (15 ) minutes. Place the ingredients into a large kettle. Add three (3) cups water to the baking pan and stir, over moderate heat, to dissolve the particles on the bottom and sides of the baking pan. Pour this liquid into the kettle and add tomato puree. Add remaining water and parsley and bring to a boil. Simmer two (2) hours, skimming occasionally. Strain. It may be frozen and used as desired.

## BROWN CHICKEN SAUCE

2 1/2 pounds bony chicken parts

2 1/2 pounds veal bones
5 carrots, chopped
3 cloves garlic, unpeeled
4 cups onions, chopped
3 large leeks, trimmed,
    cut into 1 inch pcs.
4 stalks celery, chopped

1/2 pound fresh mushrooms,
    cut up
11/2 Tbls. peppercorns, bruised
3 bay leaves
2 Tbls. thyme
9 quarts water
6 sprigs parsley

1 can tomato puree
    ( approx. 10 oz. )

Preheat oven to 465 F. Place chicken and veal bones in a large baking pan, sprinkle with carrots, garlic, onions, leeks, celery, mushrooms, peppercorns, bay leaves and thyme. Bake forty-five (45) minutes. Reduce heat to prevent burning if need to do so. Transfer all to a large kettle. Add four (4) cups water to baking pan. Place over moderate heat and stir with spoon to dissolve brown particles on bottom and sides of pan. Pour this liquid over the contents of the kettle. Add remaining water. Add parsley, tomato puree. Cook over medium heat for five (5) hours. Stir occasionally. Strain. Cool. This sauce may be frozen and defrosted as needed.

## BROWN COGNAC SAUCE

3 Tbls. butter
2 Tbls. flour
1 Tbls. beef base
1 cup light cream

1/2 cup diced ham
3 Tbls, cognac
salt and fresh ground pepper

Melt butter in a saucepan. Add flour, whisk until bubbly. ( about three (3) minutes ). Do not let the mixture take on color. Add beef base, cream, ham, cognac. Salt and pepper to taste. Stir constantly while cooking over medium heat until sauce is thickened and smooth.

## SIMPLE BROWN SAUCE

In a saucepan brown lightly one (1) finely chopped onion in two (2) Tbls, virgin olive oil. Add two (2) Tbls. flour. Cook. Stir until roux is brown. Add two (2) cups brown stock, three (3) Tbls. tomato puree. Continue cooking, stirring until sauce is thickened. Continue cooking until sauce is reduced to about one (1) cup. Season to taste with salt and pepper.

## QUICK BASIC BROWN SAUCE

3 Tbls. butter
1 small onion, chopped
1 cup dry red wine
1 1/2 cup beef broth
1/4 tsp. dried thyme

1 small bay leaf
3 sprigs parsley
3 Tbls. flour plus 2 Tbls. butter
salt and pepper

Melt butter in saucepan. Add chopped onion. Cook until golden brown. Add wine, broth. Bring to boil. Add thyme, bay leaf, parsley. Boil briskly until liquid is reduced by one—third (1/3). Knead together flour and butter to form a ball. Break off small pieces and add these a few at a time to the boiling mixture. Stir constantly until sauce reaches desired consistency—between light and heavy cream. Salt and pepper to taste. Strain.

## BROWN SAUCE QUICK

In a saucepan melt 1 1/2 Tbls. clarified butter, adding a 1 1/2 Tbls. flour. Cook this roux over low heat, stirring occasionally, until thoroughly blended and browned. Add two (2) cups strong beef stock gradually. Bring mixture to a boil. Stir constantly for about three (3) to five (5) minutes. Lower heat and simmer sauce gently thirty (30) minutes. Stir occasionally. Skim off fat. Strain through fine sieve.

## BUTTER SAUCE

| | |
|---|---|
| 2 cups butter | 1/2 tsp. Tabasco sauce |
| 3 Tbls. lemon juice | 1 Tbls. Worcestershire sauce |

Melt butter over low heat. Add remaining ingredients and beat well with whisk.


## ALMOND BUTTER SAUCE

In a saucepan melt 1/2 cup butter. Add generous 1/2 cup sliced, blanched almonds. Cook over low heat, stir occasionally, until almonds lightly browned. Stir in one (1) tsp. each finely chopped olives, onion juice, lemon juice. Heat sauce, stirring gently, until sauce comes to a boil. Season with salt, pepper, dash of nutmeg to taste.


## BEURRE BLANC SAUCE

In a saucepan cook three (3) shallots, chopped fine, in six (6) Tbls. of liquid that fish has been cooked in, 1/4 cup wine vinegar, salt, pepper, until liquid is reduce to about 1/4 cup. Partially remove pan from heat and add, small piece by small piece, 1/2 pound sweet butter. Beat constantly with whisk until butter is melted and sauce is creamy white, thick and foamy.

## BEURRE BLANC SAUCE

| | |
|---|---|
| 1/4 cup white wine vinegar | 1/2 tsp. salt |
| 2 Tbls, lemon juice | 2 Tbls. dry vermouth |
| 1/8 tsp. white pepper | 1 Tbls. minced scallions |
| 3 sticks butter, cut into | 1/4 inch pcs. |

Boil vinegar, lemon juice, vermouth, scallions, salt and pepper until liquid is reduced to 1-1/2 Tbls. Remove from heat and immediately beat in two pieces of butter—chilled—with whisk. As butter softens and creams in the liquid, add another piece. Return to very low heat, beating constantly, keep adding pieces of butter until all three (3) sticks are in. Sauce should become thick, creamy. Remove from heat. Season to taste.

## BEURRE NOIR

2 Tbls. butter
1 Tbls. white vinegar

Heat butter over a high flame until it is rich brown. Dash in the vinegar quickly and swirl the pan or whisk. When spitting ends sauce is ready to serve.

## BEURRE BROWN

Cook about 1/2 cup butter in saucepan until it foams and becomes light brown. Remove from heat. Add two (2) Tbls. lemon juice, 1/4 tsp. salt, touch of pepper. Add two (2) Tbls. each chopped parsley, chives.

## DILL BUTTER SAUCE

1 cup butter
1 tsp. dill weed
1/4 tsp. salt

In saucepan, over low heat, melt butter. Stir in dill weed. Salt to taste. Serve hot.

## DRAWN BUTTER SAUCE

Blend well three (3) Tbls. flour, three (3) Tbls. melted butter. Add 1/2 tsp. salt, pinch of white pepper to taste. Pour in gradually 1 1/2 cups fish stock, stirring occasionally. Stir in three (3) more Tbls. butter, small piece by small piece, alternating with one (1) tsp. lemon juice.

## IRISH BUTTER SAUCE

Blend thoroughly 1/4 cup cream, 1/4 cup butter, six (6) Tbls. ketchup. Season to taste with salt, pepper, touch of nutmeg. Heat but do not boil.

## LEMON BUTTER SAUCE

Melt 1/2 cup butter. Remove from heat and add two (2) Tbls. lemon juice

## LEMON BUTTER SAUCE

| | |
|---|---|
| 1/4 cup butter | 1/2 tsp salt |
| 1 Tbls. lemon juice | 1 Tbls. chopped parsley |
| 1/8 tsp. cayenne | |

Over medium heat melt butter. Stir in lemon juice, chopped parsley, salt, cayenne.

## ONION BUTTER SAUCE

Combine 1/2 cup butter with 1/4 cup lemon juice, 1/4 cup chopped green onions, 1/4 cup chopped parsley. Simmer one (1) minute to blend.

## BUTTER SHRIMP SAUCE

In a saucepan cook one (1) Tbls. chopped shallots in three (3) Tbls melted butter quickly. Drain butter and discard shallots. Add 2 1/2 Tbls. flour. Blend well. Gradually add one (1) cup strained shrimp stock—( the water in which the shrimp have been cooked )—1/2 cup dry white wine. Stir sauce constantly over low heat until it thickens. Season to taste with salt, pepper, dash of nutmeg. Stir in one (1) Tbls. lemon juice that has been mixed with one (1) tsp. dry mustard, well blended. Remove from heat. Just before serving stir in two (2) egg yolks, one at a time, beating well after each addition. Bring sauce to hot without boiling. Serve at once.

## WORCESTERSHIRE BUTTER SAUCE

Brown 1/2 cup butter.           Add 1/2 tsp. Worcestershire sauce.

## CALYPSO SAUCE

| | |
|---|---|
| 1/2 cup light brown sugar | 2 garlic cloves |
| 1/4 cup fresh lime juice | 1/4 tsp. salt |
| 2 Tbls. light rum | 1/4 tsp. Tabasco |
| 1 inch piece fresh ginger, peeled, minced | 1/8 tsp. ground cloves |

In saucepan combine sugar, with remaining ingredients. Cook over medium heat, stirring until sugar is dissolved.

## NOW GOOD DIGESTION WAIT ON APPETITE, AND GOOD HEALTH ON BOTH
Shakespeare

## CAMBRIDGE SAUCE

Pound together four (4) hard boiled eggs, two (2) sponged anchovy fillets, one (1) tsp. drained capers, 1/3 tsp. each chopped tarragon, chives, chervil, shallots. Moisten with 1/4 cup olive oil, two (2) tsp. tarragon vinegar, 1/2 tsp. prepared mustard. Beat mixture to a paste. Season with salt and pepper to taste, a dash of cayenne. This sauce should be made just before serving. It will not keep.

## CAPER SAUCE

| | |
|---|---|
| 1/4 cup butter | 3 Tbls. capers |
| 2 Tbls. chopped onions | 1 Tbls parsley, minced |
| 3 Tbls. soy flour | 1 Tbls. cider vinegar |
| 1 1/2 cups beef stock | salt and pepper |

Melt butter. Add onion. Cook until tender, not brown. Stir in flour until smooth. Add beef stock. gradually stirring constantly until smooth. Add capers, parsely, vinegar. Season to taste.

## CAPER SAUCE

| | |
|---|---|
| 1/4 cup butter | 2 cups seasoned beef broth |
| 1/4 cup flour | 3 Tbls. capers |

Melt butter in saucepan and add flour. Whisk until smooth. Bring broth to a boil and add all at once to butter mixture, whisking vigorously. Simmer fifteen (15) minutes. Stir often. Add capers just before serving.

## CAPER SAUCE

| | |
|---|---|
| 3 Tbls. butter | 1/2 cup heavy cream |
| 3 Tbls. flour | 2 plus Tbls. capers |
| 1 1/2 cups beef broth | salt and pepper |

Melt butter. Add flour. Whisk until well blended. Bring broth to boil. Add at once to mixture. Stir vigorously with whisk. Season to taste.

## CAPER SAUCE

Blend together two (2) Tbls. each melted butter and flour. Over moderate heat stir this roux until slightly brown. Gradually add two (2) cups clear stock—made from the bones of roasted lamb—

stirring constantly until mixture is boiling and smooth. Add two (2) thin slices of lemon, 1 1/2 Tbls. heavy cream, two (2) Tbls. wine vinegar, 1/4 tsp. dry mustard. Cook for a minute and, just before serving, add two (2) tsp. butter and 1/4 cup chopped capers.

## BUTTER CAPER SAUCE

Melt 1/2 cup butter over low heat. Skim off foam. Add one (1) Tbls. lemon juice, 1/4 cup capers. Salt to taste.

## CAPER CREAM SAUCE

To one (1) cup of Bechamel sauce, ( see pages 47-50 ), add 1/4 cup chopped capers, one (1) Tbls. butter, 1/2 tsp. lemon juice.

## WHAT, YOU EGG ! YOUNG FRY OF TREACHERY
Macbeth, IV, ii

## EGG AND CAPER SAUCE

1 Tbls. butter
1 Tbls. flour
1/3 cup chicken stock
1 hard boiled egg, chopped

1/4 tsp. Dijon mustard
1/3 cup sour cream
1-2 tsps. capers

Melt butter in saucepan over medium heat until frothy. Stir in flour. Heat until frothy again. Do not brown. Blend in chicken stock. Cook and stir until thickened and smooth. Remove from heat. Add sour cream all at once blending immediately. Stir in mustard. Salt and pepper to taste. Fold in capers and hard boiled egg.

## CARDINALSAUCE

Add two (2) or three (3) Tbls. fish fumet to two (2) cups hot fish veloute. ( see pages 148-150 ). Stir in one (1) Tbls. chopped truffle, a little truffle juice and 1/4 cup lobster butter.

## CARDINAL SAUCE

1 cup fish stock                  1 1/2 cups Bechamel sauce
1 truffle                         ( see pages 47-49 )
1/2 cup heavy cream               4 Tbls. lobster butter

Using high heat reduce fish stock to 1/2 cup. While reducing add truffle. Combine stock with cream and Bechamel sauce. When thickened and smooth, remove from heat, stir in lobster butter.

## CASANOVA SAUCE

To one (1) cup mayonnaise add one (1) large black truffle—which has been put through food chopper—one (1) tsp. mince shallot, white of one (1) hard boiled egg—chopped—and two (2) hard boiled egg yolks, rubbed through a fine sieve. Season with salt, pepper, a little curry powder, to taste. Serve cold.

## CELERY SAUCE

2 cups celery, diced              1 Tbls. dry onion flakes
1 cup chicken bouillon            1/4 cup evaporated skimmed milk

Place celery, bouillon, onion flakes, salt and pepper to taste, in blender until smooth. Heat, in a saucepan, over medium heat for one half (1/2) hour. Add milk and heat thoroughly but do not boil.

## CELERY SAUCE

1 can condensed cream of celery soup     1/4 cup milk
1 tsp. prepared mustard                 3 Tbls. sweet relish
1 hard boiled egg, chopped

In a saucepan blend mustard and milk with condensed milk. Add relish, egg. Heat over low heat.

## NORTHUMBERLAND CELERY SAUCE

Cut two (2) stalks of celery into 1/2 inch pieces. Cover in saucepan with one (1) cup chicken stock. Bring to a boil and strain into another saucepan. Add more stock if necessary to make 3/4 cup of liquid. Add a scant tsp. of mace, the prepared celery. Simmer gently forty (40) to forty-five (45) minutes. Rub the mixture through a fine sieve into another saucepan. Stir in cup of Bechamel sauce, ( see pages 47-49 ), into what is now a puree. Season to taste. When ready to serve stir in one (1) Tbls. sweet butter and the livers of the game birds being served that have been chopped and lightly sauted.

## CELERY SAUCE FOR PARTRIDGE (GROUSE)

Dice a large bunch of celery, cover with water. Simmer until celery is tender. Add one (1) cup cream, 1/4 tsp. mace, 1/4 tsp nutmeg. Roll two (2) Tbls. butter in flour. Add to mixture. Continue to simmer until smooth.

## CHASSEUR SAUCE

1 cup mushrooms, sliced           1 1/2 cups beef stock
2 Tbls. butter                       1 cup tomato sauce

1 Tbls. shallots, chopped          1/2 tsp. cornstarch
1 cup dry white wine               1 Tbls parsley, chopped

Saute mushrooms in butter. Add shallots, white wine, stock, tomato sauce. Simmer five (5) minutes. Stir in cornstarch mixed with a little water. Add parsley

## CHASSEUR SAUCE

2 Tbls. butter                2 Tbls. brandy
3 shallots, chopped           1 1/2 cups Brown sauce ( see pages 55-58 )
1 cup mushrooms, sliced       1/2 cup tomato sauce
1/2 cup dry white wine        fresh parsley, minced

Saute shallots gently in butter. Add mushrooms. Cook for five (5) minutes. Add white wine, brandy. Increase heat. Cook until sauce is reduced one third (1/3rd). Add brown sauce, tomato sauce and simmer until heated through.

## CHASSEUR SAUCE

Cut off the stems of one (1) pound mushrooms. Dry. Cut into thin slices. (Save caps for other uses). Saute the mushrooms in 1/4 cup butter until golden brown. Add shallots, chopped, and 1/2 cup dry white wine. Cook until reduced by one half (1/2), Add one (1) cup Brown sauce, ( see pages 55-58 ), two (2) Tbls. tomato sauce, 1/2 tsp. each tarragon, chopped parsley.

## CHASSEUR SAUCE

1 Tbls. chopped mushrooms          1 cup Bordelaise sauce
1 tsp.butter                       ( see pages 51-53 )

Lightly saute chopped mushrooms in one half (1/2) the butter. Stir into simmering Bordelaise sauce. Continue to simmer very gently over very low heat five (5) minutes. Remove from heat. Stir in remaining butter until mixture is smooth.

## CHASSEUR SAUCE

Cook two (2) Tbls. sliced mushrooms and a tsp. minced shallots in a little butter until tender. Add 1/2 cup dry white wine and reduce liquid over high heat to one half (1/2). Stir in one (1) Tbls. tomato puree, one (1) cup Brown sauce, ( see pages 55-58 ). Boil up twice, remove from heat. Beat in one (1) Tbls. sweet butter and 1/2 tsp. each minced parsley. tarragon.

## CHEESE SAUCE

| | |
|---|---|
| 1 Tbls butter | 1/8 tsp. black pepper |
| 1 Tbls. soy flour | 3/4 cup grated sharp Cheddar cheese |
| 1 cup milk | 1 tsp. lemon juice |
| Salt | |

Melt butter. Blend in flour. Stir in milk, salt and pepper to taste. Cook until slightly thickened. Add cheese, lemon juice.

## CHEESE SAUCE

To one (1) cup Medium Bechamel sauce, ( see pages 47-49 ), stir in 1/2 cup Cheddar cheese until melted.

## NOBBY CHEESE SAUCE

| | |
|---|---|
| 4 Tbls. butter | 1/4 tsp. pepper |
| 4 Tbls. flour | 1 tsp. Worcestershire sauce |
| 2 cups milk | 1/4 cup Sharp Cheddar Cheese (cubed) |

Melt butter in skillet over low heat. Add flour. Blend. Do not brown. Remove from heat. Add milk. Blend. Add salt, pepper, Worcestershire sauce. Return to low heat. Cook, stirring, until mixture is smooth and thickened. Just before serving stir in Cheese.

## PAREMSAN CHEESE SAUCE

| | |
|---|---|
| 1/4 cup butter 1 | 1/2 cups water |
| 1/4 cup flour | 2 chicken bouillon cubes |
| 1 1/2 cups half and half cream | 1/2 cup grated Parmesan cheese |

In a saucepan over medium heat, stir flour into hot butter until well blended. Gradually stir in half and half, water, chicken bouillon cubes. Cook, stirring constantly until sauce is thickened. Stir in grated Parmesan cheese and heat until melted.

## PEPPERY BLEU CHEESE SAUCE

| | |
|---|---|
| 1 Tbls. butter | 1/2 cup crumbled Bleu cheese |
| 1 Tbls. flour | 1/2 tsp salt |
| 3/4 cup milk | 1/4 tsp. ground pepper |

In saucepan over medium heat stir flour into hot butter until blended. Gradually stir in milk. Cook, stirring constantly until mixture is thickened. Remove from heat. Stir in cheese and remaining ingredients.

## PIMENTO CHEESE SAUCE

| | |
|---|---|
| 3 Tbls. butter | 1 1/2 cups grated sharp Cheddar cheese |
| 3 Tbls. flour | 1/3 cup chopped pimentos |
| 1 1/2 cups milk | salt and cayenne pepper to taste |

Melt butter in top of double boiler over direct heat. Add flour and stir with whisk until blended. Bring milk to boil and add all at once to the mixture, stirring vigorously with whisk. Add cheese to sauce, place over boiling water. Cook, stirring often until cheese melts. Add pimentos. Salt and cayenne to taste.

## RICH CHEESE SAUCE

To one (1) cup thick cream sauce add two (2) egg yolks, well beaten, 1/4 cup grated cheddar cheese. In the top of a double boiler, over hot water, heat sauce without boiling it until the cheese melts.

## SPEEDY CHEESE SAUCE

1 cup evaporated milk

1 1/2 cups cut up processed cheese

few drops Tabasco sauce

1/4 tsp. dry mustard

1/2 tsp. Worcestershire sauce

Heat milk over low heat. Add cheese and stir constantly until cheese melts. Season.

## CHERRY SAUCE

8 ounces pitted dark cherries

1 Tbls sugar

1/4 tsp.ground ginger

1/2 tsp. cornstarch

1 Tbls Kirsch

dash salt

Drain cherries, reserve syrup. Pour 1/3rd cup syrup into saucepan. Add sugar, ginger, salt. Bring to a boil. Blend cornstarch into Kirsch. Gradually add this mixture to simmering cherry syrup. Cook and stir until thickened and clear.

## CHERRY SAUCE

1/2 pound Bing cherries, pitted

1/4 cup minced onion

1/4 cup butter

2 Tbls. brandy

1 Tbls. flour

2 cans consomme

1/3 cup sherry wine

Cook onions in butter until wilted. Stir in flour and cook for a few minutes. Boil consomme until reduced to one half (1/2). Add onions. Add sherry wine and brandy. Cook five (5) minutes. Add cherries and heat through.

## CHEVREUIL SAUCE

Bring to a boil 1 1/2 cups Poivrade sauce, (see page 151-152 ), and add 1/2 cup each red wine and strained marinade. Cook mixture for thirty (30) to forty (40) minutes. Remove scum as it accumulates. Add one (1) tsp. sugar and continue cooking until sauce is reduced to 1-1/4 cups. Remove from heat. Add two (2) Tbls. butter. Strain.

## CHEVREUSE SAUCE

After removing whatever bird you are roasting from the broiler, skim the fat from the pan drippings. You need about 1/2 cup lean drippings. Add 1/2 cup dry white wine and two (2) Tbls. tomato paste. Reduce this mixture over high heat, stirring constantly, until one half (1/2) left. Remove from heat. Add three (3) Tbls. Madeira wine, one (1) Tbls. quince jelly, and one (1) tsp. each grated horseradish, finely chopped truffles. Taste for seasoning. Bring just to boil. Serve.

## CHIFFON SAUCE

Stir one (1) egg yolk into one (1) cup warm medium Cream Sauce, (see pages 80-83 ) Add salt and pepper to taste. Let sauce stand for ten (10) minutes. Add two (2) Tbls. tarragon vinegar. Fold into sauce one (1) egg white that has been stiffly beaten. Serve well chilled.

## CHINESE OMELET SAUCE

In a saucepan bring 3/4 cup chicken stock to a boil. Stir in alternately two (2) tsp. soy sauce, two (2) tsp. cornstarch ( mixed with a little water). Cook over low heat until thickened. Salt and pepper to taste. Add 1/4 cup sliced mushrooms, sauted in butter.

## TEMPERANCE AND LABOR ARE THE TWO BEST PHYSICIANS OF MAN; LABOR SHARPENS THE APPETITE, AND TEMPERANCE PREVENTS FROM INDULGING TO EXCESS
Rousseau

## CHIVRY SAUCE

Cook 1/2 cup white wine, one (1) Tbls. chopped watercress, one (1) tsp. each chopped chervil, tarragon, chives in saucepan until reduced by two-thirds. Add two (2) cups Cream sauce, ( see pages 42-46 ). Strain through a fine sieve. Add one (1) Tbls. chopped cooked spinach that has been cooked in butter with a little chopped tarragon and chervil and then rubbed through a fine sieve.

## CHORON SAUCE

1 cup Bearnaise Sauce (see pages 42-46 )
1/4 cup tomato sauce ( see pages 181-188 )

In a double boiler, over low heat, stir the two sauces together until well blended.

## CHUTNEY SAUCE

| | |
|---|---|
| 1/2 cup chutney | 2 Tbls lemon juice |
| 1/2 cup sugar | 1/4 cup water |

Mix all ingredients. Simmer until syrupy

## CIDER SAUCE

3/4 cup cider                    1/3 cup flour
2 Tbls. butter                   1 1/2 cups beef broth
1/2 cup apple jelly

Melt butter. Add flour and blend. Add broth. Stir while bringing to
a boil. Add cider and apple jelly. Remove from heat.


## CLARE de LUNE SAUCE

Rub six (6) hard boiled egg yolks through fine sieve. Add one (1)
Tbls. prepared mustard. Season to taste with salt, pepper and
cayenne. Add one (1) cup mayonnaise, Stir. Add one (1) Tbls. each
fine chopped dill pickle, capers, chervil, parsley, shallots, fresh
tarragon, one (1) hard boiled egg white chopped. Add 1 1/2 Tbls.
chopped black truffles. Mix well. Chill.


## CLAM SAUCE

6 ounces minced clams            1 tsp. minced parsley
1 cup clam juice                 1 Tbls. olive oil
1 garlic clove, minced

Combine all ingredients but olive oil in saucepan. Bring to boil.
Simmer (15) minutes. Stir in olive oil


## MINCED CLAM SAUCE

Heat four (4) Tbls. each olive oil, butter. Add one (1) garlic clove,
chopped, three (3) Tbls. chopped shallots. Saute over low heat until
shallots are slightly golden. Add 1/2 cup clam juice. Simmer five (5)
minutes. Stir in one (1) cup clams, minced, and 1/2 cup chopped
parsley. Bring to boil. Serve

## WHITE CLAM SAUCE

| | |
|---|---|
| 24 ounces minced clams | 2 Tbls. white wine |
| 1/4 cup olive oil | 1 tsp. basil |
| 1 garlic clove, minced | 1/2 tsp. salt |
| 3/4 cup parsley, chopped | |

Drain juice from clams, reserve. In saucepan, in hot oil, over medium heat, cook garlic until tender. Stir in clam juice, all other ingredients, except clams. Cook ten (10) minutes. Stir occasionally. Add clams until heated through.

## COCHER de FRANCE SAUCE

Over medium heat cook two (2) cups fresh, peeled tomatoes chopped, with three (3) Tbls. grated onion, one (1) tsp. each chopped thyme leaves, powdered mace, one (1) garlic clove, one (1) whole clove, four (4) crushed peppercorns, a bouquet garni. Cook for twenty (20) minutes. Stir frequently. Remove from heat and rub through a fine sieve. Chill thoroughly. Separately, fork rapidly 1/2 cup mayonnaise, 1/3 cup prepared mustard, a cube of ice, until mixture is fluffy and thoroughly blended. Remove ice cube. Add, drop by drop, alternately with three (3) Tbls, chopped capers, and two (2) Tbls. each fresh, grated horseradish, gherkins fine chopped, the cold tomato mixture. Blend. Salt to taste

## ARGENTINE COCKTAIL SAUCE

To the recipe for Oyster Sauce, (see page 110 ), add 1/4 cup whipped cream, one (1) tsp. ginger

**PEOPLE WHO MUST WORK DON'T KNOW HOW TO FISH**

## COCKTAIL SAUCE

To 2/3 cup chili sauce add one (1) Tbls. grated horseradish, one (1) Tbls. lemon juice, 1/3 tsp. salt, touch of cayenne, 1/2 tsp. Worcestershire sauce, two (2) drops Tabasco. Chill.

## COCKTAIL SAUCE

1/2 cup chili sauce
1 Tbls. Worcestershire sauce
1/2 cup ketchup
1/2 tsp. dry mustard

1/2 tsp. salt
1 Tbsl. horseradish
1 tsp. fresh ground black pepper

Blend all ingredients well.

## COCKTAIL SAUCE

6 tomatoes, peeled, seeded, chopped
1 green pepper, seeded, chopped
4 shallots, chopped
1 tsp. dry mustard

1 Tbls. horseradish
1 Tbls. fresh black pepper
2 tsp. lemon juice
1/2 cup olive oil

Mix all ingredients thoroughly. Chill.

## OYSTER COCKTAIL SAUCE

To one (1) cup mayonnaise add 1/4 cup chili sauce, two (2) Tbls. tomato paste, one (1) Tbls. each tarragon vinegar, chopped parsley, chives, one (1) tsp. each onion juice, Worcestershire sauce. Salt and pepper to taste.

## RED COCKTAIL SAUCE

| | |
|---|---|
| 1 cup ketchup | 1 tsp. Worcestershire sauce |
| 1/4 lemon juice | dash Tabasco |
| 1 tsp. salt | 4 tsp. prepared horseradish |

Combine all ingredients. Chill

## SEAFOOD COCKTAIL SAUCE

| | |
|---|---|
| 1/4 tsp. Tabasco sauce | 1/2 tsp. salt |
| 1 cup ketchup | 1 Tbls. horseradish |
| 2 Tbls. lemon juice | |

Mix all well. Chill

## COCKTAIL SAUCE SUPREME

| | |
|---|---|
| 2 tsp. grated onion | 2 tsp. horseradish |
| 1 Tbls. lemon juice | 1/2 tsp. Worcestershire sauce |
| 1/4 cup chili sauce | dash Tabasco |

Combine all ingredients. Salt to taste. Chill.

## YELLOW COCKTAIL SAUCE

1/2 cup mayonnaise
1/4 cup chopped pickled onions
1 Tbls. lemon juice

Combine. Chill

## CRABMEAT SAUCE

4 Tbls. butter          1/2 cup dry sherry wine
4 Tbls. flour           1 cup crabmeat
2 cups milk

Heat butter, Whisk in flour. Cook for two (2) minutes, whisking, until bubbly. Remove from heat. Add milk all at once, whisking vigorously to blend well. Return to heat and cook until sauce is thick and smooth. Add sherry wine and crabmeat. Salt and pepper to taste.

## CRANBERRY SAUCE

2 cups sugar
16 ounces cranberries
1 1/2 cups water

Over medium heat bring sugar and water to a boil. Add cranberries and return to boiling. Reduce heat to low. Simmer seven (7) to ten (10) minutes until cranberries pop open.

## CRANBERRY ORANGE SAUCE

2 Tbls. cornstarch          1 1/2 cups orange juice
1 tsp. grated lemon peel    1 tsp. lemon juice
1/2 tsp. ground cloves      1 can whole cranberry sauce
1/4 tsp. salt

In saucepan combine cornstarch, lemon peel, cloves, salt, orange, lemon juice. Stir all until smooth. Cook over high heat until sauce is smooth and thick. Stir constantly. Add cranberry sauce. Stir while heating through.

## SPICY CRANBERRY SAUCE

1 can whole cranberry sauce        1 Tbls. horseradish
2 Tbls. butter                     1/2 tsp. dry mustard
1 Tbls. light brown sugar          1/4 tsp. ground allspice

In saucepan bring all ingredients to boil over medium heat. Reduce
heat. Simmer five (5) minutes.


## WHAT WAS SAUCE FOR THE GOOSE
## WAS SAUCE FOR THE GANDER
R. Head and F. Kirkman
English Rogue, II (1671)


## CREAM SAUCE

3/4 cup heavy cream
1 cup Bechamel sauce ( see pages 47-49 )
3 Tbls. butter

Over very low heat, add cup of Bechamel sauce to 1/2 cup cream.
Stirring constantly, reduce one third (1/3rd). Remove from heat.
Stir in butter and remaining cream vigorously until smooth.


## CREAM SAUCE

2 Tbls. butter                     2 Tbls. whipping cream
2 Tbls flour                       1 Tbls. sherry wine
1/2 cup chicken stock              2 Tbls. grated Parmesan cheese

Melt butter in saucepan over medium heat until frothy. Stir in
flour. Cook until frothy again. Stir in chicken stock. Add whipping
cream. Continue cooking, stirring, until sauce is thickened and
smooth. Stir in sherry wine and cheese. Cook very gently, stirring
constantly until cheese is melted and sauce is smooth. Salt and
pepper to taste.

## CREAM SAUCE

| | |
|---|---|
| 1 cup milk | white pepper |
| 1 Tbls. flour | dash nutmeg |
| 1 thin slice onion | 1 sprig parsley |
| 2 Tbls. heavy cream | 2 Tbls. butter |

Combine milk with onion, parsley. Bring to boil. Melt butter. Whisk in flour. Strain hot milk into butter mixture, stirring vigorously with whisk. When thickened and smooth then simmer for five (5) minutes. Stir occasionally. If sauce gets too thick add a little milk. Salt and pepper to taste

## CREAM SAUCE

In the top of a double boiler over low heat melt two (2) Tbls. butter and gradually add two (2) Tbls. flour. Stir roux constantly three (3) to five (5) minutes. Gradually add 1 cup scalded milk until well blended. Season with salt and pepper. Finish sauce over hot water.

## BERCY CREAM SAUCE

Add one (1) cup thick Veloute sauce, (see pages 191 ), to 1/2 cup fish stock. Bring this mixture to a boil. Add two (2) Tbls. butter, a little chopped parsley. Spread this sauce on your fish and proceed to broil the fish

## BOMBAY CREAM SAUCE

Stir 1/2 cup chopped celery, one (1) tsp. minced onion, 1/4 tsp. curry powder into one (1) cup plain yogurt. Salt and pepper to taste.

## CARAWAY CREAM SAUCE

Stir one (1) tsp. caraway seeds, one (1) tsp. Worcestershire sauce, 1/4 tsp. salt into one (1) cup plain yogurt

## CURRIED CREAM SAUCE

To one (1) cup Cream sauce, ( see pages 80-83 ), add two (2) tsp. curry powder mixed with a little milk. Stir constantly until almost to boil. Serve very hot.

## CREAM SAUCE

After roasting small game birds pour off pan juices and cook over reduced heat for about a minute. Add one (1) egg yolk for each bird and one (1) cup of heavy cream. Stir until thickened but do not bring to boil. Season to taste. At serving pour three (3) Tbls. brandy into sauce and flame.

## QUICK CREAM SAUCE

2 Tbls. butter　　　　　　　　1 tsp. lemon juice
2 tsp. shallots, minced　　　　1 1/2 cup cream
2 tsp flour　　　　　　　　　　2 tsp. raspberry jelly

Melt butter, stir in onion and flour. Cook two (2) minutes then add lemon juice. Add cream slowly, stirring until blended and thickened. Season to taste.

REGIMEN IS BETTER THEN PHYSIC. EVERY ONE SHOULD BE HIS OWN PHYSICIAN. WE SHOULD ASSIST, NOT FORCE NATURE. EAT WITH MODERATION WHAT YOU KNOW BY EXPERIENCE AGREES WITH YOUR CONSTITUTION. NOTHING IS GOOD FOR THE BODY BUT WHAT WE CAN DIGEST.

Voltaire

## MEDIUM CREAM SAUCE

2 Tbls. butter　　　　　　　　1/4 tsp. salt
2 Tbls. flour　　　　　　　　　1 cup milk

Melt butter in double boiler top. Add flour, salt. Cook until bubbly. Slowly add milk, stirring briskly. over hot water, until sauce is thick and smooth.

## TARRAGON CREAM SAUCE

| | |
|---|---|
| 3 Tbls. butter | 1 Tbls. fresh tarragon, minced |
| 2 Tbls. flour | 1 Tbls. butter at room temperature |
| 1 cup milk | |

Heat butter in a saucepan. Whisk in flour. Cook slowly stirring constantly until well blended and frothy. Do not let color. Remove from heat. Add milk all at once, stirring vigorously. Increase heat to medium and continue cooking until sauce is thickened and smooth. Remove from heat. Add tarragon, salt, pepper to taste and the remaining butter. Stir until added butter is melted.

## TOO MANY COOKS SPOIL THE BROTH
Balthazar Gerbier
Discourse of Building (1662)

## CREAM SAUCE

After removing veal or chicken from the pan, skim off all fat. Add one (1) cup heavy cream to the pan, bring to a boil and cook until reduced by half. Stir constantly and scrape off all brown bits of meat. Add one (1) cup Bechamel sauce, ( see pages 47-49 ), correct with salt to taste. Strain through a fine sieve. Add a few drops of lemon juice.

## VENISON CREAM SAUCE

When venison is roasted, remove meat from pan and pour off fat. To the drippings in the pan add one (1) cup cream, one (1) Tbls. white wine vinegar. Scrape and stir in all the little bits of brown meat from bottom of pan. Reduce mixture by one third. Add 1/4 cup Cream sauce, (see pages 80-83 ), Season to taste. Strain.

## CREOLE SAUCE

2 cups tomato juice
1 medium cucumber, peeled, diced
1 medium green pepper, diced
3 Tbls. parsley, minced
2 Tbls. onion flakes
1 cup celery, diced

1 garlic clove
1 cup clam juice
1 chicken bouillon cube
tsp. salt
1/2 tsp. pepper

Cook tomato juice in pan until reduced by half. Add remaining ingredients. Bring to boil. Simmer for twenty (20) minutes until vegetables are crisp-tender.

## CREOLE SAUCE

1/2 medium onion, sliced
1/2 medium green pepper, sliced
2 Tbls. butter

1 can condensed tomato soup
1 tsp. vinegar
dash Tabasco

In saucepan cook onion, green pepper in butter until tender. Blend in soup, vinegar, Tabasco, pepper.

## CREOLE SAUCE

2 Tbls. safflower oil
1/2 cup onion, chopped
1 clove garlic, chopped
1/4 cup green pepper, chopped
1 large can tomatoes

1 tsp. celery seed
1 bay leaf
1 tsp. salt
2 tsp. honey

In hot oil, saute onion, garlic, pepper until tender. Add remaining ingredients. Simmer forty-five (45) minutes until sauce is thickened. Stir occasionally. Strain.

## CREOLE SAUCE

In a skillet saute one (1) small onion, one (1) small green pepper, finely diced, in 1/4 cup butter five (5) minutes. Stir often. Add 1/2 cup sliced mushrooms, eighteen (18) green olives, pitted and chopped. Cook for five (5) minutes. Add two (2) cups strained stewed tomatoes, one (1) cup fish stock [ you may also use beef or chicken stock]. Add one (1) small bay leaf, one (1) crushed garlic clove, a touch of cayenne, a pinch of thyme, salt and pepper to taste. Simmer twenty (20) minutes. Add Tbls. Sherry wine.

## au CRESSON SAUCE

Rub a handful of water cress through a fine sieve. Add to 3/4 cup mayonnaise mixed with two (2) Tbls. chili sauce. Taste for seasoning. Chill.

## CUCUMBER SAUCE

| | |
|---|---|
| 2 medium cucumbers, peeled, seeded, chopped | 1 1/2 tsp grated lemon peel |
| 1 cup water | 1 tsp. lemon juice |
| 2 1/2 Tbls. butter | 2 egg yolks |
| 2 1/2 Tbls flour | chopped parsley |
| | tsp. salt |

In saucepan simmer cucumbers in water until tender-crisp. Drain. Add water to liquid to make 1 3/4 cups. Set aside. In same saucepan melt butter over medium heat. Add flour. Stir until smooth. Slowly add reserved liquor, stirring constantly, until sauce is thickened. Add salt, lemon peel, juice and cooked cucumber. Cook until just boiling. In a separate bowl beat egg yolks slightly. Stir in some of the hot liquid, slowly add mixture to pan and cook, stirring constantly until sauce is thickened.

## CUCUMBER SAUCE

3 Tbls. non-fat dry milk　　　　　　2 Tbls. vinegar
1 medium cucumber, peeled, chopped　1/4 tsp. salt
pinch cayenne

Combine ingredients. Let stand 1/2 hour before serving.


## CUCUMBER SAUCE

1 Large cucumber　　　　　　1/3 tsp. salt
3/4 cup heavy cream　　　　　1/8 tsp. paprika
2 Tbls. lemon juice

Peel, seed, chop cucumber. Whip cream until stiff, slowly add lemon juice. Season with salt and paprika. Add cucumber. Serve cold.


## CUCUMBER SAUCE

2 Tbls. Mayonnaise　　　　　　　8 tsp. salt
2 Tbls. sour cream　　　　　　　1 tsp. lemon juice
1/4 cup peeled, seeded, minced　　cucumber pepper

Combine all ingredients. Chill.


## CUCUMBER SAUCE

1 cup sour cream　　　　　　　　　　　Tbls. chopped dill
1/2 cup peeled, seeded, grated cucumber　2 Tbls. chopped chives
1/2 tsp. salt　　　　　　　　　　　　　1/2 tsp. pepper

Blend all ingredients. Chill couple of hours before serve.

## CUCUMBER SAUCE

| | |
|---|---|
| 3 Tbls. butter | 1 cup milk |
| 3 Tbls. flour | 1/4 cream |
| 1/4 cup clam juice | 1/4 cup cucumber, chopped |

Melt butter. Add flour. Cook, stirring for three (3) minutes. Do not let flour brown. Bring clam juice, milk to a boil. Add butter-flour mixture, whisking vigorously until thick and smooth. Cook over low heat for ten (10) minutes. Just before serving add cream and cucumber, stirring in.

## CUCUMBER CREAM SAUCE

Add 1/2 cup grated cucumber to one (1) cup Bechamel sauce, ( see pages 47-49 ), dash of cayenne. Simmer gently ten (10) minutes

## CUCUMBER CREAM SAUCE

Blend two (2) Tbls. each mayonnaise and lemon juice into one (1) cup plain yogurt. Add one (1) Tbls. honey, 1/2 tsp. onion salt, a few drops of red pepper seasoning. Fine chop one (1) medium sized peeled, seeded cucumber. Stir in.

## CREAMY CUCUMBER SAUCE

| | |
|---|---|
| 1 medium cucumber, peeled, seeded. | 1 tsp. grated onion |
| 1 cup sour cream | 1/4 tsp. salt |

Shred cucumber. Pat dry. Mix cucumber and other ingredients until well blended. Chill.

## CUCUMBER DILL SAUCE

8 ounces sour cream
1 medium cucumber, peeled, chopped
1 tsp. dill weed

1 tsp. sugar
3/4 tsp. salt
1/8 tsp. pepper

Mix all well. Chill

## CUCUMBER DILL SAUCE

1 large cucumber, grated
1 cup plain yogurt
1/2 tsp. dill salt

1 Tbls. lemon juice
1/2 tsp. prepared mustard

Combine. Chill.

## CUCUMBER SAUCE

1 cup cucumber, peeled, chopped
1/2 salt
1 Tbls. sugar

1 Tbls. cider vinegar
1/8 tsp. white pepper
1/2 cup cream, whipped

Combine cucumbers with salt. Refrigerate one (1) hour. Drain. Add sugar, cider vinegar, pepper. Just before serving fold in whipped cream.

## HERBED CUCUMBER SAUCE

2 cucumbers chopped coarse
1 onion, sliced thin
1/4 tsp. celery seeds
1 tsp. mint
1 Tbls. dill weed salt

1 Tbls. parsely, minced
1 tsp. dulce
1 tsp. lemon juice
1/4 cup plain yogurt

Blend. Chill.

## SOUR CREAM CUCUMBER SAUCE

1 cup sour cream
1 Tbls. white vinegar
1 1/2 Tbls. lemon juice
1/2 tsp sugar

1 tsp. sugar
pepper
1/2 onion grated fine
1 cucumber, peeled, seeded, diced

Blend. Chill

## CUMBERLAND SAUCE

1 cup currant jelly
1 Tbls. hot water
1/4 tsp. grated orange rind

1 tsp. dry mustard
1 Tbls. orange juice

Heat jelly to simmering. Add hot water and whisk until well combined. Remove from heat. Dissolve mustard in a little water, stir to a smooth paste, add to mixture. Add orange juice, rind. Serve slightly warm.

**ANIMALS FEED; MAN EATS. ONLY THE MAN OF INTELLECT AND JUDGMENT KNOWS HOW TO EAT.**
Savarin

## CUMBERLAND SAUCE

1/2 cup currant jelly
1 grated lemon rind and juice
1 grated orange rind

1 Tbls. confectioners' sugar
1 tsp. prepared mustard
2 Tbls. Port wine

Melt jelly. Stir in all other ingredients and heat through.

90 EDWARD A. MEANY

## CUMBERLANDSAUCE

Parboil three (3) chopped shallots. Drain. Cut meat of one (1) orange, one (1) lemon in fine strips, parboil five (5) minutes in just enough water to cover. Drain. Mix fruit and shallots. Add orange juice and 1/2 lemon juice. Add pinch each ground ginger, cayenne. Add six (6) Tbls. melted red currant jelly mixed with five (5) Tbls. Port wine. Combine thoroughly. Add 1/2 tsp. prepared mustard. Blend.

## EAST CUMBERLAND SAUCE

Heat one (1) cup currant jelly. Add 2 Tbls. horse radish sauce, juice of 1/2 lemon, 1/2 tsp. dry mustard, two (2) Tbls. grated orange peel. Heat. Serve.

## CUMBERLAND GLAZE

1/4 cup currant jelly          1 tsp. grated orange peel
1/2 tsp. Dijon mustard         1/8 tsp. ground ginger
1/8 tsp. allspice

Melt currant jelly. Blend in remaining ingredients. Use to glaze chicken

## CURRY SAUCE

1 Tbls. butter                 Can of cream of celery soup
1 Tbls. onion                  1/3 tsp. curry powder

Melt butter. Saute onion until golden brown. Blend in soup. Add curry powder. Heat thoroughly. Serve at once.

## CURRY SAUCE

| | |
|---|---|
| 1 medium onion, chopped | 1/2 cup butter |
| 1 clove garlic | 1/4 pound ham, chopped |
| 1 stalk celery, diced | 2 Tbls. flour |
| 1 small bay leaf | 1/2 tsp. mace |
| sprig parsley | 1 1/4 tsp. curry powder |
| 1/4 tsp. powdered mustard | 1 1/4 tsp. chicken broth |
| 1 tart apple, peeled, diced | |

For eight (8) minutes cook together onion, garlic, celery, bay leaf, parsley, mustard, apple butter, ham. Stir occasionally. Add flour, mace, curry powder and cook about five (5) minutes longer. Add broth. Simmer one (1) hour. Strain. Rub solids through fine sieve.

## CURRY SAUCE FOR FISH

Melt one (1) Tbls. butter. Saute one (1) onion, chopped until soft, not browned. Add small bay leaf, a pinch of thyme, one (1) Tbls. curry powder. Mix well. Add 1/4 cup fish stock. Bring mixture to a boil. Add 1/2 cup Veloute sauce, (see pages 191 ), made with fish stock. Boil ten (10) to fifteen (15) minutes. Strain through fine sieve. Add 1/2 cup cream.

## CREAM CURRY SAUCE

Blend one (1) cup sour cream in one (1) tsp. curry powder. Season with salt and pepper to taste.

## CURRY SAUCE

5 Tbls. butter 1
1 medium onion, diced
1 red bell pepper, diced
2 cloves garlic, minced
dash cayenne pepper
1 1/2 Tbls. turmeric
1 1/2 Tbls. ground ginger salt
1 1/2 Tbls. ground coriander

1/2 tsp. cinnamon
3 Tbls. flour
1 1/2 cups chicken stock
1/2 tsp. sugar
1/2 Tbls. lemon juice
1/2 cup coconut milk

Heat two (2) Tbls. butter in saucepan. Add chopped onion, diced bell pepper, garlic, dash of cayenne. Saute these until tender. Stir often. Add turmeric, ginger, coriander, cinnamon. Mix well. Add remaining butter. Stir until melted. Mix in flour. Blend well. Cook for about two (2) or three (3) minutes. Add chicken stock. Cook and stir until thickened and smooth. Add lemon juice, salt and pepper to taste. Stir in coconut milk and heat all for a few minutes. Strain through fine sieve. Correct seasoning. Serve warm.

## CURRY SAUCE

2/3 cup grated coconut
1 cup milk
1 apple. cored but not peeled
2 tomatoes, peeled, seeded

4 Tbls. butter
2 Tbls. curry powder
1 cup white wine
salt

Put coconut to soak in milk. Chop onions, tomatoes, apple. Melt butter in a skillet and cook onion until soft. Add apple, tomatoes, curry powder. Cook slowly until vegetables are tender. Add wine. Simmer fifteen (15 ) minutes. Add coconut milk. Simmer another fifteen (15) minutes. Strain through sieve. Return to heat and cook for a few minutes until sauce is well blended and thickened. Season to taste.

## FRENCH CURRY SAUCE

2 cups Veloute sauce ( see pages 191 )          1/2 cup cream
curry to taste

Combine Veloute with cream and as much curry as you like. Heat.
Blend.

## DAIKON SAUCE

1/3 cup soy sauce                    1 cup grated daikon
1 cup chicken broth                  1 tsp. sugar
dash lemon juice

Combine all in a saucepan and simmer for fifteen (15 ) minutes.

## FISHERMAN'S DEVIL SAUCE

Melt 1/2 cup butter. Do not brown it. Add 1/2 cup ketchup, one (1)
Tbls. each Worcestershire sauce, grated onion, one (1) tsp each
prepared mustard, chopped parsley, chives, tarragon, one (1) small
garlic clove—grated—a good pinch of thyme. Bring slowly to boil.
Remove from heat. Cool. Season to taste. Dash Tabasco. Serve very
cold.

## DEVILED SAUCE

Place 1/2 cup wine vinegar, 1/2 tsp. black pepper, five (5) red pepper
seeds, in saucepan. Simmer until vinegar is reduced to half. Add
one (1) cup chicken bouillon, one (1) tsp. tomato paste. Continue
simmer ten (10) minutes. Blend in one (1) Tbls. butter. one (1) Tbls.
flour, little by little. Stir. Heat well but do not boil.

## DIABLE SAUCE

Three (3) shallots, chopped, eight (8) crushed peppercorns, 1/3 cup dry white wine cooked until reduced to a thick paste. Add one (1) cup Brown sauce, (see pages 55-58 ), one (1) tsp. Worcestershire sauce, 1/2 tsp. chopped parsley. Blend.

## DIABLE SAUCE

| | |
|---|---|
| 6 shallots, minced | 1 tsp. salt |
| 1 clove garlic, minced | cayenne pepper |
| 3 Tbls. butter juice of | 1/2 lemon |
| 2 Tbls. Dijon mustard | 1/2 tsp. Tabasco |
| 1/2 cup fish broth | 1 tsp. fresh ground black pepper |
| 1/2 cup white wine | 2 Tbls. tomato paste |

Saute shallots, onion, garlic in butter. Add mustard. Slowly add broth and wine. Blend well. Season to taste.

## DIANE SAUCE

Fold into 1 1/4 cups hot Poivrade sauce, (see page 151-152 ), one (1) cup whipped cream, one (1) Tbls. chopped truffles, one (1) Tbls. hard boiled egg, chopped.

## DUVAL SAUCE

Combine six (6) egg yolks, unbeaten, one (1) cup chilled beef stock, one (1) Tbls. chopped shallots, 1/4 tsp. meat extract, pinch each powdered bay leaf, thyme, nutmeg. Blend thoroughly. Cook, stirring constantly, until sauce has consistency of thick cream. Remove from heat. Stir in two (2) Tbls. melted butter, one (1) tsp. tarragon vinegar. Season to taste with salt and pepper. Add 3/4 cup tartar sauce. Serve cold.

## EGG SAUCE

Add two (2) chopped hard boiled eggs, one (1) tsp. chopped parsley to one (1) cup medium Bechamel sauce, (see pages 47-49 ).

## EGG SAUCE FOR FISH

Add two (2) Tbls. butter in small bits, while stirring, into 1 1/2 cups fish Veloute sauce, (see pages 191 ), one (1) tsp. lemon juice, two (2) chopped hard boiled eggs. Serve hot.

## EGG SAUCE PARISIAN FOR FISH

Combine two (2) egg yolks, two (2) tsp. tarragon vinegar. Heat two (2) Tbls. olive oil in top of double boiler over hot but not boiling water. Briskly stir in mixture. Cook, stirring constantly, until consistency of thick cream. Season with salt, pepper, nutmeg. Remove from heat. Stir in one (1) hard boiled egg, chopped, one (1) tsp chopped chervil. Fold in stiffly beaten whites of two (2) eggs. Serve warm.

## ESPAGNOLE SAUCE

| | |
|---|---|
| 2 1/2 quarts strained beef stock | 1/2 onion |
| 1/4 cup butter | 1 sprig thyme |
| 1/4 cup flour | 1 bay leaf |
| 1 thick slice bacon | 1/4 cup white wine |
| 1/2 carrot | 1 cup tomato paste |

Reduce two (2) quarts beef stock to one half. Skim as needed. Heat butter. Sprinkle flour in. Stir until flour browns. Add reduced beef stock. Stir until smooth. Simmer ten (10 ) to fifteen (15) minutes. Stir occasionally. Cook bacon until brown. Mince carrot, onion. Simmer them in bacon fat until soft and brown. Add thyme, bay leaf. Pour off excess fat. Over very low heat pour wine over mixture in skillet, blend thoroughly. Mash carrot and onion pieces. Cook ten (10) minutes. Add beef stock in small amounts. Simmer one (1) hour. Add remaining beef stock. Simmer another hour and a half. Stir occasionally. Strain. Refrigerate until all fat rises. Skim and discard fat. Return liquid to heat to simmer. Add tomato puree. Simmer one half hour. Strain. Sauce should be like a thick creamed soup.

## EXTINGUISHER SAUCE

6 Tbls. plain yogurt  
1 medium cucumber,  
    peeled, seeded, diced  
1/2 tsp sugar

1 Tbls. minced fresh mint  
1 tsp. fresh lemon juice

fresh ground pepper

Mix yogurt, cucumber, mint, lemon juice, sugar and pepper. Refrigerate for at least two (2) hours.

## FLEMISH OLIVE SAUCE

Melt without browning 1/4 cup butter. Stir in two (2) Tbls. each chopped parsley, chopped onions, one (1) Tbls. chopped green pepper. Stir constantly. Sprinkle 1 1/2 Tbls. flour. When mixture is well blended but not browned, gradually stir in one (1) cup dry white wine. Stir constantly. When boils and is smooth add a bit of anchovy paste the size of a pea. Add 1/2 cup chopped green olives. Season to taste with salt, pepper, nutmeg. Serve hot.

## FLEMISH SAUCE FOR POACHED FISH

1/4 cup butter  
2 tsp. Dijon mustard  
juice of a lemon  
4 egg yolks

1/4 tsp. nutmeg  
2 tsp. chopped parsley  
1 tsp. chopped chives

Combine butter, mustard, lemon juice, seasonings, herbs in saucepan. Place in a double boiler top. Whisk until butter has melted. Beat egg yolks until thick. Stir egg yolks into mixture.

Continue whisking vigorously over barely simmering water until sauce is thick. Serve at once.


## FLORENTINE SAUCE

1 cup basic bread sauce, (see pages 54 )       Worcestershire sauce
1/2 cup chopped, cooked spinach               grated nutmeg
marjoram                                      lemon juice

Add spinach to sauce. Season with nutmeg, Worcestershire sauce, lemon juice. Cook eight (8) to ten (10) minutes. Add pinch of marjoram.


## SAINT FLORENTINE SAUCE

Chop the bones of several game birds into small pieces and put them into a soup kettle. Add two (2) cups Espagnole sauce, (see page 62 ), 1/3 cup sherry wine, one (1) Tbls, walnut chutney, one (1) onion sliced thin, a carrot and a small turnip, both chopped, one (1) leek, one (1) slice garlic, eight (8) peppercorns, a bouquet garni and a pinch of salt and nutmeg. Bring this mixture to a boil. Add two (2) cups chicken stock. Simmer over very low heat 1 1/2 to 2 hours until there is very little liquid left. Discard garni bouquet, bones and other solids. Rub remainder of mixture through a sieve. Add enough chicken stock—fat free—to make mixture consistency of a medium cream sauce. Bring to a boil. Correct seasoning. Add two (2) Tbls. mango rubbed through a fine sieve. Serve hot, one (1) portion of this sauce mixed with one (1) portion Espagnole sauce.


## FRENCH QUARTER SAUCE

12 Tbls. cider vinegar          1 garlic clove, mince
6 Tbls. olive oil               6 anchovy fillets, mashed
3 Tbls. prepared mustard        1/2 tsp. salt
1 Tbls. chives, chopped         1 Tbls. chopped parsley
1 hard boiled egg

Combine all ingredients. Mix well. Chill thoroughly.

## GARLICSAUCE

Cook two (2) cloves chopped garlic in 2/3 cup olive oil. Do not burn.

## GENEVOISE SAUCE

Combine one (1) Tbls. butter with one (1) each diced carrot, diced onion, three (3) sprigs parsley, a bay leaf, a pinch of thyme. Cook slowly fifteen (15) to twenty (20) minutes. Shake pan to prevent burning. Mix in the head, trimmings and bones of whatever fish you are serving. Cook five (5) minutes. Add two (2) cups red wine. Cook mixture until wine is reduced one fourth (1/4th). Add one (1) cup Brown sauce, (see pages 58-58 ). Cook gently thirty (30) minutes. Strain. Season to taste. Finish off with two (2) Tbls. butter.

## ONE MEAL A DAY IS ENOUGH FOR A LION, AND IT OUGHT TO BE FOR A MAN.
G. Fordyce

## GRAND VENEUR SAUCE

Bring to a boil two (2) cups Poivrade sauce, ( see page 151-152 ). Add two (2) Tbls. truffles, julienned. Thicken with the blood of the rabbit or hare you are preparing, swirling it in slowly off the heat. Serve at once.

## A L'AMERICAINE GRAPE SAUCE

Melt two (2) Tbls. butter mixed with 1 1/2 tsp. lemon juice, blend in two (2) Tbls. flour. Gradually add one (1) cup chicken stock, stirring. Cook, stirring often, until sauce begins to thicken. Remove from heat. Beat in two (2) egg yolks, one (1) at a time, beating vigorously after each addition. Season to taste, salt, pepper, cayenne. Add 1/2 cup halved, seedless grapes.

## WILD GRAPE SAUCE

| | |
|---|---|
| 4 cups wild grapes | 3 cloves |
| 4 Tbls. butter | 1 Tbls. lemon juice |
| 1/4 cup Sherry wine | 1 Tbls. grated lemon rind |

Cover grapes with boiling water. Simmer five (5) minutes. Drain. Put through sieve. Melt butter. Add Sherry wine, cloves, lemon juice. Simmer five (5) minutes. Remove cloves. Add grape puree, lemon rind. Heat to serve.

## GREEN GODDESS SAUCE

| | |
|---|---|
| 1 cup mayonnaise | 1 Tbls. lemon juice |
| 1 minced garlic clove | 1 Tbls. tarragon vinegar |
| 3 anchovies, chopped | 1/2 tsp. salt |
| 1/4 cup chives, chopped | 1/2 cup sour cream |
| 1/4 cup parsley, chopped | fresh ground black pepper |

Blend ingredients except sour cream. Fold in sour cream. Serve chilled.

## GRIBICHE SAUCE

| | |
|---|---|
| 1 hard boiled egg | 1 tsp. chopped capers |
| 1/4 cup mayonnaise | 1 tsp. parsley, minced |
| 1 tsp. sweet pickle relish | 1/4 tsp. tarragon |

Mash egg yolk. Blend in mayonnaise. Add remaining ingredients except egg white. Add chopped egg white.

## GRIBICHE SAUCE

Separate three (3) hard boiled eggs. Crush yolks until they are smooth. Add one (1) tsp. mustard, 1/2 tsp. salt, a pinch of black pepper. Add 1 1/2 cups olive oil a little at a time, stirring vigorously after each addition. Gradually add 1/2 cup vinegar. Chop egg whites. Chop 1/2 cup sour pickles pressing out moisture. Chop one (1) Tbls. each parsley, chervil, tarragon, chives. Add egg whites, pickles, herbs. Mix well.

## HERB SAUCES

### BASIL SAUCE

Mince together a handful each of parsley, freed of stems, basil, one (1) garlic clove. Add six (6) Tbls. olive oil to make a thick, smooth paste.

### PESTO—BASIL SAUCE

1/2 cup basil leaves, minced
1 Tbls. olive oil
1/2 clove garlic
1 tsp. parsley, minced

1 ounce Pecorino cheese
fresh pepper
salt

Combine ingredients. Let stand one (1) hour before serving.

### DILL SAUCE

Add a tsp. chopped fresh dill to one (1) cup Bechamel sauce, (see pages 47-49 ). Season to taste with salt, pepper, nutmeg. Add two (2) tsp. lemon juice, 1/4 cup Rhine wine, pinch of sugar.

### FENNEL ROCHELOISE SAUCE

Simmer two (2) mackerel roe gently in three (3) Tbls. water for ten (10) minutes. Drain. Mash roe to a paste. During mashing, add two

(2) egg yolks that have been well beaten. Season with salt, cayenne, a pinch of thyme. Mix well. Add one (1) tsp. chopped fennel leaves. Stir into one (1) cup hot cream sauce, (see pages 80-83 ). Heat sauce over double boiler, stirring, until comes to a boil.

## PARSLEY SAUCE

| | |
|---|---|
| 2 Tbls. butter | 3/4 tsp. salt |
| 2 Tbls. flour | 1/8 tsp. black pepper |
| 1 cup chicken stock | 2 egg yolks |
| 1/2 cup light cream | 3/4 Tbls. chopped parsley |

Melt butter. Remove from heat and blend in flour. Stir in chicken stock and 1/4 cup of the cream. Return to heat. Cook. Stir constantly over medium heat until mixture begins to thicken— five (5) minutes. Salt and pepper to taste. Beat egg yolks in remaining cream. Stir into sauce. Cook over very low heat two (2) minutes. Add parsley just before serving.

## ENGLISH PARSLEY SAUCE

Melt two (2) Tbls. butter. Add two (2) Tbls. flour. Blend until roux bubbles. Do not brown. Gradually add one (1) cup chicken stock that has been mixed with 1/2 cup scalded milk. Stir constantly. Cook gently until mixture thickens. Stir often. Season to taste with salt, pepper. Add 1/4 cup chopped parsley, two (2) well beaten egg yolks just before serving.

## ROSEMARY SAUCE

Steep one (1) tsp. dry rosemary in 1/4 cup boiling red wine four (4) to five (5) minutes. Strain into two (2) cups boiling Grand Veneur sauce, (see page 98 ).

## FRESH HERB SAUCE FOR RAW SEAFOOD

2 Tbls. minced green onions        3 Tbls. safflower oil
2 Tbls. minced parsley             3 Tbls. lemon juice
1 Tbls. chopped chives             1/2 tsp. salt
1 Tbls. chopped chervil            1/2 tsp. Worcestershire sauce
touch Tabasco

Mix all ingredients well. Chill.


## AUX FINES HERBES A L'AMERICAINE SAUCE

Saute one (1) Tbls. chopped onion in one (1) tsp. butter until onion colors, stirring constantly. Add one (1) tsp. flour. Blend. Gradually add 3/4 cup vegetable stock. Stir constantly until sauce thickens. Cook three (3) to four (4) minutes. Add one (1) tsp. each chives, chervil, tarragon, basil, minced. After a few minutes add one (1) Tbls. shallot butter.


## AUX FINES HERBS SAUCE

Reserve the leaves and add chopped stems of three (3) sprigs each tarragon, chervil, parsley, and one (1) tsp. chopped chives to 1/3 cup boiling dry white wine. Let mixture steep ten (10) minutes. Strain. Melt one (1) Tbls. butter and add one (1) tsp. chopped shallots. Add to herb mixture. Cook until reduced by one half. Add one (1) cup Brown sauce, ( see pages 55-58 ). Cook ten (10) to fifteen (15) minutes longer. Add juice of a lemon, one (1) Tbls. butter. Blend by swirling pan. Add chopped tarragon, chervil leaves.


## HOLLANDAISE SAUCE

Divide 1/2 cup butter into three (3) parts. In top of double boiler place four (4) egg yolks and one (1) part of the butter. Stir mixture rapidly over hot, not boiling, water until butter is melted. Add second part of butter. As mixture thickens add third part of butter, stirring constantly. Do not allow water in bottom of double boiler to boil. When butter is all melted and well mixed remove from heat and continue to beat sauce two (2) minutes. Add two (2) tsp. lemon juice, pinch of salt, white pepper. Replace over hot but not boiling water and beat vigorously two (2) minutes. Should mixture curdle, immediately beat in one (1) or two (2) Tbls. boiling water, vigorously beating constantly.

## HOLLANDAISE SAUCE

| | |
|---|---|
| 1/2 cup butter | 1 1/2 Tbls. lemon juice |
| 2 egg yolks | 1/2 cup boiling water |
| cayenne pepper | salt |

Divide butter into three (3) pieces. Beat egg yolks slightly, add lemon juice and 1/3 of the butter. Cook over boiling water, stirring constantly, until butter is melted. Add another 1/3 of the butter. Stir constantly until sauce thickens Slowly add water, salt, cayenne, stirring constantly. If mixture curdles add two (2) Tbls. boiling water.

## HOLLANDAISE SAUCE

| | |
|---|---|
| 6 egg yolks | 1 cup butter |
| 1/4 cup lemon juice | |

In top of double boiler over hot, not boiling water, combine egg yolks, lemon juice. Whisk in three (3) Tbls. butter until completely melted. Add remaining butter two (2) Tbls. at a time, whisking constantly. until sauce is smooth and thick. Touch of salt.

## HOLLANDAISE SAUCE

Mix two (2) egg yolks with one (1) Tbls. cream, two (2) Tbls. tarragon vinegar, dash of salt, cayenne pepper. Place container over deep pan of warm water. Do not allow container to touch water. Stir constantly over low heat until yolks begin to thicken. Add remaining butter two (2) Tbls. at a time, whisking constantly until sauce is thick and smooth.

## HOLLANDAISE SAUCE

| | |
|---|---|
| 1 egg yolk | 2 tsp. water |
| 2 tsp. lemon juice | 1/4 cup butter |

Blend egg yolk, lemon juice, water, salt. Add two (2) pieces of butter. Over very low heat whisk mixture constantly. Do not over cook. Raise pan from heat if need to slow cooking. After first pieces of butter are blended add remaining butter a piece at a time, constantly stirring. When thickened and smooth add more lemon juice and salt to taste. Serve at once.

**IN GENERAL, MANKIND, SINCE THE IMPROVEMENT OF COOKERY, EAT TWICE AS MUCH AS NATURE REQUIRES.**

Benjamin Franklin

## HOLLANDAISE SAUCE

| | |
|---|---|
| 4 egg yolks | 1/2 pound butter |
| 1/2 tsp. salt | 2 1/2 Tbls. lemon juice |
| cayenne | 1/2 Tbls. white wine vinegar |

Place egg yolks, salt, cayenne in blender. Melt butter—do not brown. Add lemon juice and vinegar to the eggs in the blender. Turn on at low speed, five (5) seconds. Begin to pour in the melted butter, in a steady stream. The minute the sauce thickens turn off the blender.

## HOLLANDAISE SAUCE

| | |
|---|---|
| 1/2 cup butter | 2 Tbls. lemon juice |
| 1/4 cup hot water | 1/4 tsp. salt |
| 4 egg yolks cayenne | |

Melt butter in top of double boiler over simmering water. Stir in hot water. Remove from heat. Add unbeaten egg yolks all at once. Beat with electric beater two (2) to three (3) minutes until mixture is double in bulk. Stir in lemon juice, salt, cayenne. Replace over simmering water, stirring constantly. Do not let bottom of pan touch water beneath. Remove from heat. Stir until thick and fluffy smooth.

## HOLLANDAISE SAUCE

| | |
|---|---|
| 1/4 cup white wine vinegar | 1 Tbls. lemon juice |
| 5 egg yolks salt, pepper | |
| 1/2 pound butter | |

Over medium heat simmer the vinegar with 1/4 cup cold water until reduced 2/3rds. Transfer to top of double boiler. Beat in egg yolks, one (1) at a time, beating thoroughly between each addition to keep mixture creamy and smooth. Then begin beating in butter vigorously, a little at a time. When mixture is creamy add lemon juice, salt and pepper to taste.

## HOLLANDAISE SAUCE

| | |
|---|---|
| 3 egg yolks | 1/3 cup butter |
| 2 Tbls. lemon juice | 1/2 tsp. salt |

Add egg yolk and lemon juice in double boiler top. Whisk until well blended. Place top over bottom pan containing hot, not boiling, water. Add one third (1/3rd) butter. Cook, beating constantly until butter melted. Add another third (1/3rd). Add remaining third (1/3rd) until sauce thickens. Salt to taste.

## HOLLANDAISE SAUCE

4 egg yolks                     1/2 tsp. salt
1 cup unsalted butter, in small pieces    1/4 tsp. white pepper
juice of a lemon

Lightly whisk egg yolks. Place over very low heat and whisk until mixture thickens and becomes nice and creamy. Remove from heat occasionally even as you beat to prevent scrambling. Remove from heat and whisk in butter, a small piece at a time. Blend completely before adding more pieces. Sauce is done when consistency of light mayonnaise. Stir in salt, pepper, lemon juice.

## EASY HOLLANDAISE SAUCE

Cream 1/2 cup butter. Gradually beat in three (3) egg yolks, 1 1/2 Tbls. lemon juice, 1/2 tsp. salt, dash paprika, touch of cayenne. Blend well. Slowly stir in 1/4 cup boiling water. Place in top of double boiler. Cook five (5) minutes. Do not let bottom of top touch water in bottom of double boiler. Remove from heat and beat for a minute.

## HOLLANDAISE SAUCE

3 egg yolks                  1/4 tsp. salt
1 Tbls. cold water         1 Tbls. lemon juice
1/2 cup softened butter

Combine egg yolks and water in top of double boiler and whisk vigorously over hot, not boiling, water until fluffy. Add a few spoonfuls of butter and whisk continuously until melted and starts to thicken. Slowly add all butter in same manner. Remove from heat. Add salt and lemon juice.

## HOLLANDAISE SAUCE

1/3 cup water juice of      1/3 lemon
1/2 pound sweet butter      3 egg yolks
cold salted water      salt, pepper

In a saucepan mix water, lemon juice, 1/4 tsp. salt, pepper to taste. Cook over medium heat until about two (2) Tbls. of liquid is remaining. Melt butter. Keep luke warm. Remove saucepan from heat. Add egg yolks, one (1) at a time, whisking very fast and vigorously. Continue until form a heavy foam. Gradually add butter, piece by piece. When thickened. Serve.

## HOLLANDAISE SAUCE

3 egg yolks      salt, cayenne pepper
1-2 tsp. water      tarragon vinegar
1/2 cup butter in small pieces

Combine egg yolk and water in top of double boiler and whisk over hot water until eggs are well blended and slightly thickened. Gradually add butter whisking vigorously all the time. Be sure water does not boil under sauce. When all blended and smooth add lemon tarragon vinegar and salt to taste.

## HOLLANDAISE SAUCE

3 egg yolks      1/4 tsp. salt
1 Tbls. cold water      1/2 tsp. lemon juice
1/2 cup softened butter

In top of double boiler combine egg yolks and water, whisking, over hot, not boiling water, until fluffy. Add butter a piece at a time, beating continually until all butter is melted and sauce is thickened. Salt and lemon juice added last.

## ELECTRIC BLENDER HOLLANDAISE SAUCE

3 egg yolks                    1 stick butter, bubbling hot.
2 Tbls. lemon juice            1/4 tsp. salt
pinch white pepper.

Place egg yolks, lemon juice, salt, pepper in blender. Blend at high speed thirty (30) seconds. Uncover and, while still at high speed, pour in hot butter by droplets. When two thirds (2/3rds) of the butter is in, sauce should be thick and you can add balance of butter more quickly.

## MOCK HOLLANDAISE SAUCE

2 Tbls. margarine              1 Tbls. lemon juice
1 Tbls. mayonnaise             1/4 tsp. salt
1/4 tsp. paprika

Heat margarine in a small sauce pan set in hot water. When melted, stir in mayonnaise, lemon juice, salt, paprika. Stir vigorously. Serve immediately.

## NEVER FAIL HOLLANDAISE SAUCE

1/ 4 pound butter              1/2 tsp. salt
2 egg yolks                    1 1/2 Tbls. lemon juice
dash cayenne

Melt butter. Whip eggs until thick. Add salt, cayenne, three (3) Tbls. melted butter. Whisk until well mixed and stiff. Continue beating while adding lemon juice and the rest of the melted butter, a little of each alternately, until all added. Heat in top of double boiler over hot, not boiling water, stirring constantly. Serve at once.

## QUICK HOLLANDAISE SAUCE

Heat 1/2 cup butter to bubbling. Do not let brown. In blender put three (3) egg yolks, two (2) tbls. lemon juice, 1/4 tsp. salt, pinch cayenne. At low speed add hot butter gradually. Blend fifteen (15) seconds.

## QUICK HOLLANDAISE SAUCE

| | |
|---|---|
| 1/2 cup butter | 3 egg yolks |
| 1/4 tsp. salt | lemon juice to taste |
| cayenne | |

Heat butter to bubbling in saucepan. In blender put egg yolks, lemon juice, salt, pinch cayenne. At low speed pour in hot butter in a steady stream. When all butter added, turn off.

## QUICK HOLLANDAISE SAUCE

| | |
|---|---|
| 3 egg yolks | dash tabasco |
| 2 Tbls. lemon juice | 1/2 cup sweet butter, melted |
| 1/2 tsp. salt | |

Combine egg yolks, lemon juice, salt, tabasco sauce in blender until eggs are foamy—five (5) seconds. Heat butter until it sizzles but do not brown. Remove cap of blender and, with blender running, pour in butter in a thin, steady stream. Sauce will thicken quickly. Season to taste.

**A WELL-GOVERNED APPETITE IS A GREAT
PART OF LIBERTY.**

Seneca

## HONGROIS SAUCE

1/4 cup chicken broth
3/4 cup Bordelaise sauce, (see pages 51-53 )
1/4 tsp. paprika

Simmer the broth and Bordelaise together five (5) minutes. Add paprika

## HORSERADISH SAUCE

Bring 1/4 cup freshly grated horseradish to a boil in one (1) cup strained fish stock. Simmer gently over low heat twenty (20) minutes. Add 1/2 cup drawn butter sauce, ( see page 62 ), one (1) cup bread crumbs, one (1) Tbls. cream. Bring to boil. Remove from heat. Season with salt and pepper to taste. Add, a little at a time, two (2) egg yolks that have been beaten with a little cream.

## HORSERADISH SAUCE

1/4 cup horseradish, drained      1/4 tsp. prepared mustard
1 Tbls. white vinegar      1/2 cup whipped cream
1 tsp. sugar      1/2 tsp. salt

Mix all ingredients except whipped cream. After blending fold in whipped cream.

## HORSERADISH SAUCE

3 Tbls. butter      1 1/2 cups boiling beef stock
3 Tbls. flour      horseradish to taste

Melt butter in saucepan, add flour, whisk until blended. Add boiling liquid all at once. Stir vigorously until mixture is thick and smooth. Add horseradish to taste.

## HORSERADISH SAUCE

1/3 cup mayonnaise                      1 Tbls. milk
1/4 cup dill pickles, minced            1/8 tsp. pepper
2 Tbls. horseradish

Combine mayonnaise, dill pickles, horseradish. Add milk, pepper. Blend well.

## HORSERADISH SAUCE

1/2 cup grated fresh horseradish                      juice of 1/2 lemon
1 cup Bechamel sauce ( see pages 47-49 )

Add horseradish to Bechamel sauce. Blend well. Add lemon juice.

## HORSERADISH SAUCE

3 Tbls. butter                      1 1/2 cups beef bouillon
3 Tbls. flour                       horseradish

Melt butter. Add flour and whisk until blended. Add boiling liquid all at once, whisking vigorously, until sauce is smooth and thick. Season with horseradish to taste.

## APPLE HORSERADISH SAUCE

2 cups applesauce                   1/2 tsp. salt
1/4 cup prepared horseradish        1/8 tsp. pepper
1/8 tsp. basil

Combine ingredients.

## HORSERADISH SAUCE

1/4 cup grated fresh horseradish          1/4 tsp. salt
1 Tbls. lemon juice                        cayenne pepper
1 tsp. wine vinegar                        1/2 cup heavy cream

Remove any excess liquid from horseradish. Mix horseradish, lemon juice, wine vinegar, salt, dash cayenne pepper. Chill. Fold in whipped cream just before serving.

## A LA DRESDEN HORSERADISH SAUCE

1/2 cup fresh grated horseradish          1 cup heavy cream
2 tsp. sugar                               salt, pepper

Mix all ingredients. Chill.

## HORSERADISH CREAM SAUCE

Stir into one (1) cup plain yogurt, one (1) Tbls. each prepared horseradish, chili sauce, one (1) tsp. prepared mustard. Add salt and pepper to taste

## HORSERADISH CREAM SAUCE

To one (1) cup Bechamel sauce, ( see pages 47-49 ), add one (1) Tbls. drained, prepared horseradish, small dash prepared mustard.

## HORSERADISH CREAM SAUCE

1/2 cup heavy cream              1 Tbls. vinegar
1/4 cup prepared horseradish    1/2 tsp. salt

Whip cream stiff. Mix horseradish, vinegar, salt and fold into whipped cream.

## HORSERADISH SAUCE

8 ounce cream cheese
1 Tbls. confectioner's sugar
1 Tbls. lemon juice

1 Tbls. Worcestershire sauce
2 Tbls. prepared horseradish
1/2 cup heavy cream

Soften cream cheese. Blend in all ingredients except heavy cream. Whip the heavy cream. Fold into cream cheese mixture.

## HORSERADISH SAUCE

1 Tbls. chopped onion
3 Tbls. butter
2 Tbls. flour

2 Tbls. flour
1 cup light cream
1/4 cup prepared horseradish

Brown onion slightly in butter. Add flour. Add cream. When thick add horseradish.

## HORSERADISH VINAIGRETTE SAUCE

Mix two (2) Tbls. dry mustard in one (1) cup wine vinegar. Stir in, vigorously, 1/4 cup grated fresh horseradish, one (1) tsp. confectioner's sugar. Add salt to taste. Add chopped parsely

## YOGURT HORSERADISH SAUCE

1 cup plain yogurt
2 Tbls. horseradish

1/2 tsp. salt
3 Tbls. chopped, stuffed olives

Mix all ingredients. Chill

## HUNGARIAN SAUCE

Saute a small onion, chopped, in 1/4 cup butter until onion is transparent. Stir in two (2) Tbls. flour, 1 Tbls. paprika. Cook, stirring constantly until mixture is blended. Gradually add one (1) cup chicken stock, one (1) cup dry white wine. Continue cooking until sauce is thick and smooth, stirring often. Place over boiling water, Cook for fifteen (15) minutes. Season to taste.

## IABBLE VERTE au BEURRE SAUCE

Cream 1/4 cup butter with one (1) Tbls. dry mustard, one (1) Tbls. Worcestershire sauce. Melt butter, stirring occasionally. Stir in 1/4 cup each chopped parsely, chives, two (2) Tbls. each chopped watercress, spinach, celery tops, two (2) chopped tarragon leaves. Blend mixture thoroughly. Season to taste with salt, pepper, pinch of cayenne. Bring to boil. Stir in one (1) cup beef stock.

## IMPERIALE SAUCE

Mix together 3/4 cup mayonnaise, 1/4 cup ketchup, one (1) Tbls. Worcestershire sauce, one (1) tsp. confectioner's sugar, touch cayenne, salt to taste. Mix well. While mixing add 1/2 cup dry champagne. Fold in 1/2 cup whipped cream, two (2) Tbls. Brandy.

**TAKE THINE EASE, EAT, DRINK AND BE MERRY**
New Testament
Luke, xii, 19

## INDIAN SAUCE

| | |
|---|---|
| 1 coconut | 1/4 cup raisins |
| 2 onions | salt, pepper |
| 6 Tbls. butter | pinch cinnamon |
| 1 1/2 tsp. curry powder | 2 whole cloves |
| 1/4 cup cashews | |

Punch two (2) holes in coconut. Drain juice into one (1) quart measuring cup. ( If you do not get 1 1/2 cups of coconut juice, scrape some coconut meat, put in a blender adding as much boiling water as needed to make 1 1/2 cups coconut milk. Press pulp hard to get coconut milk.) Peel onions and slice thin. Heat butter. Add onion slices. Brown slightly. Remove to a plate where you can squeeze out butter. Add curry powder to pan and cook two (2) to three (3) minutes. Add cashews, raisins, coconut milk, cinnamon and crush the clove heads. Bring to boil. Reduce heat and simmer three (3) to four (4) minutes. Correct seasoning.

## A L'INDIENNE SAUCE

Cook 1/2 cup chopped onion in three (3) Tbls. butter with one (1) cup cubed green apples until apples are tender and onions transparent. Stir frequently. Remove from heat. Sprinkle apple mixture with two (2) Tbls. flour sifted with two (2) tsp. curry powder, 1/2 tsp. salt, pinch nutmeg, cayenne. Mix well. Add slice of garlic, small bay leaf, four (4) sprigs parsley, six (6) slices onion to 1 1/2 cups chicken stock. Simmer until somewhat reduced. Strain. Gradually stir this mixture into apple mixture. Bring to boil stirring constantly until thickens. Place pan over hot water and simmer for five (5) to six (6) minutes. Stir occasionally. Season to taste. Serve very hot.

## INDIENNE SAUCE

| | |
|---|---|
| 1/2 cup butter | 2 hard boiled eggs |
| paprika | 1/2 tsp. curry powder |

Melt butter. Chop eggs. Add. Add curry powder, sprinkle with paprika.

## IRISH TART SAUCE

In top of double boiler combine three (3) egg yolks, 1/2 cup light cream, three (3) Tbls. lemon juice, one (1) tsp. grated onion, salt, pepper, nutmeg to taste. Cook over hot water three (3) minutes, stirring constantly until thickens. Stir in 1/2 cup whipped cream, Tbls. minced parsley.

## ITALIAN SAUSAGE SAUCE

| | |
|---|---|
| 1 pound sweet fennel flavored Italian sausage | 1/2 cup chopped celery |
| 2 Tbls. water | 1 Tbls. chopped parsley |
| 1 large onion, chopped | 1 large can Italian tomatoes |
| 2 eight ounce cans tomato puree | 2 bay leaves |

Cook sausages in water until they begin to fry. Add onion, celery, parsley. Cook until sausage is brown, turning often. Add tomatoes, tomato puree, bay leaves. Simmer one (1) hour, stirring occasionally. Uncover and continue cooking until attain desired thickness.

## ITALIENNE SAUCE

Cook two (2) tomatoes—peeled, seeded, chopped—, one (1) tsp. chopped shallots, in 3/4 cup Marsala wine until tomatoes are soft and mixture is reduced by half. Add 1/2 cup Brown sauce, ( see pages 55-58 ), two (2) Tbls. each diced mushrooms, chopped ham, seasoned with salt, pepper, lemon juice. Boil five (5) minutes and add one (1) tsp. chopped parsley.

## ITALIENNE SAUCE

| | |
|---|---|
| Brown roux | 3/4 cup fish stock |
| 12 mushrooms | 2 Tbls. each chopped tarragon, |
| 3 Tbls. butter | chervil, dill |
| 1 cup tomato paste | |

Make a brown roux. Brown four (4) Tbls. flour and four (4) Tbls. butter.) Chop mushrooms. Cook them in the butter until they are a paste. Heat tomato paste, fish stock. Reduce this a little. When this mixture has reached almost the boiling point, stir in the roux and the mushrooms. Stir until thickened. Add herbs and correct seasoning.

## IVORY SAUCE

To one (1) cup Bechamel sauce, (see pages 47-49 ), add 1/2 rounded tsp. meat extract. Stir in one (1) Tbls. butter.

## LAMB SAUCE ANITA

| | |
|---|---|
| 1/2 cup brown sugar | 1 Tbls. dry mustard |
| 1/2 cup currant jelly | 3 egg yolks |
| 1/2 cup vinegar | |

Mix brown sugar, jelly, mustard and egg yolks. Cook in double boiler until thickened. Add vinegar slowly beating after each addition.

## LEMON DILL SAUCE

| | |
|---|---|
| Juice and rind of a lemon | 3 Tbls. safflower oil |
| 2 sprigs dill | 1/2 tsp. salt |
| 1 Tbls. chopped chives | 1 tsp. dill seeds |
| 1 sprig parsley | 1 tsp. dulce |

Quarter lemon. Blend all ingredients in blender.

## LEMON SAUCE

| | |
|---|---|
| 14/ cup sugar | 1/2 tsp. salt |
| 1/4 cup lemon juice | 1/8 tsp. ginger, ground |
| 4 tsp. cornstarch | drop yellow food coloring |
| 1 Tbls. grated lemon peel | 1 cup water |

I saucepan mix well all ingredients. Blend. Cook over medium heat, stirring constantly, until mixture is slightly thickened. Serve hot.

## GREEK LEMON SAUCE

Juice of a lemon          2 cups chicken broth
3 eggs, separated          salt

Beat egg whites and yolks separately. Then together until blended. Gradually whisk in lemon juice and two (2) cups boiling chicken broth. Heat but do not boil.

## LOBSTER SAUCE

1 slice bread, cubed          1/4 cup chicken bouillon
1 cup evaporated skim milk          dash paprika
6 ounces cooked lobster meat, diced

Combine ingredients. On very low heat, gently cook in double boiler.

## NORWEGIAN LOBSTER SAUCE

Make one (1) cup medium cream sauce of two (2) cups milk and one (1) cup cream. Season to taste with salt, pepper. Stir in one (1) cup lobster meat cut in small pieces, two (2) Tbls. butter. In double boiler, over hot water, cook for about fifteen (15) minutes. Do not let sauce boil. Stir occasionally. Stir in 1/4 cup Sherry wine.

## LOUIS SAUCE

2 Tbls. butter          Worcestershire sauce
1 Tbls. minced onion          1 cup milk
2 Tbls. flour          1/2 cup mayonnaise
1/2 tsp. salt          1/3 cup chili sauce
2 Tbls. chopped stuffed olives          1/2 tsp. grated horseradish

Melt butter, add onion and saute until tender but not brown. Stir in flour, salt, pepper, dash Worcestershire sauce, milk. Cook, stirring constantly until mixture comes to boil. Remove from heat. Stir in mayonnaise, chili sauce, olives, horseradish. Serve hot.

LOUIS SAUCE

1 cup mayonnaise
2 Tbls. French dressing
1/3 cup chili sauce
1 Tbls. grated onion

1 Tbls. chopped parsley
2 Tbls. chopped stuffed olives
1 tsp. grated horseradish
1/2 tsp. Worcestershire sauce

Combine all ingredients. Chill.


LYONNAISE SAUCE

Melt two (2) Tbls. butter. Saute two (2) onions, chopped, until
brown. Add 1/3 cup dry white wine. Cook until mixture is reduced
in half. Add one (1) cup Brown sauce, (see pages 55-58 ). Cook slowly
fifteen (15) minutes. Add one (1) tsp. chopped parsley. Serve.


MAITRE D'HOTEL SAUCE

To one (1) cup Veloute sauce, (see pages 191 ), add 1/4 cup water.
Heat in saucepan. Add, a little at a time, 1/4 cup butter. Add juice
of a lemon, one (1) Tbls. each chopped parsley, tarragon. Serve hot.


MALTAISE SAUCE

1 orange
3 egg yolk
salt

1 lemon
1 cup butter, melted

Grate orange rind. Add three (3) egg yolks. Vigorously whisk until
mixture is thick and sticky. Squeeze juices of orange and lemon
into a bowl. Beat two (2) Tbls. of juice into egg yolk mixture. Over
moderate heat stir mixture constantly until a smooth cream
consistency. Remove from heat. Whisk in butter, a few drops at a
time, then by tsps. Season to taste.

## MARINARA SAUCE

Saute two (2) onions, sliced, one (1) garlic clove in four (4) Tbls. olive oil for five (5) minutes. Discard garlic. Stir in 2 1/2 cups cooked tomatoes, some basil. Cook over medium heat for five (5) more minutes. Lower heat. Simmer one (1) hour. Add two (2) anchovy fillets, cut up, 1/4 tsp. sugar, salt and pepper to taste. Simmer ten (10) minutes. Add 1/4 tsp. oregano.

## MARINARA SAUCE

1 clove garlic, minced          1/2 cup chopped parsley
1/2 cup onion, chopped          4 Basil leaves
1/4 cup olive oil               4 cups canned Italian tomatoes
1/2 tsp. oregano                salt, pepper

Cook the garlic and onion until golden brown in olive oil. Put tomatoes through food mill. Combine all ingredients. Simmer until thickened, one and one half hours.

## MARINARA SAUCE

2 Tbls. olive oil               6 ounces tomato paste
2 garlic cloves, minced         1 Tbl. sugar
small onion, chopped            2 tsp. basil
16 ounces canned tomatoes       1 1/2 tsp.salt

Over medium heat, in the oil, cook garlic and onion until tender. Stir in tomatoes and tomato liquid along with all other ingredients. Reduce heat to low. Cook twenty (20) minutes until thickened. Stir occasionally.

THE INTENTION OF EVERY OTHER PIECE OF PROSE MAY
BE DISCUSSED AND EVEN MISTRUSTED;
BUT THE PURPOSE OF A COOKERY BOOK IS ONE AND
UNMISTAKABLE. ITS OBJECT CAN CONCEIVABLY
BE NO OTHER THAN TO INCREASE THE
HAPPINESS OF MANKIND.

Joseph Conrad

## SALSA MARINARA SAUCE

Brown two (2) chopped garlic cloves in 1/3 cup olive oil. Add four (4) cups tomatoes peeled, seeded, chopped, two (2) Tbls. chopped parsley, one (1) tsp. each chopped sweet basil, salt, one (1) tsp. fresh ground black pepper. Cook over low heat thirty (30) minutes. Add three (3) Tbls. grated cheese, (Parmesan), 1/8 tsp. oregano. Cook fifteen (15) minutes until thick. Stir often.

## MARINIERE SAUCE

Melt one (1) Tbls. butter. Add two (2) shallots, chopped, 1/2 cup cream. Cook until reduced in half. Stir in 1/2 cup Veloute sauce, (see pages 191 ). Bring to boil, correct seasoning. Stir in two (2) egg yolks that have been beaten with 1/4 cup cream. Cook over low heat, stirring constantly, until thickened. Do Not Boil. Add juice of half a lemon.

## MATELOTE SAUCE

To one (1) cup red wine court bouillon for fish, add 1/4 cup chopped mushrooms. Reduce bouillon over high heat to half. Add 3/4 cup Brown sauce, (see pages 55-58 ). Boil rapidly one (1) minute, taste for seasoning, stir in One (1) Tbls. sweet butter. Serve at once.

## MAYONNAISE SAUCE

| | |
|---|---|
| 1/4 tsp. unflavored gelatin | 1 Tbls. mayonnaise |
| 2 Tbls. evaporated milk | |

Sprinkle gelatin over evaporated milk in saucepan and let stand until softened. Immerse in hot water bath. Heat gently to dissolve gelatin. Stir well. Add mayonnaise. Stir well


## MAYONNAISE SAUCE

| | |
|---|---|
| 2 egg yolks | 1 pint olive oil |
| 1 tsp. salt | lemon juice |
| 1/2 tsp. dry mustard | |

Beat egg yolks, salt, mustard together. Gradually add olive oil whisking constantly until thickened and stiff. Thin with lemon juice to taste.


## COGNAC MAYONNAISE SAUCE

| | |
|---|---|
| 3/4 cup mayonnaise | 1 Tbls, cognac |
| 1 tsp. tomato paste | |

Combine ingredients thoroughly. Chill.


## HERB MAYONNAISE SAUCE

| | |
|---|---|
| 1 1/2 cups mayonnaise | 1 tsp. tarragon |
| 1/2 cup chopped parsley | 1/2 tsp. salt |
| 1/4 cup chopped watercress | 1/4 tsp. pepper |
| 1/4 cup chopped chives | 2 tsp. chervil |

In blender, at high speed, blend all ingredients until well mixed and mayonnaise is green. Chill.

## MAYONNAISE CAPER SAUCE

In a double boiler top, one (1) cup mayonnaise. Heat, do not boil. Stirring constantly, add 1/4 cup capers, chopped, three (3) Tbls. chopped onions, two (2) Tbls. blanched, chopped almonds.

## MAYONNAISE RAVIGOTE SAUCE

To two (2) Tbls. each chopped capers, chervil, parsley, shallots, onions, add 1/4 cup dry white wine, one (1) Tbls. lemon juice. Cook over low heat fifteen (15) minutes. Cool. Stir mixture into one (1) cup mayonnaise, a touch of anchovy paste, one (1) chopped hard boiled egg. Blend thoroughly. Chill.

## MAYONNAISE SAUCE

| | |
|---|---|
| 1 egg yolk | 1 Tbls. heated vinegar |
| 2 Tbls. Dijon mustard | 2/3 cup olive oil |
| 1/4 tsp. salt | 1 Tbls. hot water |
| 1/8 tsp. white pepper | |

Mix egg yolk and mustard. Add salt, pepper, hot water. Let stand a minute. Mix well. Gradually add olive oil, whisking vigorously, slowly until begins to thicken. Finally whisk in hot water.

**THE PLEASANT TALK OF A DINNER TABLE PROMOTES DIGESTION, AND PREVENTS THE MIND FROM DWELLING ON THE GRINDING OF THE DIGESTIVE MILL THAT IS GOING ON WITHIN US**

Jerdan

## MEAT SAUCE

Saute one (1) onion, one (1) garlic clove, chopped, in two (2) Tbls. olive oil until onion is tender and golden. Add can of tomato paste.

Stir. Cook three (3) minutes. Add 2 1/2 cups warm water, 1/2 pound chopped lean beef, a bay leaf. Simmer 1 1/2 hours.

## MEAT SAUCE

| | |
|---|---|
| 2 Tbls. olive oil | 4 tsp. sugar |
| 1 pound ground beef | 2 tsp. oregano |
| 1 onion, chopped | 1 3/4 tsp salt |
| 1 garlic clove, minced | 1/8 tsp. cayenne pepper |
| 16 ounces canned tomatoes | bay leaf |
| 12 ounces tomato paste | |

In a Dutch oven, over medium heat, in hot olive oil, cook ground beef, onion, garlic until meat is well browned. Skim off fat. Add tomatoes, their liquid and all other ingredients. Reduce heat to low. Simmer thirty five (35) minutes until very thick. Stir occasionally.

## BASIC BEEF SAUCE

| | |
|---|---|
| large onion | 1/3 cup flour |
| 1 garlic clove, chopped | 1 tsp. salt |
| 2 Tbls. olive oil | 1/4 tsp. pepper |
| 10 ounces beef consomme | 2 pounds stew beef |
| 1/2 cup dry red wine | 2 tsp. Worcestershire sauce |

In a large saucepan saute onion and garlic until tender. Add consomme, wine, Worcestershire sauce. Bring to simmer. Mix flour, one (1) tsp. salt and pepper. Cut meat into 1/2 inch cubes. Dry. Heat 3/4 inch olive oil in a small saucepan over medium heat. When oil is hot add some meat cubes that have been dusted well with flour mixture. Stir occasionally until meat is browned on all sides. Add more meat cubes and follow suit until all are browned. Adjust heat so broth steams but does not bubble. Cook for four (4) to five (5) hours until meat is tender. Remove from heat. Skim fat. Add salt to taste

## GAMESAUCE

| | |
|---|---|
| 1/2 cup grape jelly | orange juice |
| 1/2 cup currant jelly | 2 Tbls. grated lemon rind |
| 1/4 cup butter | 2 Tbls. grated orange rind |
| 1/2 cup Sherry wine | |

Melt jellies with butter. Add orange juice and rinds. Bring to boil. Remove from heat. Add Sherry wine. Serve at once.

## HAM SAUCE

| | |
|---|---|
| 1 tsp. salt | 1/2 cup milk |
| 4 tsp. dry mustard | 1/2 cup vinegar |
| 1 1/2 cups sugar chunk of butter egg sized | |
| 2 eggs, slightly beaten | |

Mix all ingredients. Cook one half hour. Stir often. Use warm.

## VARIETY IS THE VERY SPICE OF LIFE
### Cowper

## BEEF STYLE SAUCE

| | |
|---|---|
| 1 can tomato sauce | 1/2 cup brown sugar |
| 1/2 cup vinegar | 1 onion, chopped |

Mix ingredients. Simmer two (2) hours.

## HUNTER'S SAUCE

4 Tbls. butter
2 onions, chopped
3 tomatoes. peeled, seeded, chopped
1/4 cup Red wine

6 mushrooms, sliced up
2 cups beef stock
2 Tbls. flour

Melt two (2) Tbls. butter and saute onions until transparent. Add tomatoes, mushrooms. Add stock. Simmer one (1) hour, stirring occasionally. Blend flour and two (2) Tbls. butter thoroughly. Thicken sauce with this mixture. Add wine. Serve warm.

## STEAK SUPREME SAUCE

1/2 pound mushrooms
flour

3 Tbls. butter
1/2 tsp. soy sauce

Slice mushrooms. Dust with flour. Cook in butter over low heat until tender. Add soy sauce.

WHEN I BEHOLD A FASHIONABLE TABLE SET OUT IN ALL ITS MAGNIFICENCE, I FANCY THAT I SEE GOUTS AND DROPSIES, FEVERS AND LETHARGIES, WITH OTHER INNUMERABLE DISTEMPERS, LYING IN AMBUSCADE AMONG THE DISHES. NATURE DELIGHTS IN THE MOST PLAIN AND SIMPLE DIET. EVERY ANIMAL, BUT MAN, KEEPS TO ONE DISH. HERBS ARE THE FOOD OF THIS SPECIES, FISH OF THAT, AND FLESH OF A THIRD. MAN FALLS UPON EVERYTHING THAT COMES IN HIS WAY; NOT THE SMALLEST FRUIT OR EXCRESENCE OF THE EARTH, SCARE A BERRY OR A MUSHROOM CAN ESCAPE HIM.

Addison

## SWEDISH MEATBALL SAUCE

1 1/2 cups ketchup            1 Tbls. vinegar
1 1/2 Tbls. dry onion flakes  3 Tbls. Worcestershire sauce
1 1/2 Tbls. brown sugar

Blend all ingredients and simmer with meatballs.


## MENAGERE SAUCE

In a cup of rich Cream Sauce, (see pages 80-83 ), add four (4) hard boiled egg yolks rubbed through a fine sieve, 1/2 tsp paprika, salt to taste. Bring to boil, stirring constantly. Remove from heat. Add one (1) Tbls. chopped gherkins.


## MEUNIERE SAUCE

2 Tbls. butter               pan juice from baked fish
2 tsp. lemon juice           Tbls. chopped parsley

Combine butter, lemon juice, and pan juices. Boil until syrupy. Stir in parsley.


## MILANAISE SAUCE

Heat two (2) Tbls. butter in pan and saute 1/4 cup sliced mushrooms, 1/4 pound diced ham.


## MINT SAUCE

Mix 1/2 cup fresh mint leaves, chopped, 1/4 cup sugar, one (1) cup hot vinegar. Chill.

## MINTSAUCE

1/3 cup wine vinegar          1 cup fresh mint leaves, chopped
1/4 cup boiling water         3 Tbls. brown sugar

Heat vinegar and water. Pour over mint leaves. Add brown sugar. Let stand several hours.


## MINT SAUCE

2 bunches mint, chopped       4 tsp. sugar
1/4 cup cider vinegar         2 Tbls. boiling water

Combine ingredients. Let stand an hour before serving.


## MINT SAUCE

1/4 cup lemon juice           1/4 tsp. salt
1/2 cup water                 1 tsp. chopped fresh mint
2 Tbls. sugar                 1/4 tsp. mint extract

Combine ingredients. Heat. Add mint extract and mint


## CURRANT MINT SAUCE

10 ounces red currant jelly   2 Tbls. chopped mint
2 Tbls. shredded orange peel

Mix all ingredients thoroughly.


## CURRANT MINT SAUCE

Add 1 1/2 Tbls. fresh mint leaves to a jar of currant jelly. Mix with a fork. Add one (1) Tbls. grated orange rind, one (1) tsp. grated lemon rind. Mix well.

## MINTCURRANTSAUCE

Mix one (1) cup currant jelly with two (2) Tbls. chopped mint leaves and two (2) Tbls. grated orange rind.

## DRIED MINT SAUCE

Boil one (1) cup wine vinegar for five (5) minutes with three (3) garlic cloves and three (3) Tbls. dried mint leaves. Stand for thirty (30) minutes. Bring to boil and reduce to one half. Strain. In saucepan blend two (2) Tbls. each butter, flour and cook roux over moderate heat until brown, stirring constantly. Gradually add 1 1/4 cups beef stock, cook, stirring constantly, until sauce is thick. Reduce heat to simmer for five (5) minutes. Add strained vinegar mixture. Serve hot.

## MINT GARLIC YOGURT SAUCE

| | |
|---|---|
| 1 garlic clove, minced | 3 Tbls. chopped, fresh mint |
| 3/4 cup plain yogurt | 2 small chili, seeded, chopped |
| 1/2 cup scallions, chopped | 1 tsp. coriander |

Combine all ingredients. Chill.

## GRAPE MINT SAUCE

To a jar of softened grape jelly add 1/4 cup chopped fresh mint leaves, two (2) Tbls. prepared horseradish, drained, 1/3 tsp. grated lemon rind. Heat to luke warm to serve.

## ORANGE MINT SAUCE

Combine 1/2 cup each fresh chopped mint leaves, strained orange juice, 1/4 cup strained lemon juice, one (1) Tbls. confectioner's sugar, salt to taste, touch of nutmeg. Let stand for an hour. At serving add 1/2 tsp. grated lemon rind.

# WOULD YE BOTH EAT YOUR CAKE AND HAVE YOUR CAKE?

John Heywood
Proverbs, I, ix (1546)


## MORNAY SAUCE

3 Tbls. butter
2 Tbls. flour
1 cup chicken broth
1 cup cream

1 egg yolk
1/2 cup shredded Swiss cheese
1/4 cup Parmesan cheese, grated

Over medium heat, melt butter. Stir in flour until smooth. Gradually add chicken broth and cream, stirring constantly, until thickened. Remove from heat. In a bowl whisk egg yolk and add a small amount of the hot sauce. Slowly add this back to the main sauce, stirring vigorously. Add cheeses over low heat stirring constantly until just thickened. Serve hot.


## MORNAY SAUCE

Heat two (2) cups Bechamel sauce, (see pages 47-49 ), over low heat. Stir constantly. When boiling point has been attained, add one (1) Tbls. each grated Parmesan cheese, grated Gruyere cheese. Whisk constantly until sauce is smooth and thick. Remove from heat and add two (2) Tbls. butter gradually.


## MORNAY SAUCE

5 Tbls. butter
5 Tbls. flour
2 1/2 cups cream

1 cup shredded Cheddar cheese
1/2 cup grated Parmesan cheese

Melt butter in a saucepan. Whisk in flour, Stir for three (3) minutes until frothy but do not let flour take on any color. Remove from heat and add cream all at once, whisking vigorously. Blend well. Return to moderate heat. Cook and stir until sauce is thick and smooth. Remove from heat. Add cheeses, stir until melted and thoroughly blended.


## MORNAY SAUCE

In two (2) cups Bechamel sauce, (see pages 47-49), mix three (3) egg yolks that have been lightly beaten with a little cream. Cook, stirring constantly, until boiling point. Add two (2) Tbls. each butter, grated Parmesan cheese.


## MORNAY SAUCE

1/2 cup light cream                        1/2 cup grated Parmesan
                                                       cheese
1 cup Bechamel sauce (see pages 47-49)   3 Tbls. butter
1/2 cup grated Gruyere cheese

Over very low heat add cream to simmering Bechamel sauce. Stir often. Reduce sauce to one third. Add Gruyere and Parmesan. Stir until thoroughly blended. Remove from heat. Stir in butter until smooth


## MORNAY SAUCE

1 1/2 cups Veloute sauce (see pages 191)      1/2 cup cream
1/2 cup grated Parmesan cheese                cayenne pepper

When Veloute sauce has thickened stir in grated cheese until melted. Add cream. Season with cayenne.


## MORNAY SAUCE

Two (2) cups Bechamel sauce, ( see pages 47-49 ). Add three (3) egg yolks beaten with a little hot cream. Cook to boiling point, stirring constantly. Stir in two (2) Tbls. grated Parmesan cheese.

## MOSCOVITE SAUCE

Simmer one (1) tsp. juniper berries in 1/4 cup water for fifteen (15) minutes. Strain. Add to sauce 1 1/2 cups hot Poivrade sauce, (see page 151-152 ). Add 1/2 cup Malaga grapes, two (2) Tbls. each shredded almonds, seedless raisins ( which should be plumped in beef stock). Blend well.

## MOSCOVITE SAUCE

Bring to boil two (2) cups Poivrade sauce, ( see page 151-152 ). Cook for ten (10) minutes. Remove from heat. Add 1/2 cup Maderia wine. Add two (2) Tbls. blanched, slivered almonds, 1 1/2 Tbls. raisins which have been sauteed in a little butter.

## COLD MOUSSELINE RUSSE SAUCE

Pound together in a mortar a good handful of spinach and celery leaves. Rub this mixture through a fine sieve. Add one (1) or two (2) Tbls. sour cream and a touch of anchovy paste. Very gently fold in 1/2 cup stiffly beaten sour cream alternately with 1/4 cup mayonnaise. Stir in very gently three (3) Tbls. each Sherry wine, caviar, one (1) tsp. chopped fresh tarragon, a touch of cayenne.

## MOUSSELINE SAUCE

1 cup butter, soft           juice of a lemon
3 egg yolks           1/2 cup whipped cream
1/2 tsp. salt

Cut butter into three (3) equal parts. In double boiler combine one(1/3rd) third of the butter with beaten egg yolks. Place over very hot water and whisk until butter has melted. Add second third butter and repeat. Add third third butter, whisking vigorously and constantly. When sauce thickens season with salt and lemon juice. Fold whipped cream into sauce and serve at once.

## A FIG FOR YOUR BILL OF FARE, SHOW ME YOUR BILL OF COMPANY

Swift

## MUSHROOM SAUCE

To one (1) cup Bechamel sauce, ( see pages 47-49 ), add 1/2 cup sliced mushrooms which have been slightly cooked. Stir in one (1) Tbls. butter.

## MUSHROOM SAUCE

| | |
|---|---|
| 1 Tbls. chopped shallots | 1 tsp. lemon juice |
| 1/4 pound mushrooms, sliced | 1 1/2 cups Brown sauce |
| 3 Tbls. butter | (see pages 55-58) |

Cook shallots and mushrooms in butter, stirring occasionally, five (5) minutes. Add lemon juice, Brown sauce. Blend. Bring to boil and serve hot.

## MOREL MUSHROOM SAUCE

| | |
|---|---|
| 5 Tbls. butter | 1 1/2 Tbls. flour |
| 1/2 pound morels, sliced | 1 1/4 cups chicken stock |
| 2 Tbls. chopped onion | 1 1/4 cups milk |
| 1 chopped garlic clove | cayenne pepper, salt |

Melt four (4) Tbls. butter. Over medium heat cook morels five (5) minutes. Add onion, garlic and cook five (5) minutes more. Stir in flour. Add stock, milk. Simmer ten (10) minutes. Season to taste. Just before serving add remaining butter.

## MUSHROOM SAUCE

| | |
|---|---|
| 1/4 cup butter | 1 tsp. salt |
| 1/2 pound mushrooms, sliced | 1 Tbls. cornstarch |
| 3/4 cup beef stock | 1/4 cup Sauterne wine |

Over medium heat cook mushrooms until tender. Add beef stock and bring to boil. Blend cornstarch, Sauterne wine until smooth. Gradually add wine to mushroom sauce whisking constantly until thickened.

## ALMOND MUSHROOM SAUCE

| | |
|---|---|
| 4 Tbls. butter | 1/2 tsp. salt |
| 1 Tbls. chopped onion | 2 cups chicken stock |
| 1 cup chopped fresh mushrooms | 2 tsp. lemon juice |
| 4 Tbls. flour | 1/2 cup chopped almonds |

Melt butter. Add mushrooms and onion. Saute. Add flour and blend well. Add salt, pepper to taste, chicken stock. Cook until thick and smooth. Add lemon juice and almonds.

## DRIED MUSHROOM AND TUNA SAUCE

In skillet, 1/4 cup olive oil. Saute two (2) garlic cloves, chopped, until lightly colored. Add one (1) ounce dried mushrooms that have been soaked in water for thirty (30) minutes, one (1) cup tomato puree, dash fresh pepper. Simmer gently for an hour. Add 1 1/2 cups Tuna flakes, water packed, drained. Blend. Correct seasoning.

## MADERIA MUSHROOM SAUCE

Slice one (1) pound mushroom caps. Melt 1/4 cup butter. Add mushrooms, 1/2 tsp. salt, dash pepper. Cook until mushrooms are golden brown. Add one (1) shallot, chopped. Add one (1) cup Brown sauce, ( see pages 55-58 ). Bring to boil and cook slowly for six (6) minutes. Add 1/3 cup Maderia wine. Reheat, but do not boil. Add 1/2 tsp. chopped parsley.

## SIMPLE MUSHROOM SAUCE

| | |
|---|---|
| 1/2 pound fresh mushrooms | 1/2 cup heavy cream |
| 4 Tbls. butter | 1 tsp. cornstarch |
| 4 chopped shallots | 1/2 cup dry white wine |
| salt, pepper, lemon juice, chopped tarragon | |

Use mushrooms caps only. Heat butter. Add mushrooms, sliced. Add chopped shallots. Reduce heat and let mushrooms lose all juice. Empty juices into a separate bowl. To the mushrooms in pan add white wine and touch of lemon juice. Cook over high heat until juices are almost all gone. Return mushroom juice and keep warm over low heat. Stir in heavy cream that has been mixed with cornstarch. Stir well and let thicken. Add tarragon.

## IN GENERAL, MANKIND, SINCE THE IMPROVEMENT OF COOKERY, EAT TWICE AS MUCH AS NATURE REQUIRES.
Ben Franklin

## MOREL SAUCE

| | |
|---|---|
| 1/2 pound sliced morels | 4 Tbls. butter |
| 2 Tbls. lemon juice | 4 Tbls. olive oil |
| 1 onion, chopped | 1 bunch chopped parsley |
| large clove garlic, chopped | salt and pepper |

Sprinkle morels with lemon juice. Cook onion. garlic gently in butter and olive oil until softened without browning. Add morels, parsley. Raise heat slightly. Cook ten (10) minutes. Season to taste.

FOOD IMPROPERLY TAKEN, NOT ONLY PRODUCES
DISEASES, BUT AFFORDS THOSE THAT ARE ALREADY
ENGENDERED IN BOTH MATTER AND SUSTENANCE;
SO THAT, LET THE FATHER OF DISEASE BE WHAT IT
MAY, INTEMPERANCE IS ITS MOTHER.

Burton

## MOREL SAUCE

1/2 pound morels, sliced          1/4 cup tomato juice
6 shallots, minced                meat juices
6 Tbls. butter                    2 1/2 Tbls flour
2/3 cup dry white wine            1 1/4 cup beef stock
chopped parsley, tarragon, chervil

Brown mushrooms and shallots lightly in one half butter. Stir in
flour. Add white wine, stock, tomato juice. Cook twenty (20)
minutes. Remove from heat. Add juices of whatever meat your
are roasting. Mix in remaining butter. Season to taste. Add herbs.
Serve at once.

## MOREL SAUCE

4 Tbls. butter                    1 1/3 cups heavy cream
2 1/2 Tbls. flour                 2 egg yolks
1 1/4 cups chicken stock          salt, pepper
2 ounces chopped morels

Melt butter. Stir in flour. Heat stock. Add butter mixture, whisk
until smooth. Add morels. Simmer ten (10) minutes. Gradually stir
in cream. Beat egg yolks with a little of the sauce and add to
mixture. Thicken without boiling. Season to taste.

## MOREL WINE SAUCE

2 Tbls. butter
1 Tbls. chopped parsley
1/2 chopped garlic clove
chopped onion
1 Tbls flour

1 cup chicken stock
1/8 tsp. nutmeg
3/4 pound morels, sliced
1/4 cup dry Sherry wine

Heat one (1) Tbls. butter. Add parsley, garlic, onion. Cook over medium heat three (3) minutes. Add flour and whisk until smooth. Gradually add chicken stock, constantly stirring. Add nutmeg. In a skillet melt remaining butter. Add morels and saute. Combine mixtures. Simmer fifteen (15) minutes. Add wine. Bring to boil. Serve.

## MUSSEL SAUCE

1 1/2 cups Veloute sauce, ( see pages 191 ). Take six (6) cooked, deveined, shelled shrimp, knead them with two (2) Tbls. butter. Add to sauce. Add 3/4 cup shelled mussels that have been cooked in white wine, water.

## MUSTARD SAUCE

Mix one (1) Tbls. water with one (1) tsp. English mustard. Combine with one (1) cup hot Bechamel sauce, ( see pages 47-49 ). Add one (1) Tbls. Hollandaise sauce, ( see pages 102-107 ).

## MUSTARD SAUCE

1 1/2 cups Dijon mustard
4 tsp. dry mustard
3/4 cup sugar

1/2 cup white vinegar
1 1/3 cups olive oil
1 cup chopped fresh dill

Blend mustards and sugar. Add vinegar. Gradually whisk in olive oil. Add dill. Blend well. Refrigerate.

# REASON SHOULD DIRECT, AND APPETITE OBEY
Cicero

## MUSTARD SAUCE

| | |
|---|---|
| 1/2 cup prepared mustard | 1 tsp. sour cream |
| 1/2 cup olive oil | 1/8 tsp. salt |
| 1/3 cup sugar | 1/4 cup chopped dill |
| 1/4 cup white vinegar | |

Place all ingredients, except dill, in blender until smooth. Chill. Add dill at serving.

## MUSTARD SAUCE

Blend one (1) tsp. dry mustard, one (1) Tbls. water to a paste. Add to one (1) cup hot Bechamel sauce, (see pages 47-49 ). Serve hot or cold.

## MUSTARD SAUCE

Simmer 1/2 cup each honey, strained orange juice until reduced some what. Add 1/3 cup cider vinegar, one (1) Tbls. each dry mustard, turmeric, one (1) tsp. ginger. Mix one (1) tsp. arrowroot, two (2) Tbls. water to a paste. Add to sauce, stirring constantly until sauce is thick and clear.

## MUSTARD SAUCE

To one (1) cup of Drawn Butter sauce, ( see pages 62 ), add one (1) Tbls. prepared mustard. Blend thoroughly. Heat. Do not boil. Serve at once.

## MUSTARD SAUCE

| | |
|---|---|
| 1/2 cup mayonnaise | 1/4 tsp. salt |
| 3 Tbls. milk | 1 Tbls. prepared mustard |

Mix ingredients well. Refrigerate.


## MUSTARD SAUCE

| | |
|---|---|
| 1 beef bouillon cube | 1 cup brown sugar |
| 1/2 cup water, hot | 1/4 cup dry mustard |
| 1/2 cup vinegar | 1 Tbls. flour |
| 2 eggs well beaten | 1/4 tsp. salt |

Dissolve bouillon cube in hot water. Add vinegar Add all dry ingredients. Mix well. In top of double boiler place mixture and add beaten eggs over hot water, stirring vigorously until sauce is consistency of custard. Cool.


## BROWN DEVILED MUSTARD SAUCE

To 1/4 cup Brown sauce, (see pages 55-58 ), add two (2) Tbls. heavy cream, one (1) tsp. each lemon juice, Worcestershire sauce, 1/4 tsp. each salt, dry mustard. Cook slowly for ten (10 ) minutes.


## MUSTARD BUTTER SAUCE

| | |
|---|---|
| 1/4 butter | 1 tsp. lemon juice |
| 1 tsp. prepared mustard | |

Heat butter until light brown. Stir in mustard, lemon juice.

## CREAMY MUSTARD SAUCE

1 cup plain yogurt
1/2 tsp. dry mustard
3 Tbls. grated onion
2 Tbls. cider vinegar

1 tsp. Worcestershire sauce
1 Tbls. minced parsley
1 tsp. salt
cayenne

Combine ingredients thoroughly. Chill.

## EASY MUSTARD SAUCE

2 Tbls. butter
2 tsp. prepared mustard
5 tsp. flour
1 Tbls. lemon juice

1 tsp. salt
2 egg yolks
1 1/2 cups milk

Melt butter. Add flour, salt, mustard. Whip eggs, add milk. Add this to first mixture. Cook until thick. Add lemon juice. Serve.

## MUSTARD SAUCE FOR FISH

In double boiler over hot water blend two (2) Tbls flour, two (2) tsp. prepared mustard, one (1) tsp. sugar, pinch of salt. Add 3/4 cup fish stock, two (2) Tbls. wine vinegar. Cook over hot water, constantly stirring until smooth and begins to thicken. Remove from heat. Add beaten egg yolks. Cook, stirring constantly until sauce thickens.

## SWEET-SOUR MUSTARD SAUCE

3 Tbls. prepared mustard
1 egg
1/3 cup firmly packed brown sugar

1 tsp. paprika
1/2 cup cider vinegar
1 Tbls. butter

Combine mustard, egg, sugar, paprika with beater. Add vinegar. Beat. Melt butter. Remove from heat and cool. Blend ingredients into butter. Return to low heat. Stir until thickened. Cool.

## NANTUASAUCE

Blend one (1) cup hot Bechamel sauce, (see pages 47-49 ), with 1/4 cup scalded heavy cream. Strain through sieve. Heat without boiling. Add salt, pepper to taste. Stir in two (2) Tbls. each crayfish butter, chopped crayfish tails. ( You may use shrimp or lobster butter).

## NEWBURG SAUCE

Heat two (2) Tbls. butter. Blend in one (1) Tbls. flour. Gradually add one (1) cup hot cream, stirring constantly until thick and smooth. Do not boil. Season with salt, cayenne. Pour over two (2) well beaten egg yolks constantly stirring. Set pan over boiling water and stir for three (3) minutes. Add two (2) Tbls. dry Sherry wine.

## NEWBURG SAUCE

| | |
|---|---|
| 1 cup chicken stock | 1/4 tsp. brandy extract |
| 1/2 cup cauliflower, cooked | 1/4 cup evaporated milk |
| 1/4 cup tomato sauce | 1 tsp. fresh parsley, chopped |
| 1/4 cup clam juice | salt, pepper |
| 1/4 tsp. sherry extract | |

Put stock, cauliflower, tomato sauce, clam juice in a blender. Blend until smooth. Put into a saucepan and, over low heat, Add sherry, brandy extracts. Simmer ten (10) minutes. Season with salt and pepper to taste. Add milk. Heat but do not boil. Sprinkle in parsley.

## NEWBURG SAUCE

Heat one (1) Tbls. butter in double boiler. Blend in two (2) Tbls flour. Gradually add one (1) cup cream, stirring constantly until thick and smooth. Do not boil. Salt and cayenne to taste. Beat two (2) egg yolks. Stirring constantly, pour sauce into egg yolks, over boiling water, for three (3) minutes. Add two (2) Tbls. dry Sherry wine.

## HE HATH EATEN ME OUT OF HOUSE AND HOME
II Henry IV, II, i, 80

### NICOISE SAUCE

Cook 1/2 cup tomato puree with 1/2 crushed garlic clove, until mixture is as thick as mayonnaise. Stir constantly so sauce doesn't scorch. Chill. Combine two (2) cups mayonnaise with the puree, one (1) chopped red pepper, 1/2 tsp. each tarragon, chives.
Chill.

### NORMANDE SAUCE

Melt two (2) Tbls. butter. Stir in two (2) Tbls. flour. Cook roux until it begins to turn golden. Add one (1) cup liquor from whatever fish or shellfish you are preparing. Add liquor from one (1) cup mushrooms cooked ( save mushrooms for garnish with dish).
Cook this sauce ten (10) minutes. Mix two (2) egg yolks with 1/2 cup cream. Combine with mixture. Cook sauce until just to boil.
Strain.

## THE TURNPIKE ROAD TO MOST PEOPLE'S HEARTS, I FIND, LIES THROUGH THEIR MOUTHS, OR I MISTAKE MANKIND.
Wolcott-Peter Pindar

### NUT SAUCE

1 cup ground walnuts             1/4 cup chopped onion
1/2 cup sliced mushrooms

Blend nuts, milk and onion in blender until smooth. Add mushrooms. Cook in double boiler thirty (30) minutes. Stir often. Sauce will thicken as it cooks.

## CHESTNUT SAUCE

Roast a dozen chestnuts until tender. Shell, peel. Rub through a fine sieve or food chopper. Season with salt, pepper, cayenne, nutmeg to taste. Combine with two (2) cups light cream mixed with 1/4 scalded cream.

## CHESTNUT SAUCE

| | |
|---|---|
| 1 cup cooked chestnuts | 1 cup light cream |
| 3 Tbls. butter | 1/2 cup heavy cream |
| 3 Tbls, flour | salt, pepper, nutmeg |

Food chopper chestnuts fine. Mix cream, butter, flour heavy cream. Add chopped nuts. Blend well. Heat through just before serving

## CHINESE ALMOND SAUCE

Soak two (2) cups almonds in boiling water for five (5) minutes. Peel and dry. Heat 1/4 cup olive oil to smoking point. Fry almonds until yellow, stirring constantly. Add one (1) cup each water chestnuts, diced mushrooms, 1/3 cup each diced onions, chopped celery. Cook for twenty five (25) minutes. Stir in one (1) Tbls. soy sauce, salt and pepper to taste.

## PEANUT SAUCE

| | |
|---|---|
| 1/2 cup hot water | 1 Tbls. fresh lime juice |
| 1/2 cup smooth peanut butter | 1 Tbls. brown sugar |

Whisk peanut butter and hot water. Add lime juice and brown sugar, whisking until well blended,

## WALNUTSAUCE

1/4 cup butter
1 cup coarsely chopped walnuts
1 tsp. salt

1/2 cup milk
2 Tbls. parsley minced

Over medium heat, in hot butter, lightly brown walnuts. After five (5) minutes stir in remaining ingredients.

## WALNUT SAUCE ALBI

1/3 cup shelled walnuts
2 Tbls. Roquefort cheese
fresh ground pepper

2/3 cup olive oil
1 tsp. lemon juice

Chop nuts in food processor. Crumble Roquefort. Mash walnuts into cheese. Add little lemon juice. Gradually whisk in olive oil. Season to taste.

## OLIVES ET A L'ORANGE SAUCE

Put fat from roasted duck in pan. Mix in four (4) Tbls. each flour and cold water until smooth. Add two (2) cups hot chicken stock, stirring and scraping pan until mixture is creamy and smooth. Cook in double boiler over hot water five (5) to six (6) minutes, stirring constantly. Season with salt, pepper, cayenne to taste. Add one (1) cup strained orange juice, five (5) Tbls. orange zest, twenty four (24) sliced, ripe olives. Bring to boil until reduced to 1 1/2 cups, stirring occasionally. Whisk in two (2) Tbls. Sherry wine, one (1) Tbls. each currant jelly, sweet butter.

# TOO MANY COOKS SPOIL THE BROTH

Balthazar Gerbier

Discourse of Building (1662)

## ORANGE SAUCE

1 cup brown sugar
2 1/2 Tbls. sugar
1 Tbls. cornstarch

1 Tbls. grated orange rind
1 cup orange juice
2 drops Tabasco sauce

Cook all ingredients over low heat until thick and clear. Remove from heat. Add one (1) ounce Cointreau.

## ORANGE SAUCE

2 Tbls. flour
2/3 cup orange juice

1 tsp. grated orange peel
1 tsp. grated lemon peel

Using a little fat from pan in which you are roasting duck, add 1/2 cup hot water. Stir to incorporate. Thicken with flour. Cook, stirring until thick and smooth. Blend in orange juice. Heat. Sprinkle in the orange and lemon peel.

## ORANGE SAUCE

1/2 cup sugar
2 Tbls. flour
1/8 tsp salt
1/2 cup water

1/2 cup orange juice
2 Tbls. lemon juice
2 Tbls. grated orange rind
1 Tbls. butter

Mix flour, sigar. salt. Add water. Boil until thick. Add orange and lemon juice, rind, butter. Bring to boil. Serve hot.

## ORANGE SAUCE

| | |
|---|---|
| 1/2 cup orange juice | 1 Tbls. sugar |
| 2 Tbls. lemon juice | 1 Tbls. cornstarch |
| 1 Tbls. vinegar | 1 Tbls. water |
| salt, pepper | |

Combine in a double boiler, juices, vinegar, salt, pepper, sugar. Mix sugar and cornstarch to a paste. Add to juice. Cook until slightly thickened, stir constantly.

## ORANGE SAUCE

| | |
|---|---|
| 3 egg yolks | 1 Tbls. lemon juice |
| 2 Tbls. orange juice | 1 cup mild flavored olive oil |
| grated peel of | 1 orange salt |

Combine egg yolks, lemon and orange juice in blender. Add oil by droplets with blender running. Stir in grated peel.

## ORANGE SAUCE

| | |
|---|---|
| 3/4 cup orange juice | 1/8 tsp. nutmeg |
| 1 Tbls. lemon juice | 2 Tbls. butter |
| 1/8 tsp. salt | 2 Tbls. flour |

Combine juices, nutmeg, salt. Over medium heat melt butter. Add flour, stirring until blended. Add juices. Stir constantly until mixture is thick.

## ORANGE SAUCE

| | |
|---|---|
| 1/4 cup butter | 1/3 cup orange juice |
| 1 1/2 cups confectioner's sugar | 2 Tbls. grated orange peel |

Over low heat, melt butter. Stir in sugar, juice, peel. Cook, stirring frequently, until heated through.


## ORANGE SAUCE

| | |
|---|---|
| 2 orange rinds grated | 2 Tbls. lemon juice |
| 6 Tbls. currant jelly | 1/4 tsp. salt |
| 2 Tbls. orange juice | 2 Tbls. Port wine |
| 3 Tbls. sugar | dash cayenne |

Mix well grated orange rind, jelly, sugar. Add remaining ingredients. Stir until blended.


## ORANGE SAUCE

| | |
|---|---|
| 2/3 cup orange juice | 1 1/3 cup Brown stock |
| 1/4 cup butter | (see pages 55-58 ) |
| 1/4 cup flour | 2 Tbls. Port wine |
| 1/2 tsp. salt | grated orange rind |

Melt butter. Add flour, seasonings. Stir until well browned. Gradually add stock. Simmer five (5) minutes. Just at serving add juice, wine and rind.


## ORANGE SAUCE

| | |
|---|---|
| 3 Tbls, butter | 2/3 cup orange juice |
| 1/4 cup flour | 2 Tbls. grated orange rind |
| 1 1/3 cups water | 1 Tbls. Sherry wine |
| salt | |

Melt butter. Blend in flour. Cook until brown. Gradually add water. Stir occasionally until thick. Just before serving add juice, wine, rind.

## ORANGE SAUCE

3 Tbls. butter
3 Tbls. Cognac
2 tsp. shallots, minced
1 Tbls. grated lemon rind
3 Tbls. flour
1/4 tsp pepper
Duck liver

1/2 tsp. tomato paste
1 tsp. meat extract paste
1/2 cup orange juice
1 cup chicken stock
1/4 Tbls. orange marmalade
3 oranges, sectioned

Remove liver from Duck, chop fine. Melt butter. Add liver and brown well. Add brandy, shallots, lemon rind. Simmer three (3) minutes. Remove from heat. Remove liver. Stir in flour, pepper, tomato paste, meat extract paste. Gradually add orange juice, chicken stock, marmalade. Bring to boil. Reduce heat. Simmer, stirring occasionally, fifteen (15) minutes. Add orange slices and chopped liver.

## ORIENTAL SAUCE

1 Tbls. dry mustard
1/2 tsp. curry powder
1/2 cup ketchup

1 Tbls. vinegar
1 Tbls. soy sauce

Combine ingredients. Bring to boil. Mix well. Serve hot.

## ORIENTAL SAUCE

Melt two (2) Tbls. butter. Add Two (2) Tbls. ground mushrooms, one (1) tsp. chopped mint leaves. Cook about two (2) minutes, stirring constantly. Add 1/2 cup scalded cream. Cook, stirring constantly, another two (2) minutes. When begins to bubble add 1/4 cup stewed tomato pulp. Bring to boil. Remove from heat. Stir in two (2) lightly beaten egg yolks. Season with salt, pepper. Serve at once.

## OYSTER SAUCE

Add 1/2 cup fish stock to one (1) cup Bechamel sauce, (see pages 47-49 ), and 1/4 cup cream. Reduce a little over high heat. Add one (1) Tbls. butter and fresh shucked oysters in their own liquor.

## PAPRIKA SAUCE

Add one (1) Tbls. chopped onions to one (1) cup Bechamel sauce, (see pages 47-49 ), two (2) tsp. paprika. Strain through sieve. Add one (1) Tbls. butter.

## HOT PEPPER SAUCE

2 Tbls. crushed red pepper flakes          1 Tbls. olive oil
3 Tbls. water                              1/2 tsp.cumin

Combine flakes, water. Heat to boiling. Remove from heat. Add olive oil and cumin.

## RED PEPPER SAUCE

2 roasted red peppers, fresh          3/4 cup heavy cream

Mince 1 1/2 peppers. Place in saucepan and cook over low heat five (5) minutes. Stir in heavy cream. Simmer ten (10) minutes over low heat. Cut remaining pepper into matchstick thin pieces to garnish dish.

## PERIGUEUX SAUCE

1 Tbls grated truffle                    1 tsp. Madeira wine
1 cup Espagnole sauce (see page 95 )

Blend truffle with Madeira, stir into Espagnole sauce. Simmer ten (10 Minutes. Strain.

# IF YOU CAN'T TAKE THE HEAT, GET OUT OF THE KITCHEN
Unknown

## PERIGUEUX SAUCE

In a saucepan brown slightly two (2) chopped shallots, 1/2 sliced onion, one (1) Tbls. butter. In another saucepan heat 3/4 cup white wine. Add one (1) Tbls. brandy. Ignite. After burn out add one (1) tsp. flour to shallots, onion and saute until colored. Moisten with a little chicken bouillon. Add wine. Simmer over very low heat, stirring often ten (10)minutes. Strain through fine sieve. Add finely diced truffles. Cook three (3) minutes. At the last minute add juice of whatever meat or bird your are serving, after removing as much of the fat as possible.

## PERIGUEUX SAUCE

Chop and brown slightly two (2) shallots, 1/2 onion, in one (1) Tbls. butter. In another pan heat 3/4 cup white wine. Add one (1) Tbls. brandy. Ignite, burn off alcohol. Add one (1) Tbls. Madeira wine. Add one (1) tsp. flour to shallots and onion, brown this roux lightly. Add 1/4 cup chicken stock and wine. Simmer over low heat twenty (20) minutes. Strain. Add diced truffle. Cook another three (3) minutes.

## PICANTE SAUCE

| | |
|---|---|
| 3 tomatoes, chopped | 1 garlic clove, minced |
| 1 Tbls. onion, minced | 1/2 tsp. vinegar |
| 1 jalepeno pepper, minced, seeds removed | dash of cumin |

Mix all ingredients together. Refrigerate.

## CURRIED PINEAPPLE SAUCE

8 ounces crushed pineapple     2 Tbls. butter
1 tsp. curry powder

Over medium high heat bring ingredients to boiling. Stir occasionally. Reduce heat. Simmer five (5) minutes. Serve hot.

## PIQUANT SAUCE

1 onion, sliced          2 Tbls. butter
1 Tbls. shortening       3 tsp. soy sauce
2/3 cup water

Fry onion until crisp tender in shortening. Add water, ingredients. Mix well. Simmer two (2) minutes.

## PLUM SAUCE

1 pound canned purple plums     1/4 cup brown sugar
1/4 cup butter                  2 Tbls. chili sauce
1/4 cup chopped onion           1 tsp. Worcestershire sauce
3 Tbls. lemon juice             1/2 tsp. ginger

Drain plums. Reserve liquid. Remove pits. Puree plums in blender. Melt butter. Add onion and saute until golden. Stir in all remaining ingredients including plum liquor. Simmer thirty (30) minutes,

## POIVRADE SAUCE

To six (6) Tbls. olive oil add one each diced carrot, onion. Cook until golden brown. Stir in 1/2 cup flour and cook until flour turns golden brown. Add three (3) cups Brown stock, ( see pages 55-58 ), one (1) cup tomato puree. Whisk and cook, stirring constantly until well blended. Add three (3) sprigs parsley, a bay leaf, a little thyme.

Cook for one and a half hours, stirring occasionally. Add 1/2 cup vinegar, six (6) crushed peppercorns. Reduce liquid to two-thirds (2/3rds). Strain sauce into reduced vinegar and cook all together about thirty (30) minutes longer. Add 1/2 cup red wine.


## POIVRADE SAUCE

8 peppercorns, crushed          1 cup Brown sauce
1/2 cup vinegar (see pages 26-31 )
2 Tbls. red currant jelly

Mix vinegar, peppercorns and simmer until reduced to 1/4 cup. Add brown sauce and simmer 1/2 hour. Add jelly. Whisk well. Strain.


## POIVRADE SAUCE

1 tsp. shallots, chopped          1 cup Espagnole sauce
pinch bay leaf powder             (see page 95 )
1/2 cup red wine                  1/2 tsp. peppercorns
pinch thyme

Add shallots, bay leaf powder, thyme to simmering Espagnole sauce. Continue simmer five (5) minutes. Add vinegar, increase heat to medium, simmer five (5) more minutes. Crack peppercorns and add during last minute of cooking. Strain through very fine sieve. If sauce is too thick at this point, stir in small amount of butter.


## POULETTE SAUCE

1 cup White sauce          juice of a lemon
2 egg yolks                chopped parsley

Make a basic White sauce. Add egg yolks. Blend well by whisking. Season with lemon juice and parsley. Do not let sauce boil after egg yolks are added.

## POULETTE SAUCE

In one (1) Tbls butter saute 6-8 mushrooms, minced. When they start to brown add two (2) shallots, chopped, 1/2 cup cream. Cook until reduced by half. Add 1/2 cup Veloute sauce, (see pages 190-191 ). Bring to boil. Add salt to taste. Beat two (2) egg yolks with a little cream. Add to sauce. Bring to boil again, stirring constantly, but do not boil. Add juice of half a lemon, 1/2 tsp. parsley.

### SHE LOOKETH AS BUTTER WOULD NOT MELT IN HER MOUTH.
John Heywood
Proverbs, I, x (1546)

## LOUISIANA POULTRY SAUCE

Over low heat cook one (1) onion, sliced, two (2) Tbls. chopped celery—stalks and leaves—in 1 1/2 cups chicken stock for five (5) minutes. Season to taste with salt and pepper. Keep hot. Cream two (2) egg yolks with two (2) Tbls. flour, whisking in two (2) Tbls. hot chicken stock. Return saucepan to heat and cook, stirring constantly, until sauce thickens. Blend Tbls. butter, two (2) tsp. each chopped parsley, chervil, tarragon vinegar. Strain.

## PROVENCALE SAUCE

| | |
|---|---|
| 1 Tbls. olive oil | 1 tsp. tomato puree |
| 3 Tbls. vinegar | 1 tsp. capers, chopped |
| 1 Tbls. parsley, chopped | salt, pepper |

Mix olive oil, vinegar, salt and pepper. Stir well. Add tomato puree, capers, parsley. Stir thoroughly. Stir before serving.

## PROVENCALE SAUCE

3/4 cup onion, chopped      1/2 cup olive oil
6 cloves, chopped      32 ounces Italian plum tomatoes
1 1/2 tsp. salt      1 tsp. fresh ground black pepper
3 Tbls. fresh basil, chopped      3 Tbls. tomato paste
1/4 parsley, chopped

Saute onions, garlic in olive oil. Add tomatoes, seasonings. Bring to boil. Reduce heat. Cook slowly for fifteen (15) minutes, stirring occasionally. Correct seasoning. Add tomato paste. Simmer fifteen (15) minutes. Stir occasionally. Add parsley.

## PRUNIER SAUCE

Crumble the coral of a lobster. Add one (1) cup mayonnaise, 1 1/2 Tbls. each walnuts, ketchup, caviar, one (1) tsp. each chopped chives, parsley, chervil, shallots.

## RADZIWILL SAUCE

Beat until well blended 1/4 cup mayonnaise, three (3) Tbls. guava jelly, two (2) Tbls. fresh grated horseradish, one (1) Tbls. tarragon vinegar, one (1) tsp. prepared mustard, touch of salt, cayenne. Fold in 1/2 cup whipped cream, two (2) Tbls, Sherry wine. Serve hot or cold.

## RAISIN SAUCE

To one (1) tsp. brown sugar add one (1) tsp. vinegar. Stir in one (1) cup Brown sauce, (see pages 55-58 ). Bring to boil, stirring constantly. Remove from heat. Add 1/4 cup seedless raisins which have been plumped in Port wine and drained.

## RAISIN SAUCE

1/2 cup water

1/2 cup dark seedless raisins

1/3 cup currant jelly

1/2 tsp. grated orange peel

1/8 tsp. salt

1/8 tsp. ground allspice

1 Tbls, cornstarch

1/3 cup orange juice

Over medium heat, Bring to boil water, raisins, orange peel, salt, allspice. Blend cornstarch with orange juice. Stir this into raisin mixture, cooking until thickened and clear.

## RED RAISIN SAUCE

10 ounces red currant jelly

1/2 cup golden raisins

1/4 cup butter

1/4 tsp. ground allspice

16 ounces spiced crabapples

2 tsp. lemon juice

Combine all ingredients and cook over medium to low heat Ten (10) minutes.

## RAISIN NUT SAUCE

1/4 cup brown sugar

1 Tbls. flour

1 cup water

1/4 cup chopped walnuts

1/4 tsp. salt

3 Tbls. lemon juice

1/2 cup seedless raisins

1 Tbls. butter

Mix sugar, flour. Add water. Bring to boil. Add salt, lemon juice, raisins. Simmer five (5) minutes. Add nut meat, butter. Cook until butter melts.

**A GOOD DINNER SHARPENS WIT, WHILE
IT SOFTENS THE HEART**
Doran

## RAREBIT SAUCE

Blend three (3) Tbls. butter, three (3) Tbls. flour. Brown slightly. Slowly stir in one (1) cup light cream. Stir until smooth and thick. Add one (1) tsp. fresh black pepper, speck cayenne. Stir in 1/4 cup grated Cheddar Cheese and melt. Blend. Add dash tabasco.

## EASY WELSH RAREBIT SAUCE

4 Tbls. butter
1 tsp. salt
1/2 tsp. paprika
1/2 tsp. prepared mustard
1 cup beer

1/4 tsp. cayenne
1 tsp. Worcestershire sauce
1 pound sharp cheddar, grated
2 eggs, lightly beaten

In double boiler melt butter. Add seasonings and cheese. Cook and stir until cheese is soft. Add some of the beer, a little bit at a time, stirring gently. Mix eggs with a little of the beer. Add to mixture, stirring until smooth.

## CRAB RAREBIT SAUCE

4 ounces canned mushrooms
2 Tbls. butter
1/4 flour
tabasco sauce
1/3 cup chopped stuffed olives

1/4 cup chili sauce
1 cup evaporated milk
1 cup grated cheddar cheese
6 1/2 ounces crab meat

Save mushroom liquid. Add to mushroom liquid enough water to make 1/2 cup. Melt butter. Stir in flour until smooth. Gradually stir in mushroom liquor, tabasco, chili sauce, evaporated milk, grated cheese. Cook over low heat until cheese melts and mixture thickens. Add mushrooms, crab meat, olives. Heat but do not boil.

## RAVIGOTE SAUCE

Mix together five (5) Tbls. olive oil, two (2) Tbls. vinegar, small chopped onion, one (1) chopped hard boiled egg, one (1) Tbls. prepared mustard, one (1) tsp. of mixed chopped parsley, tarragon, chives, chervil. Salt and pepper to taste.

**VEGETARIANISM IS HARMLESS ENOUGH, ALTHOUGH IT IS APT TO FILL A MAN WITH WIND AND SELF-RIGHTEOUSNESS.**
Dr. Robert Hutchinson

## RAVIOGOTE SAUCE

| | |
|---|---|
| 1 slice bread | 1 tsp. prepared mustard |
| 2 Tbls. onion flakes | 1 tsp. chopped chives |
| 1/2 cup water | 1 Tbls. chopped capers |
| 1 pkg. instant chicken broth mix | 1 cup milk |
| tarragon | |

Make crumbs of the bread. Cook onion with chicken broth mix and water. When onions are soft and water evaporated add milk and bread crumbs. Cook until thick. Stir in remaining ingredients. Strain.

## RAVIGOTE SAUCE

| | |
|---|---|
| 3 shallots | 2 Tbls. butter |
| 1 Tbls. chives diced | 2 Tbls. flour |
| 1/2 cup vinegar | 1 1/2 cups chicken bouillon |
| 2 egg yolks | salt, pepper, tarragon, chervil, parsley |

Peel and chop shallots. Mix with chives. Add vinegar. Reduce over medium heat to about two (2) Tbls.. Strain into chicken bouillon. Heat butter, Add flour. Cook until roux becomes a light brown.

Whisk in hot bouillon. Bring to boil. Whisk until sauce is thick. Salt and pepper to taste. To egg yolks add about 1/3rd hot sauce. Whisk. Then whisk this mixture into bulk of sauce. When first bubble appears on surface remove from heat. Add one (1) Tbls. each chopped tarragon, chervil parsley. Correct seasoning to taste.

## RAVIGOTE SAUCE

Combine 1/3 cup white wine, 1/3 cup vinegar, six (6) chopped shallots. Cook until reduced by two thirds (2/3rds). Add two (2) cups Cream sauce, (see pages 80-83 ). Boil gently five (5) minutes. Remove from heat. Add two (2) Tbls. butter, one (1) tsp. mixed chopped tarragon, chervil, chives.

## BASIC RED SAUCE

| | |
|---|---|
| 1 cup chopped onion | 1/4 cup sugar |
| 1/3 cup olive oil | 1/4 cup Worcestershire sauce |
| 1 1/2 cup ketchup | 2 1/2 tsp. salt |
| 1/2 cup water | 1/2 cup lemon juice |
| pepper | tabasco sauce |

Cook onion in olive oil until soft. Add remaining ingredients. Simmer five (5) minutes. Cool.

## REMOULADE SAUCE

| | |
|---|---|
| 1 tsp. dry mustard | 1 Tbls. chopped capers |
| 1 tsp. paprika | 2 Tbls. chopped scallions |
| 1/4 tsp. salt | 2 Tbls. chopped chives |
| 1/4 tsp. pepper | 2 Tbls. chopped celery |
| 1/8 tsp. cayenne | 1/2 cup olive oil |
| 4 anchovies, chopped | 1 tsp. horseradish |

Combine dry mustard, paprika, salt, pepper, cayenne. Mix well. Add remaining ingredients and mix well.

REMOULADESAUCE

2 cups mayonnaise                1 tsp. strong mustard
1 clove garlic. chopped          1 Tbls. chopped fresh tarragon
2 hard boiled eggs, chopped      1 tsp chopped parsley
1 tsp. anchovy paste

Blend all ingredients thoroughly. Let stand two hours before serving.

**TEMPERANCE AND LABOR ARE THE TWO BEST PHYSICIANS OF MAN; LABOR SHARPENS THE APEPTITE, AND TEMPERANCE PREVENTS FROM INDULGING TO EXCESS**
Rousseau

REMOULADE SAUCE

3 Tbls. wine vinegar             1 tsp. horseradish
2 Tbls. prepared mustard         1 Tbls. chopped parsley
2 Tbls. diced scallions          1/2 cup plus 1 Tbls. olive oil
2 Tbls diced celery              sale, pepper

Combine vinegar with mustard, scallions, celery, horseradish, parsley. Whisk in olive oil, a little at a time. Season with salt, pepper, touch of red pepper.

**WHAT WAS SAUCE FOR THE GOOSE WAS SAUCE FOR THE GANDER**
R. Head and F. Kirkman
English Rogue, II, 120 (1671)

## REMOULADE SAUCE

| | |
|---|---|
| 2 cups mayonnaise | 2 cups hard-boiled eggs, chopped |
| 2 cloves garlic, chopped | 1 Tbls. chopped parsley |
| 1 Tbls. chopped tarragon | 1 Tbls. anchovy paste |
| 1 tsp. dry mustard | 1 tsp. capers |

Mix all ingredients thoroughly. Let stand two hours before serving

## REMOULADE SAUCE

| | |
|---|---|
| 2 Tbls. chopped sour pickles | 1 Tbls. chopped parsley |
| 1 Tbls. chopped capers | 1 tsp. prepared mustard |
| 1 cup mayonnaise | 1/4 tsp. tarragon |

Mix mayonnaise, pickles, capers, parsley, mustard and tarragon thoroughly.

## REMOULADE A L'INDIENNE SAUCE

Two (2) cups mayonnaise, little tomato paste, four (4) chopped, drained anchovy fillets, one (1) Tbls. each curry powder, chopped capers, onion, shallots, chervil, green pepper, dash of cayenne. Rub through sieve. Add, while rubbing, two (2) lightly beaten egg yolks. Chill.

## ROBERT SAUCE

Saute two (2) onions in one (1) Tbls. butter, until golden brown. Add 1/3 cup dry white wine, one (1) Tbls. vinegar. Reduce by three fourths (3/4ths). Add one (1) cup Brown sauce, (see pages 55-58 ), two (2) Tbls. tomato sauce. Cook slowly ten (10) to fifteen (15) minutes. Add one (1) Tbls. each prepared mustard, chopped sour pickle, one (1) tsp. chopped parsley.

## ROBERT SAUCE

Brown 3/4 cup chopped onion in 1/4 cup butter. Add can of beef gravy, one (1) Tbls. wine vinegar, 1/2 cup dry white wine, one (1) Tbls. prepared mustard. Salt and pepper to taste.

## ROBERT SAUCE

1 cup Espagnole sauce (see page 61 )          1/4 tsp. dry mustard
1/4 tsp. onion                                salt

Mix salt and mustard in simmering Espagnole until dissolved.

## ROBERT BURNS SAUCE

Melt two (2) Tbls, butter. Add one (1) tsp. chopped shallots, one (1) mashed garlic clove, pinch each sage, thyme, marjoram. Cook over medium heat until shallots begin to color. Add 1/4 cup chopped, cooked ham, a bay leaf, tsp. of parsley. Add 1 1/2 cups chicken stock. Season with salt and pepper. Bring to boil. Lower heat and simmer for fifteen (15) minutes. Stir occasionally. Strain. Add two (2) tsp. Bar-le-Duc, one (1) tsp. grated horseradish, pinch powdered juniper berry, two (2) egg yolks that have been beaten with three (3) Tbls. Madeira wine. Bring almost to boil, stirring constantly. Remove from heat.

## ROMANA SAUCE

Over low heat combine one (1) pound cooked noodles with 1/2 cup butter, two (2) Tbls. chopped parsley, one (1) Tbls. chopped basil, two (2) sliced garlic cloves. Add grated Romano cheese, pepper to taste.

## WHAT, YOU EGG! YOUNG FRY OF TREACHERY.
Macbeth, IV, 11, 83


### ROUENNAISE SAUCE

Combine 1/2 cup red wine, five (5) peppercorns, two (2) chopped shallots, a bay leaf, 1/2 tsp. thyme. Bring to boil. Reduce by two thirds (2/3rds). Add 1/2 Tbls. butter creamed with 1/2 tsp. flour. Bring to boil again. Remove from heat. Keep hot. Mix in very fine chopped duck or chicken livers. Rub sauce through sieve. Add two (2) Tbls. Cognac.


### ROUENNAISE SAUCE

Combine one (1) cup red wine, ten (10) peppercorns, a bay leaf, one (1) tsp. thyme, four (4) chopped shallots. Bring to boil. Reduce by two thirds (2/3rds). Add 1/4 cup Brown sauce, (see pages 55-58 ). Bring to boiling point. Remove from heat. Add duck or chicken livers, chopped very fine. Rub through sieve. Add 1/4 cup Cognac.


### SALMI SAUCE

Combine juice and grated rind of two (2) oranges with 1/4 cup Port wine, two (2) cups canned beef gravy. Simmer a few minutes to blend. Reduce a little bit.


### SALMIS SAUCE

To one (1) Tbls. olive oil add two (2) shallots, diced, and saute. Add one (1) Tbls. chopped mushroom stems, a little piece of bay leaf, pinch of thyme, 1/2 cup Port wine. Cook gently for five (5) minutes. Stir occasionally. Add 3/4 cup stock made from carcass of whatever game bird you are preparing. Simmer gently fifteen (15) minutes. Skim often. Strain. Skim off any scum, add salt, pepper, cayenne, nutmeg to taste. Just before serving add two (2) tsp. currant jelly and mix well.

## SHALLOT SAUCE

Combine one (1) hard boiled egg yolk, one (1) tsp. Worcestershire sauce, 1/2 tsp. dry mustard. Whisk thoroughly. Slowly add 1/2 cup olive oil, whisking briskly. Add one (1) Tbls. tarragon vinegar, salt, pepper to taste. Add cube of ice and beat until sauce thickens. While beating add 1/4 cup heavy cream, two (2) Tbls. chopped shallots. Discard ice. Serve cold.

## SHALLOT SAUCE

Combine 3/4 cup white wine, one (1) Tbls. chopped shallots. Cook this until reduced to two (2) Tbls. Add 1 1/2 cups fish Veloute sauce, (see pages 191 ). Cook slowly five (5) minutes. Remove from heat. Add one (1) tsp. lemon juice, two (2) Tbls. butter.

## SHRIMP SAUCE

Blend 1/4 cup chive cream cheese, 1/4 cup milk. Add one (1) can condensed cream-of-shrimp soup. Stir while heating. Add two (2) tsp. lemon juice.

**SIMPLE DIET IS BEST, FOR MANY DISHES BRING MANY DISEASES, AND RICH SAUCES ARE WORSE THAN EVEN HEAPING SEVERAL MEATS UPON EACH OTHER**

Pliny

## SHRIMP SAUCE

| | |
|---|---|
| 6 Tbls. butter | 1/8 tsp. pepper |
| 8 ounces shrimp | 1/4 tsp. salt |
| 6 Tbls. flour | 1 cup half and half |
| 1/8 tsp. paprika | 1/2 cup Sauterne wine |

Over medium high heat cook shrimp in butter until tender. Blend in flour, paprika, pepper, salt. Gradually add half and half, sauterne, Stir constantly until thickened.

SHRIMP SAUCE

To one (1) cup Bechamel sauce ( see pages 47-49 ), add 1/2 cup fish stock, 1/4 cup cream. Reduce this a bit over high heat. Stir in 1/3 cup hot cooked shrimp cut into cubes, one (1) Tbls. butter

## A WELL-GOVERNED APETITE
## IS A GREAT PART OF LIBERTY
Seneca

## SHRIMP MARINARA SAUCE

| | |
|---|---|
| 1 Tbls. olive oil | 1 Tbls. sugar |
| 1 chopped garlic clove | 3/4 tsp. salt |
| 15 ounces tomato sauce | 1/2 tsp. oregano |
| 6 ounces tomato paste | 1/4 tsp. pepper |
| 2 Tbls. chopped parsley | 1 pound shrimp, deveined |

In olive oil brown garlic. Add tomato sauce and all other ingredients except shrimp. Bring to boil. Reduce heat to low. Simmer over low heat ten (10 ) minutes. Add shrimp. Cook until tender. Stir constantly.

## SHRIMP OLIVE SAUCE

| | |
|---|---|
| 8 ounces tomato sauce | 1/2 cup stuffed olives, sliced |
| 1/2 pound shrimp, cooked | 1/3 cup dry wine |

Mix and heat all ingredients.

## SOUBISE SAUCE

| | |
|---|---|
| 1 cup Veloute sauce (see pages 1910 ) | onion, chopped |
| 1 Tbls. butter | |

Steam onion in butter until soft. Add to Veloute sauce.

## SOUBISE SAUCE

Cook two (2) cups chopped onion in 1/2 cup beef stock a few minutes. Drain. Melt two (2) Tbls. butter. Add onions and cook until soft. Combine onion pulp with one (1) cup Mornay sauce, ( see pages 130-131 ). [Use two (2) cups Mornay sauce for thinner sauce].

## SOUBISE SAUCE

4 ounces sliced onions          1 envelope instant chicken broth
1 1/2 cups water                salt

Cook onion in water with chicken broth until soft and liquid down to one half. Puree in blender.

## SOUBISE SAUCE

1/2 cup onions, chopped         salt—nutmeg
1 tsp. butter                   3/4 cup Veloute sauce
                                (see pages 191)

Saute onions in butter, mashing into soft paste when softened. Bring Veloute sauce to simmer over medium heat. Reduce to one third (1/3rd), stirring often. Add salt and nutmeg—dash each—onion puree. Stir until smooth.

## ANCHOVY ONION SAUCE

2 large Spanish onions, chopped     1 cup tomato paste
4 Tbls. olive oil                   1/4 cup white wine
10 anchovy pieces, cut in half      1/4 cup chopped parsley
thyme, basil

Saute onions in olive oil until golden but not browned. Add anchovy fillets. Add parsley, thyme, basil. Add tomato paste mixed with wine. Cook sauce down a little. Season to taste.

## CARAMEL ONION SAUCE

Carmelize two (2) Tbls. sugar with one (1) Tbls. butter. Add two (2) onions, sliced thin. Cook until tender. Stir often. Add one (1) cup consomme, one (1) Tbls. wine vinegar, salt to taste. Simmer twenty (20) minutes, stirring frequently

## ONION AND CURRY SAUCE

Heat three (3) Tbls. olive oil to smoking. Saute two (2) chopped onions until brown. Stir constantly. Mix together one (1) Tbls. each curry powder, flour. Stir this into onions. Gradually stir in one (1) cup scalded milk. Cook until mixture begins to thicken. Add small green pepper, julienned, two (2) Tbls. chopped red pimentos. Bring to boil. Serve.

## SOUR CREAM ONION SAUCE

Season one (1) cup sour cream with salt, pepper, grated onion.

## SOUR CREAM ONION SAUCE

| | |
|---|---|
| 2 Tbls. chopped onions | paprika |
| 1 Tbls. butter | 1 tsp. sugar |
| 1 Tbls. flour | 3/4 cup sour cream |
| 1 tsp. vinegar | 3/4 tsp. salt |

Saute onion in butter. Add flour, paprika, sugar, salt. Cook over hot water, adding cream and stirring constantly until thickened. Add vinegar. Serve hot

**I KNOW WHICH SIDE MY BREAD IS BUTTERED ON**
John Heywood (1546)

## SOUR CREAM SAUCE

| | |
|---|---|
| 1 Tbls. butter | 1/4 cup milk |
| 1 1/2 tsp. flour | 1/8 tsp. seasoned salt |
| 1/4 cup sour cream | |

Melt butter over medium heat until frothy. Stir in flour. Heat until frothy again. Blend in milk and seasoned salt. Simmer over low heat until thickened and smooth. Remove from heat. Add sour cream. Blend in one (1) tsp. Dijon mustard.

## IT IS MEAT AND DRINK TO ME
### As You Like It, V, i, 11

## SMITANE SAUCE

Saute two (2) minced onions until soft. Do not brown. Add 1/3 cup dry white wine. Reduce liquor over medium heat, stirring, to almost nothing. Add one (1) cup scalded heavy sour cream. Stir constantly until thoroughly blended. Simmer very gently five (5) minutes. Strain. Season with salt and pepper to taste. Just before serving add one (1) tsp. lemon juice.

## SMITANE SAUCE

Saute two (2) cups chopped onions until soft. Add 1/2 cup white wine. Reduce liquid over high heat to near nothing, stirring often. Add one (1) cup scalded sour cream, stirring constantly until thoroughly blended. Simmer for five (5) minutes. Strain. Add one (1) tsp. lemon juice.

## SOUR CREAM DILL SAUCE

1 egg
1 tsp. salt
2 Tbls. chopped dill
pinch sugar, pinch fresh pepper

4 tsp. lemon juice
1 tsp. grated onion
1 1/2 cups sour cream

Whip egg until fluffy. Add rest of ingredients, blend in sour cream last. Chill.

## SOUR CREAM DILL SAUCE

1 cup sour cream
1 bunch dill with stems broken into small pieces

Put sour cream in blender. Add dill and blend at high speed. Chill.

## SOUR CREAM MUSTARD SAUCE

1 cup sour cream
1/4 tsp.salt
1 Tbls. prepared mustard

1 Tbls minced onion
1/8 tsp. pepper
1 Tbls. chopped parsley

Heat all ingredients until just hot. Sprinkle parsley.

## SPADOIS SAUCE

Mix 1/4 cup dried currants in one (1) cup red wine ten (10) minutes. Add 1/2 cup bread crumbs, 1/4 cup Port wine, six (6) whole cloves, two (2) Tbls. butter stirring until all smooth. Season to taste with salt, pepper, nutmeg, touch cayenne.

## SPAGHETTI SAUCE

| | |
|---|---|
| 2 Tbls. olive oil | 2 Tbls. chopped parsley |
| 1 onion, chopped | 1 tsp. oregano |
| 1 minced garlic clove | 1 tsp. salt |
| 30 ounces tomato sauce | 1/8 tsp. pepper |
| 12 ounces tomato paste | a bay leaf |
| 2 tsp. brown sugar | |

In hot oil, over medium heat, cook garlic and onion until tender. Stir often while cooking. Add all ingredients. Bring to boil. Reduce heat to low. Simmer thirty (30) minutes.

## SPAGHETTI SAUCE

| | |
|---|---|
| 1/2 cup chopped onions | 2 cups chopped tomatoes |
| 1 tsp. chopped garlic | 2 cups tomato puree |
| 1 tsp. chopped celery | 1/8 tsp. paprika |
| 1 tsp. chopped parsley | 1/4 cup Sherry wine |
| 1/2 cup olive oil | salt, pepper |

Saute garlic, onion, celery, parsley in olive oil until celery, onions are soft. Add tomatoes, puree, paprika. Cook until thick. Season with salt and pepper to taste. Add Sherry wine at serving.

THE SATISFACTION AND RESPONSE THAT FOLLOW A
FULL MEAL TEND TO CHECK THE DISPOSITION TO
SPLENETIC ARGUMENT, OR TOO MUCH ZEAL IN
SUPPORTING AN OPINION, WHILE THE FREEDOM
AND ABANDON OF THE INTERCOURSE KEPT UP IS
EMINENTLY CONDUCIVE TO THE FEELINGS
OF GENERAL BENEVOLENCE.

Jerdan

## SPAGHETTI SAUCE

| | |
|---|---|
| 2 Tbls. olive oil | 28 ounces Italian tomatoes with juice |
| 1 chopped onion | 6 ounces tomato paste |
| 1 chopped carrot | 1 tsp. oregano |
| a chopped celery stalk | 1 tsp. salt |
| 1 minced garlic clove | 1 tsp. sugar |
| 1/4 cup fresh chopped parsley | 1 tsp. grated lemon rind |
| 3/4 pound ground beef | 1/2 tsp. pepper |
| 1/2 cup dry red wine | 1/2 tsp. basil |

Over high heat saute, in olive oil, onion, carrot, celery, garlic, parsley. Add ground beef. Stir in dry red wine. Cook until evaporated. Add all other ingredients. Bring to boil. Reduce heat. Simmer over low heat for two (2) to 2 1/2 hours. Stir often.

## SPANISH SAUCE

| | |
|---|---|
| 2 Tbls. olive oil | 1 Tbls. chopped green pepper |
| 2 Tbls. chopped onion | 1 1/2 Tbls. flour |
| 2 Tbls. chopped celery | 1 cup meat stock |
| 1/2 cup tomato puree | |

Heat olive oil. Add onion, celery, green pepper and saute until soft. Blend in flour. Gradually add stock, tomato puree. Cook ten (10) minutes, stirring.

THE INTENTION OF EVERY OTHER PIECE OF PROSE
MAY BE DISCUSSED AND EVEN MISTRUSTED;
BUT THE PURPOSE OF A COOKERY BOOK IS ONE AND
UNMISTAKABLE. ITS OBJECT CAN CONCEIVABLY
BE NO OTHER THAN TO INCREASE THE
HAPPINESS OF MANKIND.

Joseph Conrad

## SPANISH SAUCE

| | |
|---|---|
| 1 onion, chopped | a bay leaf |
| 2 Tbls. chopped green pepper | 1 tsp. salt |
| chopped garlic clove | 1/4 tsp. pepper |
| 2 Tbls. butter | pinch of cloves |
| 2 cups Italian plum tomatoes | 1/4 cup chopped stuffed olives |

Saute onion, garlic, green pepper in butter until lightly browned. Chop tomatoes and add remaining ingredients to the mixture and simmer thirty (30) minutes until thick. Add seasonings.


## SPANISH SAUCE

| | |
|---|---|
| 3/4 cup tomato puree | 1/2 tsp. salt |
| onion chopped | pinch oregano, basil |
| 1/8 tsp. pepper | 1 bell pepper, chopped |

Combine all ingredients. Refrigerate for an hour.


**HE WHO FEASTS EVERY DAY, FEASTS NO DAY.**
C. Simmons


## SPANISH OMELET SAUCE

| | |
|---|---|
| 1/ cup olive oil | 1 tsp. sugar |
| 1 cup chopped onion | 1/4 cup capers, chopped |
| 2 garlic cloves, chopped | 1/2 cup chopped parsley |
| 2 chopped green peppers | 1 cup cooked green peas |
| 4 cups peeled Italian tomatoes | 1/2 cup pimentos, chopped |
| 1/2 tsp. hot red pepper flakes | 1 cup Cheddar cheese |
| 3/4 tsp. thyme | 2 bay leaves |

Cook onions and garlic in olive oil, until wilted. Add green peppers. Cook a couple minutes. Add tomatoes, pepper flakes, thyme, bay leaves, sugar. Simmer thirty (30) minutes. Stir occasionally until thickened. Add capers, parsley, peas, pimentos. Season with salt and pepper. Use as omelet filling.

## THE PLEASANT TALK OF THE DINNER TABLE PROMOTES DIGESTION, AND PREVENTS THE MIND FROM DWELLING ON THE GRINDING OF THE DIGESTIVE MILL THAT IS GOING ON WITHIN US.
Jerdan

## SPANISH SAVORY SAUCE

| | |
|---|---|
| 1 pound chestnuts | 2 Tbls. white wine |
| 1 cup plain yogurt | 1 Tbls. butter |

Boil chestnuts until soft. Remove inner and outer skins and put through fine grinder. Blend yogurt, wine and butter. Add Chestnuts. Mix well. Cook for ten (1) to fifteen (15) minutes over low heat stirring constantly.

## SPANISH SAUCE SUPREME

| | |
|---|---|
| 3 Tbls. olive oil | 1/4 tsp. salt |
| celery stalk, leaves and all, chopped | 2 Tbls. brewer's yeast |
| onion, chopped | a bay leaf |
| 3 Tbls. whole wheat flour | 1 tsp. minced dulse |
| 1 tsp. soy flour | 1/4 tsp. basil |
| 1 cup tomato puree | 1/4 tsp. oregano |

Saute celery, onion in olive oil. Set aside. In remaining olive oil blend flours until smooth. Add celery, onion and all other ingredients. Simmer thirty (30) minutes until thick. Stir often.

## SPINACH SAUCE

1/4 cup butter                          1 cup Ricotta cheese
10 ounces cooked spinach                1/4 cup grated Parmesan cheese
1 tsp. salt                             1/4 cup milk
1/8 tsp. nutmeg

Over medium heat cook spinach in butter. Reduce heat to low and
add remaining ingredients. Cook until heated through.


## SPINACH VEGETABLE SAUCE

4 tomatoes, chopped                     1 Tbls. chopped parsley
1/2 cup cooked spinach                  1 Tbls. cider vinegar
1/2 cup diced, cooked, mushrooms        1 Tbls. dry onion flakes
a garlic clove, crushed

Combine ingredients and cook until thick, thirty (30) minutes.


## STRATFORDSHIRE SAUCE

In double boiler combine 1/2 cup Port wine, 1/4 cup Brown sauce,
(see pages 55-58 ), one (1) Tbls. lemon juice, one (1) tsp sugar, 1/2 tsp.
ketchup, one (1) Tbls. diced mushrooms, pinch cayenne, salt to taste.
Stir until blended. Bring almost to boil over hot water. Do not boil.


## SAUCE SUPREME

Combine two (2) cups chicken stock with three (3) sliced
mushrooms. Cook until reduced by two thirds (2/3rds). Add to one
(1) cup Veloute sauce, (see pages 191 ). Bring to boil. Reduce to about
one (1) cup. Gradually add one (1) cup heavy cream, stirring
constantly. Season to taste with salt, cayenne. Strain. A pat of
butter will prevent crusting if not going to use at once.

## SAUCE SUPREME

Mix two (2) egg yolks with 1/3 cup scalded heavy cream, three (3) Tbls. dry Sherry wine. Add one (1) cup Veloute sauce ( see pages 191 ), made with double strength chicken stock. Bring to boil stirring constantly. Stir in 1 1/2 Tbls. truffles, two(2) tsp. lemon juice, 1/2 tsp. paprika.


## IN GENERAL, MANKIND, SINCE THE IMPROVEMENT OF COOKERY, EAT TWICE AS MUCH AS NATURE REQUIRES.
Franklin


## SAUCE SUPREME

| | |
|---|---|
| 3/4 cup chicken stock | 1 Tbls. butter |
| 3/4 cup Veloute sauce (see pages 191 ) | 3 Tbls. lemon juice |

Add chicken stock to Veloute sauce. Simmer over medium heat to reduce mixture one third (1/3). Stir often. Remove from heat. Stir in butter until blended. Add lemon juice. Stir vigorously until smooth.


## SWEET SOUR SAUCE

| | |
|---|---|
| 2 1/2 Tbls. cornstarch | 1/2 cup sugar |
| 1/2 cup vinegar | 1 cup chicken stock |
| 3 Tbls. lemon juice | 2 Tbls. water |
| 1 Tbls.soy sauce | 1/4 tsp. salt |

Combine ingredients until smooth.

## SWEET SOUR SAUCE

| | |
|---|---|
| 2 Tbls. sugar | 3 Tbls. ketchup |
| 1 Tbls. cornstarch | 1 Tbls. cider vinegar |
| 1/2 tsp. chili powder | 1/4 cup chopped sweet gherkin |

Mix cornstarch, chili powder, sugar. Add water, ketchup, vinegar until smooth. Over medium heat cook until boils and is thick, stirring constantly. Remove from heat and stir in gherkins.

**ANIMALS FEED; MAN EATS. ONLY THE MAN OF INTELLECT AND JUDGMENT KNOWS HOW TO EAT.**
Savarin

## SWEET SOUR SAUCE

| | |
|---|---|
| 2 green peppers, chopped | 3 Tbls. sugar |
| large onion, chopped | 2 Tbls. tomato sauce |
| 3 slices canned pineapple | 1/2 cup vinegar |
| a garlic clove, minced | 1 cup pineapple juice |
| 1 Tbls. cornstarch | 1/2 tsp. salt |
| 3 Tbls. water | 2 Tbls. olive oil |

Blend cornstarch and water to a paste. Blend sugar, tomato sauce, vinegar, pineapple juice, salt. Bring slowly to a boil, stirring. Heat skillet. To hot olive oil add garlic, onion, green pepper and stir fry until slightly softened. Add pineapple pieces and heat. Add stir fried ingredients. Stir in cornstarch paste quickly over medium heat until sauce is thickened.

## SWEET SOUR SAUCE

2 Tbls. plum preserves  2 Tbls. sugar
4 Tbls. vinegar    2 Tbls. hot mustard powder

Mix plum preserves, sugar, vinegar. Add hot mustard powder with three (3) Tbls. water to form paste. Add paste to mixture to taste.


## SWEET SOUR SAUCE

3 dried mushrooms   3 Tbls. tomato sauce
2 scallions, chopped   1 Tbls. soy sauce
small bamboo shoot, shredded 1/2 tsp. salt
small carrot, chopped   3/4 cup chicken stock
2 slices ginger root    1 Tbls cornstarch
6 Tbls. sugar      2 Tbls. water
4 Tbls. vinegar     2 Tbls. olive oil

Soak mushrooms to soften. Blend sugar, vinegar, tomato sauce, soy sauce, salt and chicken stock. Blend cornstarch and water to a paste. In saucepan bring ingredients to a boil over medium heat. Heat skillet. Add olive oil. Add shredded, chopped vegetables. Stir fry until softened. Add heated sauce mixture and blend. Add paste, after re-stirring it, to thicken sauce. Garnish with scallions.


## SWEET SOUR SAUCE

3 stalks green onions, chopped 5 Tbls. brown sugar
1/2 green pepper, chopped  1 cup water
2 Tbls. olive oil     1 1/2 Tbls. cornstarch
3 slices ginger root    2 Tbls. vinegar
1 Tbls. soy sauce     cold water

Saute onions, green pepper in olive oil. Add ginger root, soy sauce, brown sugar, one (1) cup water. Bring to boil and boil for two (2) minutes. Dissolve cornstarch in a small amount of cold water. Add to thicken sauce. Add vinegar. Serve hot.

## SWEET SOUR SAUCE

In a large skillet heat three (3) Tbls. olive oil. Add three (3) slices fresh ginger root and two (2) crushed garlic cloves. Cook over high heat a minute. Stir in one (1) cup each sliced onions, strips of green and red bell pepper, one small, thinly sliced carrot. Cook over high heat three (3) minutes stirring constantly. Add juice from can of pineapple, juice from four (4) ounces sweet pickle jar, 1/2 cup each malt vinegar, water, three (3) Tbls. soy sauce, two (2) Tbls Sherry wine, one (1) tsp. each salt, pepper. Bring to boil. Add 1/2 cup sugar, three (3) Tbls. cornstarch mixed with 1/2 cup water until smooth. Stir in pineapple chunks, pickle chunks, one (1) each quartered lemon, tomato. Continue cooking until sauce is thick and clear.

## SWEET SOUR SAUCE

| | |
|---|---|
| 2 Tbls. drippings from venison roasting pan | 2 Tbls. vinegar |
| 1 tsp. shallots, chopped | 2 cups Burgundy wine |
| 1 Tbls. flour | 2 Tbls. currant jelly |
| salt and pepper | |

Remove all but two (2) Tbls. fat from roasting pan. Add chopped shallots, flour. Blend. Add vinegar and wine. Continue cooking, stirring constantly, until reduced by half. Stir in currant jelly until well mixed. Salt and pepper to taste.

## TARTAR SAUCE

To 1 1/2 cups mayonnaise add one (1) chopped dill pickle, four (4) chopped shallots, two (2) chopped anchovies, one (1) Tbls. each capers, parsley, tarragon, chervil, one (1) tsp. mustard. Thin sauce with heavy cream, 1/2 tsp lemon juice, sugar, salt, pepper to taste.

## TARTAR SAUCE

1 cup mayonnaise
1 Tbls. chopped parsley
1 Tbls. chopped, stuffed olives

1 Tbls. chopped pickle
1 Tbls. chopped capers
1 tsp. onion juice

Combine all ingredients. Chill

## TARTAR SAUCE

1/4 cup mayonnaise
1/2 tsp Dijon mustard
1 Tbls. chopped capers
1/4 tsp anchovy paste
1 chopped hard boiled egg

1 Tbls. sweet pickle relish
2 tsp. chopped parsley
1 tsp. chopped chives
1/8 tsp chervil

Combine all ingredients. Chill.

## TARTAR SAUCE

1/2 cup mayonnaise
2 Tbls. sweet relish
1 Tbls. chopped onion

1 Tbls. chopped capers
1 tsp. prepared mustard

Combine all ingredients. Chill.

## TARTAR SAUCE

1 cup mayonnaise
2 Tbls chopped parsley
1 Tbls. chopped chives
1 Tbls. chopped fresh tarragon
1 tsp. mashed garlic

1 Tbls. chopped chervil
1 tsp. chopped onion
1 Tbls, chopped capers
1 chopped sour pickle

Combine all ingredients. Chill

## TARTAR SAUCE

Mash and pound to a paste two (2) hard boiled egg yolks. Slowly
beat in one (1) cup olive oil adding in a constant stream. Add one
(1) tsp. tarragon vinegar, pinch of minced chives that have been
mixed with one (1) tsp. mayonnaise. Salt and pepper to taste.

## TARTAR SAUCE

1 Tbls. mayonnaise                1/2 tsp. chopped capers
1/2 Tbls. minced gherkins         1/2 tsp. prepared mustard
1/4 dill pickle, minced

Combine. Chill

## TARTAR SAUCE

3 Tbls. chopped onion             2 cups mayonnaise
2 Tbls. chopped dill              2 tsp. lemon juice
chopped parsley

Blend well. Let stand a couple hours.

## TARTAR SAUCE

1 cup mayonnaise                  1 Tbls. chopped chervil
1 Tbls. chopped parsley           1 Tbls. capers
1 Tbls. chopped chives            1 chopped sour pickle
1 tsp. chopped tarragon

Combine all ingredients.

## TARTAR SAUCE

2/3 cup evaporated milk      2 Tbls. relish
1/4 cup mayonnaise      1 Tbls. chopped onion

Over medium heat mix all ingredients stirring until thick. Do Not Boil.

## TARTAR SAUCE

Add one (1) cup Bechamel sauce, (see pages 47-49 ), to 3/4 cup mayonnaise, one (1) Tbls. chopped sweet pickles, one (1) tsp. each chopped onions, parsley, three (3) or four (4) green olives chopped.

## TERIYAKI SAUCE

2 Tbls. soy sauce      2 Tbls. brown sugar
2 Tbls. Sake      1/4 tsp. ground ginger
a pressed garlic clove

Blend ingredients.

## TERIYAKI SAUCE

1/2 cup soy sauce      small minced ginger root
1 tsp. sugar      mashed garlic clove
1 tsp. lemon juice

Combine all ingredients

**A FIG FOR YOUR BILL OF FARE;
SHOW ME YOUR BILL OF COMPANY.**
Swift

## TOMATO SAUCE

Four (4) cups tomato juice, one (1) cup beef bouillon, 3/4 tsp. allspice, one (1) Tbls. dry onion flakes, one (1) tsp. celery seed, sugar and cinnamon to taste.

## TOMATO SAUCE

| | |
|---|---|
| 6 ounces tomato paste | 8 minced garlic cloves |
| 2 pounds whole tomatoes | 1 Tbls. chopped oregano |
| 2 chicken bouillon cubes, dissolved | 3 Tbls. chopped basil |
| chopped onion | 1 tsp. mustard |
| 1/2 tsp. cinnamon | 1/4 cup olive oil |

Combine all ingredients. Simmer five (5) hours. Stir often.

## TOMATO SAUCE

Melt three (3) Tbls. butter. Add a small onion and a small carrot, chopped. Cook until onion is soft. Do not brown. Stir in 1/4 cup flour. Cook until roux turns golden. Add 2 1/2 cups chopped fresh tomatoes, 1 1/2 cups brown stock, two (2) crushed garlic cloves, 1/2 tsp. salt, one (1) tsp. sugar, pinch of thyme, dash of pepper, a garni of parsley, celery, bay leaves (all tied together). Bring to boil, stirring constantly. When thickens, continue cooking and skimming when necessary, for one and one half (1 1/2) hours until reduced to about two (2) cups. Discard garni and rub sauce through sieve. Bring to boil again and cook for five (5) minutes.

## TOMATO SAUCE

| | |
|---|---|
| 3/4 cup beef stock | salt, cayenne pepper |
| 3 Tbls. butter | 1 Tbls. lemon juice |
| 4 1/2 Tbls. flour | 1 tsp. chopped parsley |
| 3/4 cup chopped tomatoes | 1/2 cup cooked mushrooms, sliced |

Thicken stock with butter and flour. Add tomatoes seasoned with salt, cayenne, lemon juice. Add parsley, mushrooms.

## TOMATO SAUCE

Heat two (2) Tbls. olive oil. Add a chopped garlic, a chopped onion, one (1) Tbls. chopped celery, 1/2 tsp. chopped parsley, one (1) Tbls. chopped carrot. Cook three (3) to four (4) minutes stirring constantly. Add three (3) cups fresh chopped tomatoes, bay leaf, 1/2 tsp. basil, 1/4 tsp. oregano, 1/2 tsp. salt, 1/2 tsp. pepper. Bring to boil. Lower heat and simmer forty (40) minutes until thick. Add celery, parsley, oregano. Blend thoroughly.

## TOMATO SAUCE

| | |
|---|---|
| Stalk of celery, chopped | 1/2 tsp. salt |
| 1/4 cup chopped onion | dash pepper |
| 2 1/2 cups cooked tomatoes | 2 tsp. Worcestershire sauce |
| 2 Tbls. olive oil | 2 Tbls. flour |

Combine celery, onion, tomatoes, salt, pepper, Worcestershire sauce. Simmer ten (10 ) minutes. Press through sieve. Heat olive oil. Blend in flour. Gradually add tomato mixture. Cook, stirring constantly, until thick.

## TOMATO SAUCE

| | |
|---|---|
| 1 can cream of tomato soup | 1 tsp. ketchup |
| 1/4 cup grated Cheddar cheese | 1/2 cup sliced, ripe olives |
| 1/2 tsp. Worcestershire sauce | a little cream |

Heat soup, cheese, stirring constantly, until cheese is melted. Add Worcestershire sauce, ketchup, ripe olives. Heat thoroughly. Add a little cream.

## TOMATO SAUCE

| | |
|---|---|
| 3 cups chopped onion | 2 bay leaves |
| 3 chopped cloves garlic | 1 tsp. oregano |

1/3 cup olive oil

2 cups fresh tomatoes, chopped

12 ounces tomato paste

6 cups water

1/2 tsp. dried basil

1 1/2 tsp. salt

ground pepper

Saute onions and garlic in olive oil until onion is well browned. Add tomatoes, tomato paste, water, bay leaves. Simmer one (1) hour. Stir often. Add oregano, basil, salt, pepper. Continue cooking one (1) hour until thick.

## TOMATO SAUCE

1/4 cup tomato puree

1 Tbls. butter

3/4 cup Espagnole sauce

(see page 62)

Stir puree into Espagnole sauce. Simmer a few minutes. Remove from heat. Add butter.

## TOMATO SAUCE

2 Tbls. butter

small onion, chopped

salt, pepper

6 ounces tomato paste

3 cups tomato puree

Melt butter and saute onion until transparent. Add rest of ingredients and simmer thirty (30) minutes or until thickens. Correct seasoning.

## TOMATO SAUCE

Melt three (3) Tbls. butter and cook two (2) chopped carrots, two (2) chopped onions until onions are soft, not browned. Add 1/4 cup flour, stirring, until begins to turn golden. Add 2 1/2 cups chopped fresh tomatoes, 1 1/2 cups beef stock, two (2) crushed garlic cloves, one (1) tsp. sugar, 1/2 tsp. salt, pinch each thyme, pepper. Bring to a boil. Simmer, stirring constantly, until thickens. Lower heat and simmer, skimming often, until reduced to about two (2) cups. Strain, rubbing pulp through sieve. Again bring to boil. Simmer five (5) minutes. Add 1/4 cup dry Sherry wine.


## TOMATO BARBECUE SAUCE

46 ounces tomato juice　　　1 Tbls. Worcestershire sauce
3 Tbls. vinegar　　　　　　　1/2 tsp. garlic powder
2 Tbls. dry onion flakes　　　3 Tbls. brown sugar
2 Tbls, prepared mustard　　　1 Tbls. lemon juice

Combine all ingredients. Heat slowly until reduced by half. Use as a baste or marinade.


## TOMATO AND BASIL SAUCE

3 Tbls. olive oil　　　　　　　　1 pound chopped fresh tomatoes
2 onions, sliced　　　　　　　　3/4 cup tomato puree
garlic clove, minced　　　　　　1 cup water
3 stalks celery, chopped　　　　2 bay leaves
a carrot, sliced　　　　　　　　1/2 tsp. oregano
12 fresh basil leaves, chopped　salt

Heat olive oil and cook onions, garlic, until onions are wilted. Add remaining ingredients and simmer three (3) to four (4) hours. Press through sieve. Cook another two (2) hours.


## TOMATO AND CLAM SAUCE

In 1/3 cup olive oil saute chopped garlic clove until light brown. Add 2 1/2 cups chopped tomatoes, one (1) can tomato paste, one (1) tsp. salt, 1/4 tsp. pepper, a big pinch thyme and oregano. Bring to boil. Add three dozen small clams, ten (10) sprigs chopped parsley. Lower heat and simmer three (3) minutes.

## TOMATO CREAM SAUCE

4 Tbls. butter                     1/2 tsp. salt
1 chopped onion                    black pepper
1 chopped carrot                   pinch sugar
1 chopped celery stalk             1/2 cup heavy cream
35 ounces chopped fresh tomatoes

Melt butter in a skillet. Cook onions, carrots, celery until onion becomes translucent. Add tomatoes, salt, pepper, sugar. Cook over low heat until vegetables are tender. Puree mixture in food processor. Return to heat. Cook until thickened. Stir in cream.

## TOMATO SAUCE DIABLE

Combine 1/2 cup tarragon vinegar, one (1) tsp. each dry mustard, paprika, one (1) tsp. salt, two (2) chopped garlic cloves, a bay leaf, pinch of cayenne, 12 bruised peppercorns. Reduce liquid by half over high heat. Strain, pressing thorough sieve. Add one (1) cup tomato sauce. Bring to boil. Simmer gently ten (10) minutes. Add 1/4 cup boiling beef stock, one (1) Tbls. butter, 1/4 tsp. Worcestershire sauce.

## TOMATO SAUCE

2 pounds fresh tomatoes, peeled, seeded    salt, pepper
2 chopped cloves                           2 Tbls. mixed basil,
                                              parsley,
1/4 cup herb vinegar                       chervil, chopped

Food process tomatoes, garlic, vinegar. Over medium to high heat reduce to (2/3). Season to taste. Add herbs. Chill.

## FRESH TOMATO SAUCE

| | |
|---|---|
| 2 chopped garlic cloves | 1 1/2 tsp. salt |
| 1/2 cup chopped onion | 1/2 cup water |
| 2 Tbls. olive oil | a bay leaf |
| 1/4 cup chopped celery | 4 whole peppercorns |
| 1/2 cup chopped green pepper | 2 whole cloves |
| 2 cups chopped fresh tomatoes | 1/2 tsp. sugar |

Saute onions, garlic in olive oil. Add celery, green pepper, tomatoes, sugar, salt, pepper, water. Put bay leaf, peppercorns, cloves in cheese cloth garni and add to pot. Cook slowly twenty-five (25) minutes. Press through sieve. Add tomato paste. Reheat to serve.

## FRESH TOMATO SAUCE

| | |
|---|---|
| 1 sprig thyme | 1 1/2 pounds fresh chopped |
| small bunch parsely | tomatoes |
| small bay leaf | 2 Tbls. butter |
| 1 onion, chopped | 1 Tbls. cornstarch |
| 2 garlic cloves, chopped | |

Make garni of thyme, parsley, bay leaf. Seed tomatoes, squeeze out juice. Put tomato pulp, garni, onions, garlic, salt and pepper to taste in saucepan. Bring to boil. Reduce heat and cook for twenty (20) minutes. Remove garni. Puree sauce in food processor. Reheat and add butter. Make a paste of cornstarch and add to simmering sauce. Stir well until thick.

**IT IS NOT THE QUANTITY OF THE MEAT,
BUT THE CHEERFULNESS OF THE GUESTS,
WHICH MAKES THE FEAST.**

Clarendon

## TOMATO HORSERADISH SAUCE

1 1/4 cups condensed tomato soup    2 tsp. prepared mustard
2 Tbls. prepared horseradish    pinch cloves
pepper to taste

Combine all ingredients. Serve hot or cold.

## TOMATO KETCHUP SAUCE

Melt two (2) Tbls. butter, ( in which has been mixed a minced garlic clove). Add two (2) Tbls. flour, stirring until mixture begins to bubble. Add 1/3 cup each ketchup, Sherry wine, two (2) Tbls. beef stock, one (1) tsp. brown sugar, one (1) tsp. prepared mustard. Bring to a boil. Simmer gently five (5) minutes, stirring constantly. Add one (1) Tbls. onion juice, salt and pepper to taste, dash of ground cloves. Hot or cold.

## TOMATO AND MEAT SAUCE

1/2 chopped garlic clove    1 tsp. salt
1/4 cup chopped onion    1/2 tsp. sugar
1/2 cup chopped mushrooms    3 Tbls. olive oil
1/4 pound ground round    2 1/2 cups cooked tomatoes
2 Tbls. flour    pepper

Combine onions, garlic, mushrooms. Brown in olive oil. Add ground round, salt, pepper, sugar. Simmer fifteen (15) minutes. Stir often. Blend in flour. Add tomatoes. Simmer twenty (20) minutes.

## TOMATO MUSHROOM SAUCE

Saute two (2) chopped garlic cloves in 1/4 cup olive oil until colors. Add one (1) pound sliced mushrooms. Simmer ten (10) minutes. Add 2 1/2 cups chopped tomatoes, two (2) basil leaves, pinch cayenne, salt to taste. Simmer one (1) hour over low heat. Stir occasionally.

## TOMATO MUSSEL SAUCE

In 1/2 cup olive oil saute two (2) chopped garlic cloves. Discard garlic. Add 1 1/3 cups fresh chopped tomatoes, two (2) ounces ) Tbls. tomato paste. Bring to a boil. Add one (1) tsp. marjoram. Salt and pepper to taste. Add two (2) Tbls. chopped parsley. Cook two (2) quarts of mussels in water until open up. Drain. Reserve mussel liquor. Mix 1/2 to one (1) cup mussel liquor with tomato mixture. Blend. Remove mussels from shells. Add to sauce.

## WHAT WAS SAUCE FOR THE GOOSE WAS SAUCE FOR THE GANDER.
R.Head and F. Kirkman
English Rogue, II, 120 (1671)

## TOMATO SAUCE

Peel, seed and chop six (6) tomatoes. In a saucepan with 1/2 tsp. salt, a small onion studded with two cloves, add 1/2 cup chicken stock, a few leaves of sweet basil. Simmer forty (40) minutes until tomatoes are very soft. Strain through sieve. Add one (1) Tbls. butter.

## QUICK TOMATO SAUCE

Combine one (1) can condensed tomato soup with 1/3 cup water, one (1) Tbls. sauteed chopped onion, two (2) tsp. Worcestershire sauce. Heat to boiling. Stir often.

## TOMATO SAUCE

Saute, in three Tbls. olive oil, one chopped garlic clove, one (1) chopped Bermuda onion, 1/2 green pepper, chopped, small carrot, chopped. Stir constantly until onion browns. Add one (1) quart fresh, chopped tomatoes, a bay leaf tied to sprigs of celery tops, thyme. Season with salt and pepper to taste. Cook slowly over low heat forty (40) minutes until thickens. Strain.

## TOMATO SAUCE SPICY

1 can condensed cream of tomato soup       2 Tbls. prepared horseradish
1 Tbls. prepared mustard                   1/8 tsp. pepper

Combine and heat.


## TONGUE SAUCE

1 1/2 cups dry red wine        3 Tbls. sugar
1 1/2 cups stale bread         1/4 tsp. cinnamon
1 Tbls. prepared mustard

Combine in blender all ingredients. Bring to boil in saucepan. Stir constantly one (1) minute.


## TOULONNAISE SAUCE

In a small saucepan in 1/4 cup of clarified butter, saute three (3) slices of onion. Stir until they take on color. Discard onion. Blend in three (3) Tbls. flour. Make roux. Do not brown. Gradually add one (1) cup dry white wine, stirring until mixture thickens and is smooth. Add salt, pepper, nutmeg, cloves to taste. Remove from heat and beat in vigorously three (3) egg yolks, one (1) at a time. Beat well after each yolk is added. Strain through sieve into saucepan. Add one (1) Tbls. each washed capers, chopped sour gherkins, chopped black olives. Bring to boil. Just before serving add one (1) Tbls. butter, whisking vigorously.


## TRUFFLE SAUCE

1 small can of truffles, chopped       2 Tbls. butter
1/4 cup Madeira wine                   1 1/2 cups Brown sauce
1 Tbls. chopped shallots               (see page 26-31)
Maggi seasoning

Reserve truffle liquor. Combine truffles with Madeira wine over moderate high heat until wine is reduced to about one (1) Tbls.

Cook shallots in a Tbls. butter and add to brown sauce. Cook three (3) minutes. Strain. Add truffles and reduced wine mixture. Add truffle liquor, remaining butter, Maggi seasoning.

**REGIMEN IS BETTER THAN PHYSIC. EVERY ONE SHOULD BE HIS OWN PHYSICIAN. WE SHOULD ASSIST, NOT FORCE NATURE. EAT WITH MODERATION WHAT YOU KNOW BY EXPERIENCE AGREES WITH YOUR CONSTITUTION. NOTHING IS GOOD FOR THE BODY BUT WHAT WE CAN DIGEST.**

Voltaire

## TUNA FISH SAUCE

1 chopped clove garlic
3 ounces tuna fish, water packed
2 anchovies

1/4 cup olive oil
2 Tbls. vinegar
2 Tbls. brine in which capers come

Combine ingredients in blender for one (1) minute at high speed. Chill.

## VATEL SAUCE

In saucepan over high heat cook one (1) chopped shallot, sprig of tarragon, one (1) tsp. chopped chervil, three (3) bruised peppercorns, one (1) Tbls wine vinegar. Stir occasionally until vinegar is almost evaporated. Remove from heat. Beat in three (3) egg yolks, one (1) at a time, alternately with 1 1/2 Tbls. tomato paste. After each addition whisk briskly. Return to heat. Beat in three (3) Tbls. butter, a little piece at a time and beating briskly as added. When sauce is smooth and foamy, strain through sieve. Season to taste with salt, pepper, cayenne. Stir in 3/4 cup scalded cream. Serve hot.

## VELOUTE SAUCE

In a saucepan melt 1/3 cup butter. Stir in 1/3 cup flour. Cook roux for three (3) minute Add three (3) cups chicken stock, 1/2 tsp salt, pepper. Cook, constantly stirring, until thickened. Continue cooking until reduced to about 2 1/2 cups thick, but light and creamy.

## VELOUTE SAUCE

| | |
|---|---|
| 1 quart strained veal stock | dash salt |
| 1/2 cup butter | dash nutmeg |
| 1/2 cup flour | pepper |

Simmer veal stock. Heat butter in skillet. Sprinkle flour in it, stirring to smooth. Keep heat low so flour will not brown. About five (5) minutes to blend well. Pour stock over flour mixture. Simmer fifteen (15) minutes over lowest heat. Season to taste. Strain.

## VELOUTE SAUCE

| | |
|---|---|
| 2 Tbls. flour | salt |
| 2 Tbls. butter | 2 cups fish stock |
| pepper | |

Combine flour, butter. Cook together until slightly brown. Gradually stir in fish stock. Stir constantly until sauce thickens. Simmer ten (10) minutes. Season to taste. Separate into two(2) parts. To one (1) part add one (1) cup cream, three (3) egg yolks, which have been beaten together thoroughly, gradually, stirring until sauce is thick and heated through. Do not boil. Repeat for second part. Combine.

## VELOUTE SAUCE

Melt 1/4 cup butter. Add 1/4 flour. Mix well without letting flour take on color. Add six (6) cups boiling white stock, two,(2) cups at a time, whisking vigorously. Add one (1) cup chopped mushrooms, three (3) white peppercorns, a touch of salt, one sprig parsley. Cook, stirring often, one (1) hour. Skim from time to time, until sauce is reduced by a third (1/3rd) and is the consistency of heavy cream. Strain.

## FISH VELOUTE SAUCE

3/4 cup butter          5 cups fish stock
1 1/2 cups flour

Melt butter and stir in flour. When blended and smooth gradually add hot fish stock stirring vigorously with a whisk. When thick and smooth continue cooking for an hour, stirring occasionally.

## FISH VELOUTE

Melt two (2) Tbls. butter and mix in two (2) Tbls. flour. Cook this roux slowly until it starts to turn golden. Slowly add two (2) cups fish stock stirring vigorously with a whisk. Cook for twenty (20) minutes. Strain.

## VELVET SAUCE

2 Tbls. butter          1 cup chicken stock
2 Tbls. flour           1/4 tsp. salt
dash pepper

Melt butter. Blend in flour. Gradually add chicken stock. Stir constantly until thick and boiling. Salt and pepper to taste.

## VELVET SAUCE

Over low heat melt two (2) Tbls. butter. Stir in flour until blended. Stir until smooth and bubbly. Remove from heat. Gradually stir in one (1) chicken bouillon cube dissolved in one (1) cup hot water. Bring to a boil, stirring constantly. Boil one (1) minute. Salt and pepper to taste.

## VERTE SAUCE

Into two (2) cups mayonnaise, fold two (2) Tbls chopped parsley, one (1) Tbls. each chopped chervil, dill. Chill.

## VERTE SAUCE

| | |
|---|---|
| 2 Tbls. chopped, cooked spinach | 1/4 tsp. tarragon |
| 1 Tbls. minced parsley | 1/8 tsp. chervil |
| 2 chopped green onions and tops | 1/3 cup mayonnaise |

Mix and blend all ingredients. Refrigerate for a couple of hours.

## VILLEROI SAUCE

Over medium heat reduce three (3) cups Veloute sauce, (see pages 191 ), to two (2) cups. It should get very thick. Mix in two (2) lightly beaten egg yolks. Cook, stirring constantly, until just about to boil. Do not boil. Remove from heat and let cool to lukewarm before using.

## VINAIGRETTE SAUCE

| | |
|---|---|
| 3/4 cup olive oil | 1 Tbls. chopped capers |
| 1/4 cup lemon juice | 1 tsp. chopped sweet pickles |
| 1/2 tsp. chopped parsley | 1/2 tsp. dry mustard |
| 1/2 tsp. chopped chervil | 1/2 tsp chopped chives |
| salt and pepper to taste | |

Combine ingredients thoroughly and chill.

## VINAIGRETTE SAUCE

| | |
|---|---|
| 3/4 cup olive oil | 2 Tbls. chopped parsley |
| 1/3 cup dry red wine | 1 tsp. salt |
| 3 Tbls. sweet pickle relish | 3/4 tsp. sugar |

In blender, at low speed, blend all ingredients.


## VINAIGRETTE SAUCE

Warm in double boiler, 1/2 cup French dressing, one (1) Tbls. grated onion, one (1) tsp. each chopped parsley, chives, shallots, capers, gherkins. Mix well.


## VINAIGRETTE SAUCE

| | |
|---|---|
| 3 Tbls. wine vinegar | 1/2 tsp. chopped onions |
| 3/4 cup olive oil | 1 tsp. chopped cornichon |
| 1/2 cup chopped parsley | salt, pepper |
| 1 Tbls. chopped chives | 1 Tbls. chopped capers. |

Combine all ingredients until well mixed. Chill if you are going to use over shrimp or vegetables. Warm for other dishes.


### WOULD YE BOTH EAT YOUR CAKE AND HAVE YOUR CAKE?

John Heywood
Proverbs, I, ix (1546)


## VINAIGRETTE SAUCE

| | |
|---|---|
| 1/4 cup sweet pickle relish | 1 tsp. salt |
| 2 Tbls. chopped parsley | dash pepper |
| 1 tsp. sugar | 1/4 cup vinegar |
| 1/2 cup olive oil | |

Combine all ingredients and blend well. May be served warm, too.

## VINAIGRETTE SAUCE

Mix two (2) Tbls. vinegar, six (6) Tbls. olive oil, one (1) tsp. each salt, dry mustard, fresh ground pepper, one (1) split garlic clove, one (1) tsp. each chopped chervil, tarragon, chives, hard boiled egg.

## VINAIGRETTE SAUCE

1 Tbls. olive oil                    dash salt, pepper
3 Tbls. vinegar

Mix thoroughly.

## I WON'T QUARREL WITH MY BREAD AND BUTTER
Swift
Polite Conversation

## VINAIGRETTE SAUCE

2/3 cup olive oil                    1/2 tsp. chopped chervil
1/4 cup red wine vinegar             1/2 tsp. chopped tarragon
2 tsp. salt                          pepper

Mix ingredients thoroughly.

## VINAIGRETTE SAUCE

1 Tbls. vinegar                      pepper, salt
1/4 tsp. Dijon mustard               1/2 tsp. each basil, tarragon, dill,
1/4 cup olive oil                    thyme, marjoram

Combine all ingredients in a covered jar or bottle. Shake vigorously until salt is dissolved. Shake before using.

## CUCUMBER VINAIGRETTE SAUCE

Beat until blended one (1) tsp. each lemon juice, grated onion, 1/2 tsp. salt, dash cayenne, touch of thyme, 3/4 cup olive oil, 1/4 tsp. dry mustard. Chill. Stir in 1/2 cup diced cucumber. Serve cold.

## VINAIGRETTE SAUCE WITH HERBS

One (1) Tbls. vinegar, four (4) Tbls. olive oil, one (1) tsp. each chopped chives, parsley, tarragon, chervil, 1/4 tsp. prepared mustard. Mix well.

## HORSERADISH VINAIGRETTE SAUCE

Add two (2) Tbls. dry mustard, one (1) cup wine vinegar. Beat in 1/4 cup grated fresh horseradish, one (1) tsp. confectioner's sugar. Salt to taste. Sprinkle with chopped parsley.

## PARSELY VINAIGRETTE SAUCE

| | |
|---|---|
| 4 Tbls. olive oil | 1/4 tsp. dry mustard |
| 3 Tbls. vinegar | 2 sprigs parsley, minced |
| 1/2 envelope chicken broth mix | |

Combine in blender until thick. Chill.

## WATERCRESS SAUCE

| | |
|---|---|
| 1 sliced onion | 1 bunch watercress, chopped |
| 1/3 cup butter | 1/4 cup white wine |
| garlic clove | |

Over medium high heat melt butter and cook onion and garlic until onion is tender. Remove garlic. Stir in chopped watercress and wine. Cook about two (2) to three (3) minutes.

## WATERCRESS SAUCE

| | |
|---|---|
| 13 ounces chicken broth | 2 12/ cups chopped watercress |
| 3 Tbls. flour | 1/2 tsp. salt |
| 1/3 cup water | 1/8 tsp. pepper |

Over high heat bring chicken broth to a boil. Separately blend flour, water until smooth. Reduce heat to medium, stir in flour mixture. Stirring constantly, cook until smooth and thick, Add all other ingredients. Simmer a couple of minutes. Serve hot.

WHEN I BEHOLD A FASHIONABLE TABLE SET OUT IN ALL ITS MAGNIFICENCE, I FANCY THAT I SEE GOUTS AND DROPSIES, FEVERS AND LETHARGIES, WITH OTHER INNUMERABLE DISTEMPERS, LYING IN AMBUSCADE AMONG THE DISHES. NATURE DELIGHTS IN THE MOST PLAIN AND SIMPLE DIET. EVERY ANIMAL, BUT MAN, KEEPS TO ONE DISH. HERBS ARE THE FOOD OF THIS SPECIES, FISH OF THAT, AND FLESH OF A THIRD. MAN FALLS UPON EVERYTHING THAT COMES HIS WAY; NOT THE SMALLEST FRUIT OR EXCRESENCE OF THE EARTH, SCARCE A BERRY OR A MUSHROOM CAN ESCAPE HIM.

Addison

## WHITE SAUCE

| | |
|---|---|
| 4 Tbls. butter | 1 quart hot water |
| 4 chicken wings, chopped | a bay leaf |
| 2 chicken gizzards, chopped | sprig of thyme |
| 1 onion, chopped | 6 Tbls. flour |
| salt, pepper | |

Melt butter. Add chicken wings, gizzards and brown until golden. Remove and reserve. To remaining butter add onion and saute until translucent. Add flour. Cook three (3) minutes. Add 1/2 hot water and whisk in well. Add remaining water. Bring to a boil, stirring. Return chicken parts. Add bay leaf, thyme. Simmer thirty (30) minutes. Strain.

## VEGETARIANISM IS HARMLESS ENOUGH, ALTHOUGH IT IS APT TO FILL A MAN WITH WIND AND SELF-RIGHTEOUSNESS.
Robert Hutchinson

## WHITE SAUCE

| | |
|---|---|
| 2 Tbls. butter | 2 Tbls, flour |
| 1/8 tsp. pepper | 1/8 tsp. paprika |
| 1 cup half and half cream | 1/2 tsp. salt |

Over low heat melt butter. Add flour, salt, pepper, paprika. Stir until smooth. Gradually stir in half and half, constantly stirring, until sauce is smooth and thick.

## LIFE ISN'T ALL BEER AND SKITTLES
T. Hughes
Tom Brown's Schooldays, Ch. 2

## CREAM SAUCE

Melt two (2) Tbls. butter. Stir in gradually two (2) Tbls. flour. Stir this roux over low heat five (5) minutes. Slowly add one (1) cup scalded milk. Cook, stirring constantly, until thick and smooth. Season to taste.

## CREAM SAUCE

| | |
|---|---|
| 1 cup milk | 1 slice of onion |
| salt, white pepper | sprig of parsley |
| dash nutmeg | 2 Tbls. butter |
| 2 Tbls. heavy cream | 2 Tbls, flour |

Combine milk, onion, parsley. Bring to a boil. Separately melt butter. Stir in flour. Strain the hot milk mixture into the flour mixture, vigorously whisking. When thick and smooth, simmer gently five (5) minutes. Stir often.


## CAULIFLOWER WHITE SAUCE

| | |
|---|---|
| 1 cup milk | 1/2 tsp. salt |
| 2 cups cauliflower florets | 1/2 tsp. butter |

Heat milk to simmer. Add cauliflower. Cook until soft. Puree in blender. Add salt, butter.


## CHAUD-FROID SAUCE

| | |
|---|---|
| 3 Tbls. butter | 1/2 cup cold water |
| 1/4 cup flour | 2 egg yolks. |
| 1/2 cup cream | 1 quart chicken broth |
| 2 packets unflavored gelatin | |

Melt butter and whisk in flour. Bring chicken broth to a boil. Add to butter mixture, stirring vigorously. When thick and smooth continue cooking five (5) minutes over very low heat. Soften gelatin in cold water and add to sauce. Stir until dissolved. Remove from heat. Beat egg yolks with cream. Stir into sauce. Heat but do not boil. Cool but do not chill.


## WHITE SAUCE

| | |
|---|---|
| 2 Tbls. butter | 1/2 cup evaporated milk |
| 2 Tbls. flour | 1/4 tsp. salt |
| 1/2 cup vegetable stock | pepper |

Melt butter, blend in flour. Gradually add vegetable stock. Cook in double boiler, stirring constantly, until thick. Salt and pepper to taste.

## WHITESAUCE

| | |
|---|---|
| 1 Tbls. butter | 1 Tbls. flour |
| 1 cup milk | salt, pepper |

Melt butter, blend in flour. Add milk gradually. Cook five (5) minutes in a double boiler, stirring constantly.

## WHITE SAUCE

| | |
|---|---|
| 2 Tbls. butter | 1 cup milk |
| 2 Tbls. soya flour | 1/2 tsp. salt |
| touch pepper | |

Melt butter, blend in flour. Add milk. In double boiler, stirring constantly, cook until thickened. Then cook another five (5) minutes, stirring occasionally.

## WHITE SAUCE

| | |
|---|---|
| 4 Tbls. butter | 1 cup milk |
| 4 Tbls. flour | salt, pepper |

Melt butter, blend in flour, add milk. Over hot water, in double boiler, stirring constantly, cook until thick. Salt, pepper to taste.

**NOW GOOD DIGESTION WAIT ON APPETITE, AND HEALTH ON BOTH.**

Shakespeare

## WINE SAUCE

| | |
|---|---|
| 1 1/2 cups dry red wine | 3 Tbls. sugar |
| 1 1/2 slices firm white bread | 1/4 tsp. cinnamon |

Place red wine, bread, sugar, cinnamon in blender. Blend well. Place in saucepan and bring to a boil. Stirring constantly boil a few seconds. Remove from heat. Serve.

## WINE SAUCE

| | |
|---|---|
| 1/2 cup dry red wine | 1 Tbls. butter |
| 1/4 cup water | 1 small anchovy |
| 1 slice of onion | 1 Tbls. lemon juice |

Bring wine, water, onion, butter slowly to a boil. Reduce heat. Simmer five (5) minutes. Add anchovy and lemon juice. Remove onion. Stir well.

## CHAMPAGNE SAUCE

| | |
|---|---|
| 2 Tbls. butter | 1/2 cup milk |
| 1 Tbls. flour | 1/2 cup champagne |
| 1/4 tsp. salt | Tbls. chopped parsley |

Over medium heat melt butter. Whisk in flour and salt. Gradually add milk. Stirring constantly, cook until thickens. At serving add champagne and parsley.

## CHATEAUBRIAND SAUCE

Simmer 1/2 cup dry white wine with one (1) chopped shallot, until slightly reduced. Mix in two (2) Tbls. glace de viande. Add one (1) Tbls. butter, one (1) tsp. chopped tarragon, pinch cayenne, dash lemon juice. [ Glace de viande can be purchased as "meat extract" or "beef extract"].

## CHATEAUBRIAND SAUCE

| | |
|---|---|
| 1 tsp. chopped shallots | 6 Tbls. butter |
| 1/2 cup white wine | 1/8 tsp. cayenne |
| 3/4 cup Espagnole sauce, (see page 95 ) | 1 tsp. lemon juice |

Over medium heat simmer shallots in wine until volume reduced by half. Strain into simmering Espagnole sauce. Add butter, a little at a time, stirring thoroughly. Stir in cayenne. Remove from heat, add lemon juice, and stir until smooth.

## IRISH WHITE WINE SAUCE

Beat three (3) egg yolks into one (1) cup Bechamel sauce, (see pages 18-21 ), one (1) at a time. Beating vigorously, alternate with one (1) Tbls. grated cheese, 1/3 cup dry white wine. Simmer four (4) minutes, stirring constantly. Season to taste.

## MADEIRA SAUCE

Reduce two (2) cups Brown sauce, (see pages 55-58), to one half (1/2). Add 1/3 cup Madeira wine. Bring almost to a boil. Serve.

## MADEIRA SAUCE

| | |
|---|---|
| 1 cup Espagnole sauce, (see page 95) | 1/4 tsp. butter |
| 3 Tbls. Madeira wine | |

Simmer Espagnole sauce and Madeira wine five (5) minutes. Remove from heat and stir in butter until smooth.

## MADEIRA SAUCE

| | |
|---|---|
| 2 Tbls. butter | 1 1/2 cups Brown sauce |
| 2 Tbls. minced shallots | (see pages 55-58 ) |
| 1/4 cup Madeira wine | 2 Tbls. lemon juice |

Melt butter and saute shallots. Do not let butter brown. Add brown sauce and lemon juice. When liquor boils, add Madeira wine and simmer gently five (5) minutes.

## MADEIRA SAUCE

In the pan in which you have already cooked meat, after pouring off fat, add 1/3 cup Madeira wine. Cook, stirring to get all the browned bits of meat mixed in and the sauce is reduced by half. Add one (1) cup Brown sauce, (see pages 55-58 ), 1/4 tsp. meat extract. Cook five (5) to ten (10) minutes. Add one (1) Tbls. butter. Do not let sauce boil. Add two (2) more Tbls. Madeira wine. Serve.

## MARCHANDS DE VIN SAUCE

| | |
|---|---|
| 6 Tbls. butter | 1 1/2 cups Brown sauce, (see pages 55-58) |
| 6 diced scallions | 2 Tbls. lemon juice |
| 3/4 cup dry red wine | |

Heat four (4) Tbls. butter and slowly cook scallions until wilted. Add wine. Simmer until liquid is reduced to about 1/4 cup. Add brown sauce, lemon juice. Heat. Bit by bit add remaining butter, swirling the sauce in the pan gently.

## PERIGOURDINE SAUCE

Cook two (2) cups Brown sauce, (see pages 55-58 ), until reduced by half. Add 1/3 cup Madeira wine. Bring to boil but do not boil. Add two (2) truffles, sliced, truffle liquor, one (1) Tbls. butter. Rotate pan so butter melts and mixes into sauce.

## PIQUANTE SAUCE

Combine three (3) Tbls. dry white wine with 1 1/2 Tbls. vinegar and
one (1) tsp. minced shallots. Reduce over high heat by one half. Stir
in one (1) cup Brown sauce, (see pages 55-58 ) and bring sauce up to
a boil again. Remove from heat and add 1 1/2 Tbls. chopped sour
gherkins, one (1) Tbls. each chopped chives, chopped parsley, pinch
chopped tarragon.

## POIVRADE SAUCE

| | |
|---|---|
| 3 Tbls. olive oil | 1 cup dry red wine |
| 1/3 cup chopped carrot | 2 1/2 cups canned beef gravy |
| 1/3 cup chopped onion | 1/8 tsp. ground cloves |
| 4 Tbls chopped parsley | pepper to taste |

In a skillet saute carrot, onion, parsley in olive oil. Add wine. Simmer
until reduced by half. Add beef gravy and cook over low heat thirty
(30) minutes. Strain. Stir in cloves, pepper. Simmer five (5) minutes.

## PORT WINE SAUCE

| | |
|---|---|
| 1 cup Port wine | 1 cup chicken stock |
| 1/2 cup orange juice | 2 Tbls. cornstarch |
| 1 chopped onion | orange flesh, grated orange rind |
| 1/2 tsp. thyme | salt, pepper |

Combine wine and orange juice. Simmer with onion and thyme.
When reduced one half add chicken stock. Make paste of
cornstarch and stir into mixture until sauce is smooth and thick.
Add orange meat and rind to taste.

## PORTUGAISE SAUCE

Melt butter, add one (1) chopped shallot, 1/4 cup red wine. Reduce,
over medium heat, two thirds (2/3rds). Add two (2) peeled, seeded,
chopped tomatoes. Cook until soft. Add 1/2 cup Brown sauce, (see

pages 55-58 ), 1/2 cup tomato sauce, (see pages 181-188 ), 1/2 tsp. parsley. Salt and pepper to taste. Bring to a boil. Serve.


RED WINE SAUCE

1 1/2 cups red wine                          1/2 chopped garlic
                                                  clove
1 1/2 cups consomme                          3 Tbls. butter
1 1/2 cups Espagnole sauce, ( see page 95 )  1/2 bay leaf
pinch thyme

Over medium heat, add wine to one (1) cup simmering consomme. Add thyme, bay leaf, garlic. Simmer until reduced by half. Add Espagnole sauce. Cook until reduced by a third (1/3). Strain. Return to heat. Add remaining consomme. Reduce by a third (1/3). Remove from heat and stir in butter, a little at a time, stirring vigorously, until sauce is smooth.


SHERRY WINE SUPREME SAUCE

2 Tbls. flour                      1/2 cup grated Guyere cheese
2 Tbls. butter                     1/2 cup cream
2 Tbls. Sherry wine                1/2 cup chicken broth

Make a cream sauce with flour, butter, cream, chicken broth. Add cheese, stirring until blended. Add Sherry wine. Salt and pepper to taste.


DRY VERMOUTH SAUCE

2 chopped onions                   2 Tbls. tomato paste
3 chopped shallots                 1/4 cup dry vermouth
2 Tbls. olive oil                  1 1/2 Tbls. flour
1 cup beef bouillon                dash lemon juice
salt, pepper, cayenne to taste

Heat olive oil. Saute onions, shallots until golden. Do not brown. Whisk in flour. Cook for four (4) minutes. Add bouillon, whisking it in. Sauce should thicken instantly. Bring to a boil. Stir in tomato paste, salt, pepper, cayenne, lemon juice, (2/3) of the vermouth. Simmer twelve (12 ) minutes, stirring often. At serving add balance of vermouth.

## WHITE WINE SAUCE

| | |
|---|---|
| 2 cups white wine | 1 tsp. butter |
| 1 cup consomme | 1 tsp. flour |
| 1 Tbls. chopped chives | 1 Tbls. chopped tarragon |

Over medium heat add wine to consomme. Add chives, tarragon. Stirring often, reduce by one half. Strain. Return to very low heat. Mix butter and flour and flake it into sauce, whisking vigorously, until smooth and creamy. Simmer five (5) minutes.

## WHITE WINE SAUCE

Reduce three (3) cups strained fish stock that has been made with white wine court bouillon by half, over high heat. Knead together 1 1/2 Tbls each flour, butter. Add to the sauce, stirring constantly, until thickened. Separately cook one (1) tsp. each chopped onion, chervil, three (3) crushed peppercorns in three (3) Tbls. vinegar until vinegar is almost all absorbed, stirring often. Add this mixture to sauce and bring to a boil. Remove from heat. Beat in, one (1) at a time, three (3) egg yolks. Beat after each yolk added.
Return to heat. Bring to a boil again, stirring constantly. Strain sauce. Stir into strained sauce 1/2 tsp. each chopped tarragon, chervil, salt and pepper to taste.

**LET US EAT AND DRINK; FOR TOMORROW WE DIE.**
I Corinthians, xv, 32

## WHITE WINE SAUCE

| | |
|---|---|
| 1/2 pound chopped morels | 1 cup white wine |
| 4 Tbls. butter | 2 egg yolks |
| 1 1/4 cups fish stock | 2 Tbls. lemon juice |
| 2 Tbls. flour | 2/3 cup cream |
| salt, pepper | 1/4 tsp. sugar |

Cook morels in butter for five (5) minutes. Add 1/2 of fish stock and lemon juice. In another saucepan, melt butter, stir in flour, balance of fish stock, wine. In a separate bowl beat egg yolks and quickly add almost boiling wine mixture, a little at a time. Over a pan of simmering hot water, place bowl with this egg mixture and stir gently until thickens. Do not boil. Add mushrooms. Season. Stir in cream. Serve very hot.

## WINE VENISON SAUCE

Remove whatever game you are cooking from pan and pour off fat. To the pan add two (2) Tbls. butter, two (2) tsp. flour, two (2) tsp. chopped shallots. Combine thoroughly. Cook about two (2) minutes. Stir in 2/3 cup red wine, scraping all the bits of meat sticking to the pan. Add 1/3 cup of whatever marinade liquor you used for the game, stir in slowly. Cook until thickens. Add two (2) tsp. currant jelly. Correct seasoning.

# DESSERT SAUCES

## APRICOT SAUCE

3/4 cup sugar                          2 tsp. lemon juice
1 1/2 cups canned apricot nectar

Combine sugar and nectar. Bring to a boil. Cook five (5) minutes.
Remove from heat. Stir in lemon juice. Serve hot.

## APRICOT SAUCE

Wash 1/2 pound dried apricots. Soak in water several hours. Drain. In
saucepan, with enough water to cover the apricots, bring to a boil.
Simmer until fruit is soft. Rub through sieve. Add 1/2 cup sugar. Return
puree to heat. Cook until sugar is dissolved. Add two (2) Tbls. rum.

## APRICOT JAM SAUCE

Combine 1 1/2 cup apricot jam with 1/2 cup water, two (2) Tbls.
sugar. Bring to a boil. Cook ten (10) minutes, stirring often. Rub
through sieve and add two (2) Tbls. brandy.

## BANANA SAUCE

Mash one (1) ripe banana and rub through sieve. Combine this puree with 1/4 cup sugar, one (1) Tbls. curacao. Bring to a boil. Chill. Fold in 1/2 cup whipped cream.

## A LA BELLE INDIENNE SAUCE

In double boiler cream one (1) cup butter until fluffy. Gradually beat in 3/4 cup brown sugar, 1/4 cup blanched, toasted. ground almonds. Cook over hot water, stirring constantly until fluffy. Remove from heat. Add 3/4 cup cream, 1/3 cup rum, 1/4 tsp. almond extract. Serve warm

## BERRY SAUCE

Rub two (2) quarts fresh berries through sieve. Bring 1/2 cup water, 1/2 cup sugar to a boil. Reduce heat and simmer five (5) minutes. Combine berries with syrup and flavor with Kirsch. Serve cold.

## BERRY JELLY SAUCE

Mix 1/2 cup strained raspberry juice, 1/2 cup currant jelly. Bring to a boil. Mix two (2) Tbls. berry juice with one (1) tsp. cornstarch. Add to boiling liquid. Cook until clear and slightly thick. Serve cold.

## BLACKBERRY SAUCE

20 ounces frozen,                    1/2 tsp. ground cinnamon
    unsweetened blackberries
1/2 cup brown sugar
2 Tbls. lemon juice

Combine blackberries, sugar, lemon juice, cinnamon. Cook over medium heat, stirring occasionally, until bubbly. Chill.

## BLACKBERRY GLAZE SAUCE

2 cups fresh blackberries          1/4 cup water
1/3 cup sugar                      1 Tbls. cornstarch
1 Tbls. lemon juice

Combine berries, sugar, lemon juice over medium heat. Add water and cornstarch, stirring constantly. Cook until glaze thickens. Chill.


## BLUEBERRY SAUCE

1 cup water                        1 Tbls. cornstarch
1 pint blueberries                 1/8 tsp. salt
3/4 cup sugar                      1 tsp. lemon juice

Over medium heat bring water to boil. Add blueberries. Return to boil. Separately combine sugar, cornstarch, salt. Stir this into berries, Cook, constantly stirring, until thick. Add lemon juice.


## BLUEBERRY SAUCE

10 ounces frozen blueberries          2/3 cup sugar
1/2 cup unsweetened pineapple juice   2 tsp. cornstarch
1/4 cup water                         salt

Combine all ingredients. Cook, stirring, over medium heat until thickens. Chill.


## BLUEBERRY SAUCE

2 tsp. cornstarch                  1/8 tsp. salt
1 Tbls. water                      1 Tbls. lemon juice
1/4 cup sugar                      2 cups blueberries

Blend Tbls. of water and cornstarch. Add sugar, water, salt, lemon juice. Cook over medium heat, stirring, constantly, until clear and slightly thick. Add berries. Boil two (2) minutes. Serve warm.

## BLUEBERRY SAUCE

| | |
|---|---|
| 2 cups water | 1 tsp. cornstarch |
| 1/4 cup sugar | 1 cup blueberries |
| 1 Tbls. lemon juice | |

Bring water to a boil. Add sugar. Stir until dissolved. Add lemon juice. Mix cornstarch with a little water and add to syrup. Stir one (1) minute. Add berries. Cook about a minute. Serve warm.

### A GOOD DINNER SHARPENS THE WIT, WHILE IT SOFTENS THE HEART
Doran

## BLUEBERRY SAUCE

Combine 1/3 cup sugar, 1 1/2 Tbls. flour, 1/4 tsp. salt. Gradually add one (1) Tbls. lemon juice, one (1) cup hot water. Stir until smooth and begins to thicken. Add one (1) cup blueberries. Cook, stirring constantly, until thick. Remove from heat and vigorously whisk in two (2) Tbls. sweet butter, two (2) Tbls. rum. Serve warm.

## BLUEBERRY SAUCE

| | |
|---|---|
| 1 1/2 cups fresh blueberries | 1/4 tsp. nutmeg |
| 1/4 cup sugar | 1/2 tsp. grated lemon rind |
| 3/4 tsp. cinnamon | |

Mix ingredients. Bring to a boil. Simmer slowly five (5) minutes. Stir occasionally. Serve hot.

## SPICED BLUEBERRY SAUCE

| | |
|---|---|
| 1/4 cup sugar | 1/4 tsp. ground cloves |
| 1/4 cup water | 1/4 tsp. grated nutmeg |
| 1/2 tsp. cinnamon | 1 pint blueberries |

Combine sugar, water, cinnamon, cloves, nutmeg. Over high heat bring to a boil. Add one (1) cup crushed blueberries, whisking into syrup. Cook five (5) minutes until thick. Stir in rest of whole blueberries. Cook another two (2) or three (3) minutes. Let cool a bit before serving.

# A DINNER LUBRICATES BUSINESS
Stowell

## SPICED BLUEBERRY SAUCE

| | |
|---|---|
| 1 cup blueberries | 1/2 tsp. cinnamon |
| 1/4 cup sugar | 1/4 tsp. nutmeg |

Combine all ingredients. Bring to a boil. Cook five (5) minutes. Stir often. Serve hot.

## BRANDY SAUCE

| | |
|---|---|
| 1 cup sugar | 1 Tbls. butter |
| 1 Tbls. cornstarch | 1 cup boiling water |
| 1/4 tsp. salt | 1/4 cup brandy |

Mix all dry ingredients. Add butter and boiling water. Stir thoroughly. Cook until clear. Add brandy after removing sauce from heat. Serve warm.

## BRANDY SAUCE

| | |
|---|---|
| 2 cups milk | 1/2 tsp. dried ground ginger |
| 2 Tbls. sugar | 1/2 tsp. vanilla extract |
| 3 egg yolks | 2 Tbls. brandy |

Over low heat, combine milk, sugar. Heat gently until small bubbles begin to form at side of pan. Remove from heat. In double boiler over hot, not boiling water, whisk eggs with ginger and gradually add milk, a few tablespoons at a time. Stirring constantly, cook about four (4) minutes until sauce thickens. Remove from heat. Add vanilla and brandy. Refrigerate. Serve chilled.

## CHERRY BRANDY SAUCE

Rub two (2) cups fresh raspberries through sieve. Bring to a boil 1/ 2 cup each sugar, water. Simmer gently five (5) minutes. Add sieved berries. Add two (2) Tbls. Cherry Brandy.

## FOAMY BRANDY SAUCE

In double boiler blend one (1) cup sugar, one (1) Tbls. quick cooking tapioca, 1/4 tsp. salt. Gradually add 1 1/2 cups boiling water, stirring constantly. Beat one (1) egg until light and foamy. Add a little of the hot mixture, then stir into the sauce. Cook over hot water for five (5) minutes or until slightly thick, stirring constantly. Remove from heat. Stir in 1 1/2 Tbls. butter, 1/4 cup brandy. Serve hot.

## BRANDY GINGER SAUCE

Combine one (1) cup water, 1/4 cup sugar, one (1) tsp. ground ginger, two (2) strips of lemon rind. Bring to a boil after sugar is dissolved thoroughly. Lower heat. Simmer gently fifteen (15) minutes, stirring occasionally. Strain. Reheat without boiling and stir in three (3) Tbls. brandy that has been mixed with one (1) Tbls. spoon lemon juice. Serve hot.

## BRANDY ORANGE SAUCE

Beat two (2) egg whites with 1/4 tsp. salt until stiff. Gradually beat in 2/3 cup confectioner's sugar, stirring constantly until egg whites hold peaks. Fold in 2 1/2 Tbls. brandy, 1/2 tsp. grated orange rind, three drops rose water. Chill.

## BROWN SUGAR SAUCE

| | |
|---|---|
| 1 cup brown sugar | 1 1/2 cups hot water |
| 1 Tbls. cornstarch | 1 tsp. vanilla extract |
| 4 Tbls. butter | |

Combine brown sugar, cornstarch, butter, dash of salt, in hot water. Cook over medium heat until slightly thick. Remove from heat. Cool before adding vanilla.

## BROWN SUGAR SAUCE

Combine one (1) cup brown sugar with three (3) Tbls. flour. Add 1/2 cup each cold water, dry white wine and stir into a smooth paste. Cook over medium heat until thick, stirring often. Stir in three (3) Tbls. cream, one (1) Tbls. butter, 1/2 tsp. vanilla extract, dash salt, 1/3 cup chopped, toasted almonds.

## BUTTERSCOTCH SAUCE

| | |
|---|---|
| 1 pound brown sugar | 4 Tbls. butter |
| 1 can evaporated milk. | |

Mix ingredients in double boiler. Cook until mixture coats spoon.

## BUTTERSCOTCH SAUCE

2/3 cup brown sugar          3 Tbls. butter
2/3 cup corn syrup           2/3 cup half and half cream

Combine sugar, corn syrup, butter. Over high heat bring to a boil and cook until sugar is dissolved. Gradually add syrup mixture to cream, stirring constantly. Quickly bring to a boil. Remove from heat. Sauce will thicken as it stands. Serve hot or cold.


## BUTTERSCOTCH SAUCE

1 cup dark corn syrup        1/2 cup half and half cream
1/2 cup white sugar          1/2 cup brown sugar
1/4 tsp. salt                1 tsp. vanilla extract

Combine all ingredients except vanilla extract. Cook over medium heat, stirring constantly, until achieve a rolling boil. Boil five (5) minutes. Stir often. Remove from heat and add vanilla extract. Serve warm.


## BUTTERSCOTCH SAUCE

Blend one (1) cup brown sugar, 1/3 cup each melted butter, heavy cream. Bring to a boil for five (5) minutes. Remove from heat and beat until foamy. Serve warm.


## BUTTERSCOTCH ALMOND SAUCE

Combine 1 1/4 cups brown sugar, 2/3 cup each corn syrup, heavy cream, 1/4 cup butter, 1/8 tsp. salt. Heat mixture slowly, stirring constantly, until sugar is dissolved. Cook until temperature reaches 238 degrees F. on candy thermometer. Remove from heat. Cool. Add 1/2 cup toasted, slivered almonds. Serve very cold.

## BUTTERSCOTCH SAUCE

| | |
|---|---|
| 1 cup brown sugar | 2 Tbls. butter |
| 1/4 cup half and half cream | 2 Tbls. corn syrup |

Over medium heat bring mixture of brown sugar, half and half, butter, syrup to boiling. Stir occasionally.


## BUTTERSCOTCH SUNDAE SAUCE

| | |
|---|---|
| 1 1/3 cups brown sugar | 1/4 cup butter |
| 1/3 cup cream | 1 1/2 tsp. vanilla extract |

Combine sugar, cream, butter, dash of salt. Over low heat, stirring constantly, bring to a boil and continue boiling one (1) minute. Remove from heat. Add vanilla extract. Cool.


## CARAMEL SAUCE

| | |
|---|---|
| 2 Tbls. butter | 3/4 cup brown sugar |
| 2 Tbls. flour | 3/4 cup sugar |
| 1 1/2 cups half and half cream | 1/4 tsp. salt |

Over medium heat melt butter and stir in flour until blended. Gradually add half and half. Stirring constantly, cook until thick and smooth. Add brown sugar, sugar, salt, stirring until well mixed. Serve warm.


## COFFEE CARAMEL SAUCE

| | |
|---|---|
| 3/4 cup brown sugar | 1/3 cup heavy cream |
| 1 cup sugar | 1/2 tsp. vanilla extract |
| 2/3 cup light corn syrup | 1/2 cup strong coffee |
| 1/4 cup butter | |

Combine sugar, brown sugar, corn syrup, butter, dash of salt. Cook until sugars dissolve. Stir often. Continue cooking, without stirring, until thermometer reaches 236 degrees F. Cool a little then stir in cream, vanilla and coffee.

## GINGER CARAMEL SAUCE

| | |
|---|---|
| 1 1/4 cups brown sugar | 1/4 butter |
| 2/3 cups light corn syrup | 4 Tbls. chopped ginger |
| 1 Tbls. syrup from preserved ginger | 1/2 tsp. vanilla extract |
| 1/2 cup heavy cream. | |

Combine corn syrup, sugar, ginger syrup, butter. Stir over low heat until sugar dissolves. Continue cooking until mixture reaches 242 degrees F. on thermometer. Remove from heat. Stir in cream, vanilla extract, chopped ginger.

## QUICK CARAMEL SAUCE

1/2 pound caramel candies
1/2 cup hot water.

In double boiler heat candies and water until melted and smooth.

## RUM CARAMEL SAUCE

Melt three(3) cups sugar in skillet over low heat. Stir constantly. Slowly stir in three (3) cups boiling water. Cook until syrup reaches consistency of thick maple syrup. Remove from heat. Add two (2) Tbls. rum.

## CARDINAL SAUCE

Combine one(1) cup each mashed raspberries, mashed strawberries, one (1) cup sugar, one (1) tsp. cornstarch. Bring to a boil and cook over medium heat until thick. Rub through sieve. Serve hot.

## CHERRY SAUCE

1 pound sweet, pitted cherries
1/2 cup water
2 Tbls. Sherry wine

1 Tbls. cornstarch
1/3 cup corn syrup (white)
lemon juice

Bring cherries, 1/4 cup water, syrup to a boil. Blend in cornstarch with remaining water. Stirring, add cherries. Cook until clear. Add lemon juice to taste and Sherry wine. Serve warm.

## CHERRY SAUCE

2/3 cup boiling water
1 pound sweet cherries, pitted
1/4 cup sugar

Over medium heat put cherries into boiling water and bring to a boil. Reduce heat to low. Simmer five (5) minutes. Add sugar in last minute of cooking. Stir well.

## BING CHERRY SAUCE

1 large can Bing cherries, pitted, halved
1 Tbls. butter

1 cup cherry liquid
2 tsp. cornstarch

Combine liquid and cornstarch thoroughly. Cook over medium heat, stirring constantly, until thickened. Remove from heat. Add cherries and butter. Chill

## BLACK CHERRY SAUCE

Drain a large can of cherries. In saucepan, to the cherries, add juice of a lemon, 1/2 cup sugar, one (1) Tbls. maraschino. Stir constantly. When thickened, add cherries. Serve cold.

## BRANDIED CHERRY SAUCE

1 pound sweet. pitted cherries        2 tsp. cornstarch
1/2 cup brandy                        1/2 cup sugar
1/4 tsp. almond extract

Combine all but almond extract. Over medium heat, stir constantly until thick. When boils remove from heat and stir in almond extract. Serve warm.

## SPICED CHERRY SAUCE

2 1/2 cups sour cherries, pitted      2 sticks cinnamon
1/2 cup sugar                         2 Tbls. cornstarch
15 whole cloves                       cherry syrup

Enough cherry syrup and water to make one (1) cup liquid. Add sugar, cinnamon, cloves. Bring to a boil. Cook ten (10) minutes. Remove spices. Add a bit of hot mixture to cornstarch and mix thoroughly. Add this to sauce. Cook until slightly thickened. Add cherries.

## CHOCOLATE SAUCE

2 squares unsweetened chocolate       1/8 tsp. salt
1 Tbls. butter                        1 cup vanilla sugar
1/4 cup white corn syrup              1/2 cup boiling water

Melt chocolate, butter over hot water. Blend in corn syrup, salt, vanilla sugar. Stir in boiling water. Boil three (3) minutes over medium heat. Cool.

## CHOCOLATE SAUCE

| | |
|---|---|
| 3/4 cup brown sugar | 1/8 tsp. salt |
| 1/4 cup cocoa | 2 cups water |
| 1 Tbls. cornstarch | 2 Tbls. butter |

Combine sugar, cocoa, cornstarch, salt in iron skillet. Stir in water. Cook until begins to boil and thicken. Stir constantly. Add butter.

## CHOCOLATE SAUCE

| | |
|---|---|
| 1/4 cup sugar | 1/8 tsp. salt |
| 2 Tbls. brandy | 1 square unsweetened chocolate |
| 1 egg yolk | 2 Tbls. milk |

Mix sugar, brandy, egg yolk, salt thoroughly. In a measuring cup melt chocolate in milk. Over low heat combine mixtures, stirring constantly. Add sugar, stirring until sauce is slightly thickened.

## CHOCOLATE SAUCE

1/2 pound unsweetened chocolate
4 Tbls. butter
2/3 cup hot milk

Over low heat dissolve chocolate in milk and butter, stirring until smooth. Serve hot.

## CHOCOLATE SAUCE

Grate one (1) pound chocolate in two (2) quarts of water. Bring to a boil. Cook over hot water until smooth. Rub thorough sieve. Add two (2) Tbls. rum

## CHOCOLATE SAUCE

6 ounces semisweet chocolate pieces          1/4 cup half and half
1/2 cup light corn syrup                     1 Tbls butter
1 tsp. vanilla extract

Over low heat melt chocolate in corn syrup. Stir constantly. Remove from heat. Stir in all other ingredients until smooth.

## CHOCOLATE SAUCE

15 ounces condensed milk                     1 cup hot water
1/8 tsp. salt                                1/2 tsp. vanilla extract
2 ounces unsweetened chocolate

In double boiler place condensed milk, chocolate, salt. Over rapidly boiling water, stirring until thick, cook ten (10) minutes. Remove from heat. Vigorously whisk in, slowly, hot water. Cool. Add vanilla extract. Chill.

## BITTER CHOCOLATE SAUCE

4 squares unsweetened chocolate              7 Tbls. sugar
2 Tbls. butter                               3/4 cup milk
2 Tbls white corn syrup

Melt chocolate with butter over hot water. Add corn syrup, sugar. Blend. Add milk, dash of salt. Stirring constantly, cook ten (10) minutes.

## CHOCOLATE SAUCE

1 pound chocolate                            1/4 cup warm water
1 quart half and half                        4 cups sugar

In a double boiler melt chocolate, sugar, water. Cook until smooth. Add half and half. Stirring often, over hot, not boiling water, cook for about three (3) hours.

## CHOCOLATE FUDGE SAUCE

In double boiler, over hot water, melt 1 1/2 squares unsweetened chocolate, one (1) cup sugar, 1/2 cup boiling water, two (2) Tbls, corn syrup, one Tbls. butter, 18 tsp. salt. Stir constantly. Over direct heat bring to a boil for three (3) minutes. Remove from heat and stir in 1/2 tsp. vanilla extract.

## CHOCOLATE SAUCE

Combine one (1) package of semisweet chocolate pieces, two (2) Tbls. butter, three (3) Tbls. water in double boiler. Stirring often, cook until smooth. Add 1/4 tsp. vanilla extract.

## HONEY CHOCOLATE SAUCE

In double boiler over hot water melt four (4) ounces unsweetened chocolate, one Tbls. Cointreau. Stir until smooth. Stir in ten (10) Tbls. honey. Cook, stirring often, until smooth. Stir in 1/3 cup shredded, toasted almonds. Remove from heat, cover and let steam for fifteen (15) minutes. Stir it a couple of times. Serve lukewarm.

## MILK CHOCOLATE SAUCE

Sift together one (1) cup confectioner's sugar, 1/2 cup cocoa, 1/4 tsp. salt. Add 1/2 cup each hot water, milk. Blend to a smooth paste. Cook in double boiler over hot water twenty-five (25) minutes, stirring often. Cool. Add vanilla extract to taste.

## CHOCOLATE MINT SAUCE

10 large chocolate peppermint patties
4 Tbls. cream

Melt patties over hot water, stirring often. Add cream and blend.

## PEANUT CHOCOLATE SAUCE

4 ounces chocolate pudding mix    1/4 tsp.salt
3/4 cup water                     1 Tbls. butter
3/4 cup corn syrup                1/3 cup peanut butter
1/2 tsp. vanilla extract

To pudding mix add water until smooth. Add corn syrup, salt. Mix well. Over medium heat, stirring constantly, bring to a boil. Remove from heat and add butter, peanut butter, vanilla extract. Stir until all is melted and blended.

## CHOCOLATE PEPPERMINT CREAM SAUCE

In double boiler over hot water melt twelve (12) chocolate peppermint patties. Stir in one (1) cup heavy cream, Bring to boiling point and stir in one (1) Tbls peppermint Schnapps.

## CHOCOLATE CINNAMON SAUCE

3 squares unsweetened chocolate    3/4 cup sugar
1/2 cup water                      1/2 tsp. cinnamon
salt

Combine chocolate and water. Stirring constantly heat until chocolate is melted. Add sugar, stirring until dissolved. Remove from heat. Add cinnamon, dash salt.

## CHOCOLATE SOUR CREAM SAUCE

1 cup semisweet chocolate bits    1/2 cup sour cream
1/8 tsp. salt                     1/4 cup milk
1/2 tsp. cinnamon

Half fill a skillet with water brought to simmering. Place a saucepan in the water containing chocolate bits. Stir until melted. Add and blend in sour cream, salt, cinnamon and milk.

## CHOCOLATE SAUCE

In double boiler combine one (1) pound sweet grated chocolate. Cook until smooth. Press through a sieve.

## CIDER SAUCE

Boil together one (1) cup sugar, 1/2 cup cider for five (5) minutes.

## COFFEE SAUCE

Dissolve one (1) Tbls. instant coffee in 1/2 cup boiling water. Add 1/4 cup sugar, 1/8 tsp. salt. Pour this mixture gradually into two (2) well beaten eggs. Stirring constantly, cook over hot water until spoon is coated. Chill. Add two (2) Tbls. honey. Cook again over hot water, stirring often, and add 1/3 cup shredded. toasted almonds. Remove from heat. Cover pan and let stand for fifteen (15) minutes. Serve lukewarm.

## CRANBERRY APPLE SAUCE

3 large cooking apples              1/3 cup water
1 cup whole berry-cranberry sauce

Place peeled, cored, cut-up apples in saucepan. Over high heat, bring to boil. Reduce heat, simmer, fifteen (15) minutes, until apples are tender. Stir in cranberry sauce. Heat through.

## OREGON CRANBERRY SAUCE

1 pound cranberries              2 Tbls. water
2 cubes sugar

In a saucepan place cranberries, sugar, water. Heat until cranberries start to pop open. Stir gently, do not crush berries. Cook two (2) minutes. Bring up to a boil for one (1) minute.

## CRANBERRY SAUCE

2 cups sugar                    4 cups cranberries
2 cups water                    1/2 tsp. vanilla extract
dash ground cinnamon

Combine sugar and water, stirring to dissolve sugar. Heat to boiling, boil five (5) minutes. Add cranberries. Cook until berries pop.

## AUX FRAMBOISES A LA CREME SAUCE

Crush one (1) pint raspberries. Sprinkle with two (2) Tbls. Kirsch, one (1) Tbls. sugar. Set aside. Combine 1/3 cup sugar, one (1) tsp. flour, 1/8 tsp. salt, one (1) cup hot Sauterne. Over medium heat, stirring constantly, bring to just boil. Remove from heat. Whip two (2) egg yolks with pinch each nutmeg, ginger. Whisk this mix into sauce. Return to heat and cook four (4) minutes, stirring constantly. Add crushed berries. To serve hot, stir in 1/2 cup heavy cream. At serving, fold in 1/2 cup whipped cream. Serve cold.

## CREPES SUZETTES SAUCE

2 oranges                       3/4 cup light rum
2 ounces sweet butter           1/4 cup cognac
3/4 cup sugar                   salt

Combine butter, sugar, juice from one (1) orange, shredded rind of one (1) orange, rum in a large copper skillet. Simmer until orange rind is translucent. Add Rum. Add cognac and ignite. Serve while flaming.

## RED CURRANT SAUCE

Combine two (2) cups red currants, 1 1/2 cups sugar. Bring to a boil. Cook twenty (20) minutes. Rub through sieve.

## CUSTARD SAUCE

4 egg yolks                    2 cups scalded milk
1/4 cup sugar                  1 tsp. vanilla extract
salt

Beat egg yolks slightly in double boiler. Add sugar, salt, slowly add scalded milk. Cook over hot water, not boiling, stirring constantly, until thick. Add vanilla extract.

## CUSTARD SAUCE

3 Tbls. flour                  2 eggs
1/2 cup sugar                  2 cups milk
1 tsp. vanilla extract

Mix flour, sugar, dash of salt. Add eggs slightly beaten. Scald milk and gradually add. Cook over hot water, stirring constantly until thickens. Add vanilla extract. Chill.

## CUSTARD SAUCE

3 Tbls. sugar                  1 Tbls. cornstarch
1 3/4 cups half and half       1/8 tsp. salt
1 egg yolk                     1/2 tsp. vanilla extract

Combine all ingredients except vanilla. Over medium heat cook fifteen (15) minutes. When coats spoon remove from heat and add vanilla extract. Chill.

## CUSTARD SAUCE

3 beaten egg yolks             2 cups scalded milk
1/4 cup sugar                  1 tsp. vanilla extract
1/8 tsp. salt

Combine egg yolks, sugar, salt. Slowly mix in scalded milk. Cook over hot water, constantly stirring, until mixture coats spoon— five (5) minutes. Remove immediately to a pan of cold water to cool quickly. When cool, add vanilla extract. Chill.

## BROWN SUGAR CUSTARD SAUCE

| | |
|---|---|
| 1 cup brown sugar | salt |
| 1/3 cup water | 2 egg yolks |
| 4 Tbls. Sherry wine | |

Boil water, sugar until dissolved. Beat egg yolks and add syrup gradually, while whisking. Cook over hot water until thick. Stir constantly. Remove from heat. Add Sherry. Serve hot.

## CUSTARD SAUCE

| | |
|---|---|
| 3 Tbls. sugar | 1 Tbls. cornstarch |
| 1 3/4 cup half and half | 1/8 tsp. salt |
| 1 egg yolk | 1/2 tsp. vanilla extract |

Combine all ingredients except vanilla. Over medium heat, stirring constantly, cook until mixture coats spoon. Remove from heat. Add vanilla extract. Chill.

## CUSTARD SAUCE

| | |
|---|---|
| 3 egg yolks | 2 cups scalded milk |
| 1/4 cup sugar | 1 tsp. vanilla extract |
| 1/8 tsp. salt | |

Combine beaten egg yolks, sugar, salt. Over hot, not boiling, water, slowly stir in scalded milk, stirring constantly, until thickens. Remove from hot water and place in a pan of cold water to cool quickly. When cool add vanilla extract. Chill.

## BROWN SUGAR CUSTARD SAUCE

| | |
|---|---|
| 1 cup brown sugar | 1/8 tsp. salt |
| 1/3 cup water | 2 egg yolks |
| 4 Tbls. Sherry wine | |

Boil sugar and water until sugar dissolves. Beat egg yolks and add to syrup gradually, whisking constantly. Cook, stirring, over hot water, until thick. Remove from heat. Add Sherry wine.

## EASY CUSTARD TYPE DESSERT SAUCE

1 package vanilla pudding mix
2 12/ cups milk

Combine pudding mix and milk. Heat, stirring constantly until full boil is reached. Remove from heat. Serve warm.

## JIFFY CUSTARD SAUCE

| | |
|---|---|
| 1 egg | 1 Tbls. honey |
| 1/2 cup plain yogurt | 1/4 tsp. vanilla extract |

Combine all ingredients, beating until smooth. Refrigerate.

## JIFFY CUSTARD SAUCE

Place one (1) cup milk, 1/2 cup skim milk powder, pinch of salt, 1/4 cup honey in blender until smooth. Add two (2) eggs and blend until mixed.

## CUSTARD PUDDING SAUCE

Heat two (2) cups milk, dissolving two (2) Tbls. sugar and a pinch of salt in it. Pour over three (3) egg yolks, lightly beaten. Cook mixture over hot, not boiling water, in a double boiler, until coats spoon. Add vanilla extract to taste.

## SOFT CUSTARD SAUCE

4 egg yolks
3 Tbls. sugar
1 tsp. vanilla extract

2 cups scalded milk
2 Tbls. flour
salt

Mix egg yolks, sugar, salt, flour. While stirring, add scalded milk. In double boiler cook over hot water until thickens. Set pan in cold water for five (5) minutes. Stir occasionally. Strain. Add vanilla extract.

## DATE NUT SAUCE

8 ounces chopped, pitted dates
1/8 tsp. salt
3/4 cup water

1/2 cup dark corn syrup
1/2 cup chopped walnuts

Over medium heat bring to boiling, dates, salt, water. Remove from heat. Stir in corn syrup, walnuts. Serve warm.

## SATINY DESSERT SAUCE

1 egg white
1/2 cup confectioner's sugar
1 egg yolk

1/2 cup whipping cream
1 tsp. vanilla extract
salt

Beat egg white stiff. Gradually add sugar, whisking constantly. Whisk egg yolk, fold into mixture. Whip cream. Fold into mixture. Add vanilla extract.

## EGGNOG SAUCE

Scald two (2) cups half and half. Stir in 1/2 cup sugar. Gradually add four (4) egg yolks that have been beaten with 1/2 tsp. vanilla extract, a pinch of salt. Heat this over hot, not boiling, water, stirring constantly so that it does not boil. Add two (2) Tbls. rum.

## EGGNOG SAUCE

1/2 cups whipping cream          3/4 cup confectioner's sugar
2 egg yolks                      3 Tbls. brandy

At high speed, with mixer, beat cream until stiff. In another bowl, at high speed with mixer, beat eggs until fluffy. To egg yolk mix add sugar, brandy. At high speed blend the mixtures together. Add whipped cream gently folding in. Serve warm.

## ENGLISH TOFFEE SAUCE

In double boiler combine one (1) cup each sugar, cream, 1/3 cup butter, 1/8 tsp. salt. Bring to a boil, stirring often. Remove from heat, cover and let cool to lukewarm. Stir in 1/4 tsp. almond extract.

## FOAMY SAUCE

1 egg                            1 tsp. vanilla extract
1/3 cup butter                   1 cup whipping cream
1/2 cup sugar

Beat egg until fluffy. Add melted butter and vanilla extract. Fold in whipped cream. Chill.

## BRANDIED FOAMY SAUCE

| | |
|---|---|
| 1/2 cup butter | 2 Tbls. cognac |
| 1 1/3 cups confectioner's sugar | 1/2 cup heavy cream, whipped |
| 1 egg, separated | dash nutmeg |

Soften butter and gradually blend in sugar. Add dash of salt and egg yolk. Beat thoroughly. Cook over hot, not boiling. water, stirring constantly six (6) minutes, until fluffy. Remove from heat. Stir in cognac. Chill. Fold in egg white. Fold in whipped cream. Dash nutmeg at serving.

## FOAMY HOT SAUCE

| | |
|---|---|
| 1/2 cup milk | 2 tsp. sugar |
| 1 tsp. plain gelatin | 1/4 tsp. vanilla extract |

Sprinkle gelatin in milk to soften. Over low heat vigorously whisk until hot and foamy. Add sugar, vanilla extract. Whisk.

## FRUIT SAUCE

Combine one (1) cup unsweetened fruit juice, ( any kind you choose), 1/4 cup sugar, juice of 1/2 lemon. Bring to a boil. Mixing one (1) tsp. arrowroot with two (2) Tbls. cold fruit juice, Add to boiling juice. Cook until clear and slightly thick.

## FRESH FRUIT A LA SUISSE SAUCE

1 cup prepared fresh fruit ( whatever you choose)
1/4 cup sour cream
2 tsp. brown sugar

Blend ingredients.

## GLACED FRUIT SAUCE

Combine one (1) cup orange juice, 1/4 cup lemon juice, 1/2 cup pineapple juice, two (2) cups sugar. Cook ten (10) minutes until syrupy. Add one (1) Tbls. corn syrup, 1/2 cup chopped, mixed glaced fruits. Simmer slowly twenty (20) minutes. Fold in two (2) Tbls. slivered almonds

## HOT FRUIT SAUCE

| | |
|---|---|
| 3 nectarines | 3 plums |
| 1/2 cup orange juice | 1/2 cup sugar |
| 2 Tbls. brandy | |

Cut fruit into wedges. Cook over low heat, with juice, until tender. Stir often. Remove from heat. Stir in sugar until dissolved. Add brandy.

## FRUIT SAUCE WITH WATER CHESTNUTS

| | |
|---|---|
| 2 Tbls. butter | 1/2 cup sugar |
| 5 ounces sliced water chestnuts | 1/4 cup cornstarch |
| 20 ounces pineapple juice | 1/4 tsp. ginger |
| 6 ounces tangerine concentrate | 1/8 tsp. salt |
| 2 sticks cinnamon | 2 Tbls. lemon juice |
| 2 tsp. grated lemon rind | |

Heat one (1) Tbls. butter in a skillet. Add water chestnuts. Stir until butter is absorbed and nuts lightly browned. Remove from heat. In saucepan mix pineapple juice, enough water to make three (3) cups. Add tangerine concentrate, cinnamon sticks. Mix sugar, cornstarch, ginger, salt separately. Blend. Add to juices. Stir until smooth. Cook, stirring, until clear, thick. Remove from heat. Add lemon juice, rind, one (1) Tbls. butter. Cool to room temperature. Remove cinnamon sticks when cooled. Chill. Just before serving add water chestnuts.

## WINTER FRUIT SAUCE

| | |
|---|---|
| 1 Tbls. flour | 1 egg yolk |
| 1 1/2 Tbls. sugar | 1/2 cup orange juice |
| salt | 1/4 cup whipping cream |

Mix flour, dash salt, sugar. Beat egg yolk. add to flour mix. Add orange juice. Cook over hot water, stirring constantly until thick. Then cook ten (10) minutes. Chill. Fold in whipped cream

## FUDGE SAUCE

| | |
|---|---|
| 1 cup sugar | 1/2 cup butter |
| 1/2 cup whipping cream | 2 egg yolks |
| 4 ounce unsweetened chocolate | 1 tsp. vanilla extract |

Over medium heat, combine sugar, cream. Cook, stirring constantly until sugar dissolves and mixture boils. Add chocolate, butter. Stir until melted and smooth. Remove from heat. Pour 1/4 cup chocolate mix into egg yolks whisking quickly. Pour this mix back into chocolate mixture, whisking vigorously. Cook over low heat, stirring constantly, three (3) minutes, until sauce is shiny. Remove from heat. Add vanilla extract.

## CHOCOLATE FUDGE SAUCE

In double boiler over hot water, melt 1 1/2 squares unsweetened chocolate. Stir in one (1) cup sugar, 1/2 cup boiling water, two (2) Tbls. corn syrup, one (1) Tbls. butter, 1/8 tsp. salt. Stir constantly. Over direct heat, bring to a boil for three (3) minutes. Remove from heat. Stir in 1/2 tsp. vanilla extract.

## CREAMED FUDGE SAUCE

1 cup sugar                              1/2 cup water
1/4 cup light corn syrup                 1 tsp. vanilla extract
1/3 cup cocoa                            2 Tbls. butter
1/2 tsp. salt                            1/2 cup heavy cream, whipped

Mix sugar, corn syrup, cocoa, salt, water and cook to 228 degrees F. on thermometer. Add vanilla extract and butter. Mix but do not beat. Fold in whipped cream.

## DOUBLE FUDGE SAUCE

1 1/2 cups sugar                         1/4 cup corn syrup
1 cup cocoa                              1 cup evaporated milk
1/3 cup water                            1 tsp. vanilla extract

Mix sugar and cocoa. Stir in water and corn syrup. Cook, stirring, to a full boil. Boil, stirring, until thickens. Remove from heat. Add evaporated milk and vanilla extract. Chill

## HOT FUDGE SAUCE

1 cup light corn syrup                   1 tsp. vanilla extract
2 squares unsweetened chocolate

Combine corn syrup, chocolate. Cook over hot water, stirring constantly until chocolate melts. Remove from heat. Beat until smooth. Add vanilla extract. Serve hot.

## HOT FUDGE SAUCE

1/2 cup butter                           2/3 cup evaporated milk
2 1/4 cups confectioner's sugar          6 squares bitter chocolate

Mix butter, sugar in double boiler. Add evaporated milk,

chocolate. Cook over hot water for thirty (30) minutes. Do not stir while cooking. Remove from heat. Whisk vigorously. Chill.

## HOT FUDGE SAUCE

| | |
|---|---|
| 1/4 cup half and half | 1/4 cup chocolate chips |
| 1/4 cup sugar | 1/2 tsp. vanilla extract |
| salt | |

Combine half and half, sugar, chocolate chips, salt. Bring to a gentle boil over medium heat. Stir constantly. Cook two (2) minutes until thick and smooth. Stir in vanilla. Cool before serving.

## HOT FUDGE SAUCE

| | |
|---|---|
| 1 1/2 cups sugar | 1 Tbls. butter |
| 1/2 cup milk | 1 tsp. vanilla extract |
| 1/3 cup light corn syrup | 2 squares unsweetened chocolate |
| 1/8 tsp. salt | |

Over medium heat bring sugar, milk, corn syrup, chocolate to a boil. Stir constantly. When thermometer reaches 228 degrees F. remove from heat. Immediately stir in butter, vanilla extract, salt. Serve hot.

## HOT FUDGE SAUCE

| | |
|---|---|
| 11/2 cup cocoa | 1/4 tsp. salt |
| 1 cup sugar | 3 Tbls. butter |
| 1 cup light corn syrup | 1 tsp. vanilla extract |
| 1/2 cup light cream | |

Combine all ingredients except vanilla extract. Cook over medium heat, stirring constantly, to a full boil. Continue boiling three (3) minutes. Stir occasionally. Remove from heat. Add vanilla extract.

## GRAND MARNIER SAUCE

Scald one (1) cup milk with a one (1) inch piece of vanilla bean. In double boiler beat four (4) egg yolks, gradually adding 1/2 cup sugar. Stir in 3/4 cup heavy cream. Gradually add scalded milk, 1/3 tsp. salt, beating vigorously until well blended. Cook over hot water, stirring constantly, until coats spoon. Remove from heat and stir in three (3) Tbls. Grand Marnier.

## GRAND MARNIER SAUCE

1/2 cup milk
1/2 cup cream
1 inch piece vanilla bean
2 egg yolks

1/4 cup sugar
1/2 tsp. cornstarch
2 ounces Grand Marnier
1/2 cup heavy cream, whipped

Scald milk and cream with vanilla bean. Discard bean. Beat egg yolks with sugar. Add cornstarch and liquid. Cook until thick, stirring constantly. Strain. Chill. Add Grand Marnier. Fold in whipped cream.

## HARD SAUCE

1/3 cup butter
1 tsp. vanilla extract

1 cup confectioner's sugar

Cream butter. Add confectioner's sugar, whisking until fluffy. Add vanilla extract. Mix

## HARD SAUCE

1/4 cup butter
1 tsp. milk

1 cup confectioner's sugar
1/4 tsp. nutmeg

Cream butter, add sugar and milk gradually. Beat until light. Add nutmeg. Chill.

## HARDSAUCE

1 pound confectioner's sugar           2 Tbls. brandy
1 cup butter, room temperature

Blend sugar into softened butter until smooth. Add brandy.

## HARD SAUCE

1/2 cup butter                         1 cup confectioner's sugar
1/2 tsp. vanilla

Beat butter, sugar with mixer until fluffy and creamy. Add vanilla, whip in. Chill.

## HARD SAUCE

1 stick butter                         1 egg white
1 cup confectioner's sugar             1 tsp. brandy

Cream butter and sugar. Add egg white, brandy. Chill

## HARD SAUCE

4 Tbls. butter                         1 Tbls. brandy
1/2 cup heavy cream                    2 3/4 cup confectioner's sugar
salt

Cream butter. Whip cream. Alternately add sugar to butter, whipped cream to butter, whisking well after each addition. Add brandy. Chill.

## HARDSAUCE

Cream 1/2 cup sweet butter. Gradually beat in 1 1/2 cups confectioner's sugar, two (2) Tbls. rum. Chill.

## HARD SAUCE

1 cup sweet butter, softened      1/4 cup Sherry wine
1 cup confectioner's sugar      nutmeg

Cream butter and sugar. Add Sherry wine and few drops at a time, whisking until luffy. Add nutmeg. Chill

## BRANDY HARD SAUCE

1/4 cup butter      1 Tbls. brandy
3/4 cup confectioner's sugar      1/4 tsp vanilla extract

In mixer bowl, at medium speed, beat butter until fluffy. Gradually add confectioner's sugar, brandy, vanilla. Refrigerate.

## CIDER HARD SAUCE

Cream together six (6) Tbls. sweet butter, three (3) Tbls. sugar. Slowly add three (3) Tbls. Calvados. Blend.

## COFFEE HARD SAUCE

Cream 1/2 cup sweet butter. Gradually beat in 1 1/2 cups dark brown sugar. Slowly add four (4) Tbls. strong, black coffee, pinch of nutmeg.

## LEMON HARD SAUCE

1/4 cup heavy cream            1 tsp. grated lemon peel
1/2 cup butter                 1 Tbls. lemon juice
1 1/4 cup confectioner's sugar

Whip cream. Cream butter. Add sugar until light and fluffy. Add lemon juice and peel. Fold in whipped cream. Chill.

## MOCHA RUM HARD SAUCE

Cream 1/3 cup sweet butter. Gradually add one (1) cup sugar, stirring constantly until mixture is light. Add one (1) Tbls. strong, black coffee, a drop at a time alternately with three (3) Tbls. rum. Cream and knead mixture until thoroughly blended. Chill.

## HONEY CREAM SAUCE

Combine 1/2 cup each honey, light cream, two (2) Tbls. butter. Cook over medium heat ten (10) minutes until smooth and syrupy. Stir in two (2) Tbls. Curacao. Serve hot.

## WHIPPED HONEY SAUCE

Beat three (3) egg whites with a pinch of salt until stiff. Very slowly whip in 1/2 cup honey until thick. Serve at once.

## LEMON SAUCE

1 Tbls. cornstarch            1 cup water
1/2 cup sugar                 1 Tbls. grated lemon rind
2 Tbls. lemon juice           2 Tbls. butter
salt

Mix cornstarch, sugar, lemon rind, dash salt. Gradually add water. Cook over low heat, stirring constantly until thick. Over hot water continue cooking five (5) minutes. Stir often. Add lemon juice, butter.

## LEMON SAUCE

2 eggs
1/2 cup sugar
1/2 cup butter

3/4 cup grated lemon peel
1/2 cup lemon juice

Combine eggs, sugar at high speed in mixer five (5) minutes until fluffy. Gradually add lemon peel, juice, butter. Thoroughly mix. Put in double boiler. Cook over hot, not boiling, water, stirring constantly, for eight (8) minutes until consistency of sour cream. Cool.

## LEMON SAUCE

In a double boiler combine 1/2 cup sugar, three (3) Tbls. flour. Stir in two (2) egg yolks that have been beaten with 3/4 cup cold water. Cook over hot water ten (10) minutes, stirring constantly. Add 3/4 cup lemon juice, one (1) Tbls. sweet butter, grated rind of 1/2 lemon, 3/4 tsp. grated orange rind.

## CLEAR LEMON SAUCE

Mix 1/2 cup sugar, one (1) Tbls. cornstarch. Add one (1) cup water slowly. Cook over low heat five (5) minutes until thick. Stir constantly while cooking. Add three (3) Tbls. each lemon juice, butter, one (1) tsp. grated lemon peel, 1/8 tsp. salt.

## LEMON MOUSSELINE SAUCE

Make clear lemon sauce, ( see above ). Cool and fold in one (1) cup whipped cream.

## LEMON PEACH SAUCE

1/2 cup sugar
1 Tbls. cornstarch
salt
1 cup canned peach syrup

1/4 cup seedless raisins
1 egg yolk
3 Tbls. lemon juice
2 Tbls. butter

Mix sugar, cornstarch, dash salt. Gradually add peach syrup. Bring to boiling point, stirring constantly. Add raisins. Cook over boiling water, stirring often. Beat egg yolk. Add to peach syrup. Add lemon juice, butter. Stir until butter melts. Serve hot.

## LEMON ORANGE YOGURT CHEESE SAUCE

1 cup yogurt cream cheese
1 cup honey
1 Tbls. grated lemon peel
dash salt

2 Tbls. lemon juice
1 Tbls. grated orange peel
2 Tbls. orange juice

Combine all ingredients and, at medium speed, with mixer, blend until smooth and creamy. Chill.

## FRESH LINGONBERRY SAUCE

2 cups fresh lingon berries
1 cup water

1/2 cup sugar

Over high heat bring water, sugar to a quick boil. After a half minute of boiling add berries. Reduce heat. Simmer gently twenty (20) minutes. Cool.

## MAPLE SYRUP SAUCE

Pour one (1) cup heated maple syrup over two (2) egg whites that have been stiffly beaten. Mix lightly until foamy. Serve at once.

## CHOCOLATE MARSHMALLOW SAUCE

242 cups miniature marshmallows

242    EDWARD A. MEANY

2 cups miniature marshmallows    1 1/2 squares unsweetened
  chocolate
1/3 cup heavy cream              1/8 tsp. salt
1/3 cup honey

Ove low heat cook marshmallows, cream, honey, chocolate, salt, stirring constantly until chocolate and marshmallows are melted. Serve hot.


## MAPLE MARSHMALLOW SAUCE

3/4 cup maple syrup             8 big marshmallows

Heat maple syrup to boiling point. Quarter marshmallows and stir in until melted. Serve hot.


## ORANGE MARSHMALLOW SAUCE

4 cups miniature marshmallows   1 1/4 cups orange juice
1/2 cup water                   2 Tbls. lemon juice
3 tsp. orange rind              salt

Heat marshmallows and water to boiling. Remove from heat, stir to melt marshmallows. Add rind, juices, dash salt. Chill until congeals then beat until airy and light using beater. Chill.

## MELBA SAUCE

10 ounces frozen raspberries    1 Tbl. lemon juice
1/2 cup currant jelly           1/4 tsp. grated lemon peel
1/4 cup sugar                   salt

Thaw berries. Gently simmer fifteen (15) minutes. Strain. Get as much of the juice as possible. Add water to juice to make 2/3 cup. Return juice to heat. Add remaining ingredients. Simmer until jelly melts, sugar dissolves and all is smooth. Cool.

## MELBA SAUCE

2 tsp. cornstarch
2 Tbls. sugar
1/4 cup corn syrup

1 cup crushed raspberries
1 pint crushed strawberries
1 Tbls. lemon juice

Mix cornstarch, sugar, syrup. Add raspberries and cook until clear and slightly thick. Cool. Strain. Mix then with strawberries, lemon juice.

## MELBA SAUCE

1/4 cup red currant jelly
10 ounces frozen raspberries
red food coloring

2 Tbls. cornstarch
1 Tbls. cold water

Over low heat melt jelly, stirring constantly. Add frozen berries and heat. Mix cornstarch with water and add to berry mixture. Over medium heat cook until thick, stirring occasionally. Stir in a couple drops food coloring. Refrigerate.

## MELBA SAUCE

Blend one (1) cup thawed raspberries, one (1) tsp. sugar, one (1) tsp. cornstarch. Cook over low heat, stirring constantly, until clear. Strain. Cool. Add 1/2 cup currant jelly, heat until melts. Cool.

## MINT SAUCE

1/2 cup corn syrup
1/2 cup packed mint leaves

2 Tbls. lemon juice
1/8 tsp. salt

At high speed in blender mix all ingredients until well blended. Stir before serving.

## MOLASSES ALMOND SAUCE

Blend one (1) Tbls. flour, 1/2 cup each unstrained orange juice, light molasses to a smooth paste. Over low heat cook, stirring constantly, until spoon is coated. Remove from heat and add one and one-half (1 1/2) Tbls. sweet butter, 1/2 tsp. each grated orange peel, lemon peel, 1/3 cup slivered, toasted almonds. Just before serving add 1/4 tsp. vanilla extract, dash salt, 1/3 tsp. almond extract. Do not boil. Serve hot.

## MOUSSELINE LORETTE SAUCE

In double boiler beat four (4) egg yolks thoroughly. Gradually add 1/2 cup sugar, whisking until well blended. Cook over hot water six (6) minutes, stirring constantly. Remove from heat and whisk vigorously while adding 1/4 cup brandy and a dash salt. Add 1/3 tsp. orange flower water. Cool. When sauce is quite cold, fold in 3/4 cup whipped cream. Serve very cold.

## ORANGE SAUCE

| | |
|---|---|
| 1 cup sugar | 1 cup orange juice |
| 1/4 tsp. salt | 1/4 cup lemon juice |
| 2 Tbls. cornstarch | 3/4 cup water |

Mix sugar, salt, cornstarch. Add juices. Cook, stirring constantly, until boils and thickens. Cook one (1) minute. Cool.

## A L'ORANGE SAUCE

Peel, pith, seed, dice six (6) oranges. Strain juice. Combine oranges, juice, two (2) Tbls. sugar. Bring to a boiling point. Add two (2) Tbls. Kirsch, one (1) Tbls. grenadine, Serve very cold.

## ORANGE SAUCE

1/2 cup sugar

1/2 cup orange juice

2 Tbls. flour

1 Tbls. lemon juice

1/8 tsp. salt

2 Tbls. grated orange rind

1/2 cup water

1 Tbls. butter

Mix sugar, flour, salt. Gradually add water. Stirring constantly, boil until thick. Add juices, rind, butter. Serve hot.

## ORANGE BUTTER SAUCE

1/4 cup butter

2 tsp. grated orange peel

1 1/4 cups confectioner's sugar

2 Tbls. orange juice

Cream butter until fluffy. Gradually add sugar, beating until sauce is fluffy. Add orange peel and enough juice to make sauce easily spreadable.

## ORANGE FLUFF SAUCE

1/2 cup sugar

1/8 tsp. salt

1/2 cup orange juice concentrate

2 egg yolks

1 cup whipping cream

Over low heat, cook sugar, juice concentrate, salt. Stir constantly until sugar dissolves. Remove from heat. At high speed, mix egg yolks until fluffy. At medium speed, gradually beat in orange juice mix. Return to heat. Over low heat cook, stirring constantly, until slightly thick. Cool. Fold in whipped cream. Chill.

## SOUR CREAM ORANGE SAUCE

Cream 1/4 cup confectioner's sugar, three (3) Tbls. butter until light and fluffy. Add one (1) cup sour cream, one (1) tsp. grated orange peel, three (3) Tbls. orange juice. Blend all together and serve cold.

## PEACH SAUCE

10 ounces frozen peaches, thawed     1/4 tsp. almond extract
1/8 tsp. nutmeg

Blend all together at low speed until smooth.

## PINEAPPLE SAUCE

1/2 peeled, cored, pineapple        2 Tbls. sugar
2 Tbls. water

Combine ingredients in blender. At medium speed until pineapple all chopped and sauce even in consistency.

## SPICED PINEAPPLE SAUCE

2/3 cup pineapple syrup        1/8 tsp. cloves
1/8 tsp. cinnamon        2/3 cup drained, crushed pineapple
1/8 tsp. nutmeg

Combine syrup, cinnamon, nutmeg, cloves. Bring to boiling point. Add pineapple. Heat. Chill.

## PLOMBIERE SAUCE

1/2 cup orange marmalade
1/4 cup toasted coconut
2 Tbls. water

Combine ingredients.

## NO COOK PRALINE SAUCE

1 cup corn syrup                    2/3 cup chopped pecans
2 Tbls. molasses                    2 Tbls. water
4 ounces instant butterscotch pudding mix

Blend syrup, molasses. Add pudding mix. Blend. Add water, chopped nuts. Chill. Stir before serving.


## PUDDING SAUCE

1 cup sugar                         1/2 tsp. salt
2 eggs                              1 tsp. vanilla extract
1 cup butter

Beat sugar and eggs until light and fluffy. Add remaining ingredients. Blend. Chill.


## PURPLE COW SAUCE

3/4 cup buttermilk                  2 tsp. sugar
1/2 cup blueberries                 1 tsp. lemon juice

Put all ingredients into blender until smooth.


## RAISIN ALMOND SAUCE

In enough red wine to cover, parboil one (1) cup seedless raisins, chopped, four (4) minutes or until plump. Let cool. Drain. Blanch and toast 1/2 cup almonds. Cool. Combine one (1) cup sugar, 1/2 cup water, 1 1/2 Tbls. corn syrup. Cook over low heat until boils, stirring constantly. Lower heat. Simmer gently four (4) minutes. Uncovered, cook four (4) minutes longer until barely begins to thicken. Add raisins, almonds, two (2) Tbls. Sherry wine, two (2) Tbls. lemon juice, one (1) tsp. grated orange rind.

## RASBERRY SAUCE

| | |
|---|---|
| 1 pint fresh raspberries | 2 Tbls. sugar |
| 1/4 cup black currant liqueur | |

In food processor blend ingredients. Strain through sieve. Chill.

## RASPBERRY SAUCE

| | |
|---|---|
| 2 cups fresh raspberries | 1 Tbls. lemon juice |
| 1/2 cup sugar | 1 Tbls. cognac |
| 1 Tbls. cornstarch | |

Heat raspberries, sugar, to a boil, stirring constantly. Strain. Taste to see if need more sugar. Mix cornstarch with two (2) Tbls. raspberry juice. Heat main batch and stir in cornstarch mix until thickens. When cool, add lemon juice, cognac.

## RASBERRY STRAWBERRY SAUCE

Mix equal amounts of raspberry, strawberry juices and melted red currant jelly. Bring to a boil. For each cup of mixed ingredients add one (1) tsp. arrowroot mixed to a paste with a little cold juice. Boil until clear and thick.

## RHUBARB SAUCE

| | |
|---|---|
| 1 1/4 pounds cut rhubarb | 1/4 tsp. salt |
| 1/2 cup water | 1/4 tsp. cinnamon |
| 1/2 cup sugar | |

Over medium heat bring rhubarb, water, salt, cinnamon to boiling. Reduce heat to low and cook until rhubarb is tender. Stir often. Stir in sugar.

## ROSY RHUBARB SAUCE

Bring to a slow boil one (1) pound fresh rhubarb cut in one (1) inch pieces, 1/4 cup corn syrup, dash salt. Cook five (5) minutes until rhubarb is tender. Cool. Chill.

## NEW ENGLAND RHUBARB SAUCE

Combine two (2) Tbls. each sugar, cornstarch, 1/4 cup cold water and make a smooth paste. Add 1/4 cup honey. Heat one (1) cup unstrained orange juice, two (2) Tbls. unstrained lemon juice, 1/4 tsp. each grated orange peel, lemon peel. Do not boil. Add juice mix to paste and cook over moderate heat, stirring constantly until thickens. Remove from heat and stir in 1 1/3 cups rhubarb, chopped. Simmer very gently ten (10) minutes until rhubarb is soft.

## RUM SAUCE

1 cup milk                         2 tsp. rum extract
1/2 tsp. almond extract            1/2 cup crushed ice

Combine in blender until smooth. Serve at once.

## BUTTERED RUM SAUCE

Boil together for three (3) minutes 1/2 cup water, 1/4 cup sugar. Cool to lukewarm. Add dash salt. Stir in 1/2 cup very good rum, one (1) Tbls. butter. Serve at once.

## HOT RUM SAUCE

Boil together one (1) cup each sugar, water. When thermometer reaches 230 degrees F. remove from heat. Add 1/2 cup butter. When melted, stir in 1/4 cup good rum. Serve at once.

## HOT RUM SAUCE

2 cups juice from cooked apples
2 cups sugar
4 Tbls. dark rum

Simmer juice and sugar until thick. When ready to serve add rum.
Serve hot.

## RUM MINT SAUCE

2 cups sugar            1 tsp. grated lemon rind
1 cup water            1/4 cup lemon juice
1/2 cup packed fresh mint leaves     1/2 cup rum

For two (2) minutes boil sugar, water, mint, lemon rind together.
Strain. Chill. Add lemon juice, rum.

## MOCHA RUM SAUCE

Over low heat melt six (6) ounces dark, sweet chocolate, 1/2 ounce
bitter chocolate, cut into small pieces, 1/2 cup very strong coffee.
Stir constantly. Add one (1) Tbls. rum. Stir until smooth. Serve hot.

## SABAYON SAUCE

Whip six (6) egg yolks, 2/3 cup sugar in double boiler. Add one (1) cup
Marsala wine. Stir constantly. Set pan over cold water and cook mixture
until water reaches boiling point. Stir constantly. When sauce is
creamy and thick add one (1) Tbls, Kirsch. Serve hot.

## SHERRY SAUCE

Combine 1/2 cup water, three (3) Tbls. sugar. Bring to a boil. Reduce
heat. Simmer gently ten (10) minutes. Add 1/2 cup dry Sherry wine,

two (2) Tbls. any kind of jam, a few drops of lemon juice. Bring to boil again. Strain. Serve hot.

## SHERRY FLUFF SAUCE

| | |
|---|---|
| 2 tsp. cornstarch | 3 egg yolks |
| 1/4 cup sugar | egg whites |
| 1/4 tsp. salt | 1 Tbls. Sherry |
| 2 cups milk nutmeg | |

Combine cornstarch, sugar, salt. Gradually add milk. Cook over hot water until slightly thickened, stirring constantly. Beat egg yolks and gradually add to mixture. Cook over hot water until coats spoon, stirring constantly. Beat egg whites stiff. Fold in milk mixture. Cool. Add Sherry wine and nutmeg. Serve hot.

## SHERRY FLUFFY SAUCE

| | |
|---|---|
| 2 egg yolks | 1/4 cup sugar |
| 1/8 tsp. salt | 1 Tbls. Sherry wine |
| 1/2 cup heavy cream, whipped | |

At low speed, in mixer, beat egg yolks, sugar, sherry, salt. Increase speed to high until light and fluffy. Fold in whipped cream.

## HOT SHERRY SAUCE

Rub four (4) lumps of sugar with rind of a lemon. Crush sugar cubes. Mix with 2/3 cup Sherry wine in double boiler. Add four (4) egg yolks, one (1) at a time, whisking briskly after each addition. Whisk until well blended. Cook over hot water until smooth and coats spoon. Remove from heat and beat in 1/2 cup scalded heavy cream and grated rind of 1/2 lemon. Serve hot.

## SHERRY MOUSSELINE SAUCE

In double boiler beat four (4) egg yolks. Combine one (1) cup sugar, two (2) Tbls. cake flour, 1/2 tsp. salt. Sift this mix over egg yolks. Blend thoroughly. Cream 1/3 cup sweet butter, 1/3 cup dry sherry wine, one (1) tsp. grated lemon rind. Add flavored butter, bit by bit, stirring constantly to egg mixture. Cook over hot water, stirring constantly, until sauce is thick and holds shape. Remove from heat and whisk until cool. Whip one (1) cup heavy cream until stiff. Fold in 1/3 cup slivered, toasted almonds, one (1) Tbls. Curacao. Fold cream mix into sauce. Chill. At serving sprinkle with 1/4 cup chopped mixed candied fruit.

## SHORTCAKE SOUR CREAM SAUCE

| | |
|---|---|
| 1 cup heavy cream, whipped | 3 Tbls. honey |
| 2 egg yolks | 2 Tbls. lemon juice |

Whip cream to slightly thick. Add egg yolks, one (1) at a time, continue beating. Slowly drizzle in honey, lemon juice. Sauce should be thick and creamy.

## SNOW GOLD SAUCE

| | |
|---|---|
| 1/2 cup sugar | 1/2 cup chopped dried apricots |
| 3/4 cup water | 6 Tbls. shredded coconut |

Combine water, sugar. Bring to boiling point. Add apricots. Simmer fifteen (15) minutes. Cool. Add coconut.

## STRAWBERRY SAUCE

| | |
|---|---|
| 2 cups fresh strawberries | 1/2 cup water |
| 1/2 cup sugar | Grand Marnier |

Rub berries through sieve. Combine sugar, water. Bring to a boil. Reduce heat. Simmer gently five (5) minutes. Add sieved strawberries, Grand Marnier. Chill.

## BRANDIED STRAWBERRY SAUCE

30 ounces thawed, frozen strawberries     1 Tbls. cornstarch
1/2 cup currant jelly                      1/4 cup Brandy

Drain strawberries. Reserve 1/2 cup juice. Over low heat melt jelly, stirring constantly.
Mix reserved juice, cornstarch until smooth paste. Stir this into melted jelly, stirring constantly. Increase heat to medium. Cook until thick, stirring. Stir in berries and Brandy. Add red food coloring if desired.

## ENGLISH BERRY SAUCE

Cream together 1 1/2 cups confectioner's sugar, five (5) Tbls. butter. Add one (1) egg white, stiffly beaten. Fold in 1 1/2 cups crushed ripe strawberries, one (1) Tbls. Kirsch

## SUNSHINE SAUCE

1/2 cup butter                            1/2 tsp. vanilla extract
1 egg 1 cup confectioner's sugar

Cream butter and sugar. Add egg, vanilla extract. Over hot water, whisk constantly until fluffy. Serve hot.

## TUTTI-FRUTTI SAUCE

Mix one (1) cup wild cherry syrup add one (1) Tbls. each, finely chopped, almonds, candied orange peel, candied apricot, candied pineapple, candied pear, one (1) tsp. candied angelica. Bring to a boil. Reduce heat. Simmer gently fifteen (15) minutes. Chill.

## VANILLA SAUCE

1/2 cup vanilla sugar         1/8 tsp. salt
1 Tbls. cornstarch           1 cup water
2 Tbls. butter

Combine all but butter. Cook over medium heat five (5) minutes until thick. Add butter. Cool

## VANILLA SAUCE

6 egg yolks            4 tsp. vanilla extract
4 Tbls. sugar          1/2 cup heavy cream, whipped
2 cups cream, heated

Beat egg yolks, sugar in double boiler. Add heated cream and cook until thick, stirring constantly. Remove from heat. Add vanilla extract. Cool. Whisk occasionally. When cold fold in whipped cream.

## VANILLA SAUCE

Scald one (1) cup each milk, cream, 1/2 vanilla bean. In double boiler beat four (4) egg yolks, 1/2 cup sugar. Combine this with hot milk, cream mix, whisking. Cook over hot water, stirring constantly, until thick, coating spoon. Strain. Cool.

## VANILLA A L'ANGLAISE SAUCE

In double boiler scald one (1) cup milk, one (1) cup cream, 1/2 vanilla bean. Whip four (4) egg yolks, 1/2 cup sugar, 1/4 tsp. flour until light. Add hot milk/cream mix slowly, stirring vigorously. Return custard to double boler. Cook over simmering water, stirring constantly, until thick enough to coat spoon. Strain. Cool. Stir from time to time.

## WHIPPED CREAM LIQUEUR SAUCE

Beat two (2) Tbls. of any cordial or liqueur into one (1) cup heavy cream until stiff.

## HOT WINE SAUCE

Combine 1 1/2 cups red wine, 1/2 cup sugar, grated rind of 1/2 lemon, two (2) crushed cloves, piece of cinnamon. Simmer five (5) minutes. Strain. Serve hot

## RED WINE SAUCE

Cream one (1) cup confectioner's sugar, one (1) Tbls. sweet butter, 1/2 cup light cream. Cook over direct heat six (6) minutes until thick, stirring constantly. Stirring constantly add 1/4 dry red wine, dash salt, dash nutmeg.

# COOKING TERMS

| | |
|---|---|
| ALDENTE | Referring to pasta that is cooked but firm to the bite |
| A' POINT | Referring to a medium cooked meat |
| AU BLEU | Referring to very rare meat |
| BARD | Place fat or bacon on lean meat before roasting |
| BIEN CUIT | Referring to well done meat |
| BLANCH | Boil very briefly |
| BOUCHE'E | Small puff pastry case |
| BOUILLON | Stock or clear broth |
| BOUQUET GARNI | Bunch or small bag of herbs |
| BRULE' | Glazed with a carmelized sugar |
| CHINE | Separate backbone from ribs in a joint of meat |
| CODDLE | Simmer eggs slowly |
| CRE'ME FRAICHE | Cream that is mature but not sour |
| CRIMP | Gash or score meat for crisper cooking |
| DEVILING | Grilling or roasting with highly seasoned ingredients |
| DREDGE | Coat with flour or sugar |
| EN CROUTE | In pastry |
| FARCI | Stuffed |
| FINE HERBS | Fresh, finely chopped mix of parsley, chervil, tarragon, chives |
| FLAMBE' | Served or covered with flaming spirits |
| HULL | Remove leaves and stems of soft fruit |
| INFUSE | Steep in water or other liquid |

| | |
|---|---|
| JARDINIERE | Garnished with vegetables |
| LARD | Thread strips of fat through lean meat before roasting |
| LIAISON | Thickening agent such as cream, for sauces, soups, and such |
| MACEDOINE | Mixture of fruit or vegetables |
| MACERATE | Soften by soaking in liquid |
| MARINADE | Blend of oil, wine, vinegar, herbs, spices, used to flavor |
| MARINATE | Steep in marinade |
| MEDALLION | Small cylinder cut of meat or fish |
| PARBOIL | Boil briefly to slightly cook food |
| PUREE | Mash or pulp fruit or vegetables in food processor |
| ROUX | Mixture of flour, butter, fat, used as a base for sauces |
| SAIGNANT | Referring to underdone meat |
| SAUTE' | Fry lightly |
| SHIRR | Bake eggs removed from their shells |
| SOUSED | Pickled |
| SWEAT | Cook vegetables or fruit slowly to release juices |
| ZEST | Outer, colored skin of citrus fruit |

## COOKING UTENSILS

| | |
|---|---|
| BAIN-MARIE | Double sauce-pan: or a large pan of hot water in which a smaller pan is placed |
| BROCHETTE | Small spit or skewer |
| CASSEROLE | Ovenproof dish with close fitting lid |
| COCOTTE | Small ovenproof dish |
| COQUILLE | Shell shaped ovenproof dish |
| DUTCH OVEN | Large, heavy iron pot with lid; three sided metal oven used in front of an open fire; oven that cooks by means of preheated bricks |
| GRIDDLE | Flat cooking surface |
| MANDOLINE | Vegetable slicer |

| | |
|---|---|
| OLLA | Wide mouthed earthenware pot |
| RAMEKIN | Individual ovenproof dish |
| SPATULA | Knife with a flat, blunt, pliable blade |
| TERRINE | Earthenware pot |
| TIMBALE | Cup-shaped mold |
| WOK | Large, bowl-shaped metal pan used in Chinese cooking |

# Liquid Capacity

## Equivalents

| Spoons, cups pints, quarts, gallons | Equivalent measure & fluid ounces | Approximate metric equivalent | |
|---|---|---|---|
| Pinch or dash | less than 1/8 tsp. | | |
| 1 tsp. | 1/6 fl. ounce | 5 | ml |
| 1 Tbls. | 3 tsp., or 1/2 fl. ounce | 15 | ml |
| 2 Tbls. | 6 tsp., or 1 fl. ounce | 30 | ml |
| 1/4 c. | 4 Tbls., or 2 fl. ounces | 60 | ml |
| 1/3 c. | 5 Tbls. plus 1 tsp., or 2 2/3 fl. ounces | 80 | ml |
| 1/2 c. | 8 Tbls., or 4 fl. ounces | 120 | ml |
| 1 pt. | 2 c., or 8 fl. ounces | .24 | L. |
| 1 qt. | 2 pt., or 32 fl. ounces | .47 | L. |
| 1 gal. | 4 qt., or 128 fl. ounces | 3.8 | L. |

Conversion formulae:

To covert ounces to milliliters, multiply the ounces by .30
To convert milliliters to ounces, multiply the milliliters by .03
1,000 milliliters equals 1 liter

# Weights and Metric Equivalents

| Ounces and pounds | Grams |
|---|---|
| 1/4 ounce | 7 grams |
| 1/2 ounce | 15 grams |
| 1 ounce | 30 grams |
| 2 ounces | 60 grams |
| 4 ounces-1/4 pound | 115 grams |
| 8 ounces-1/2 pound | 225 grams |
| 16 ounces-1 pound | 455 grams |

Conversion formulae:

To convert ounces into grams, multiply the ounces by 28.35
To convert grams into ounces, multiply the grams by .035

# INDEX

# DESSERT SAUCES

CPSIA information can be obtained at www.ICGtesting.com
Printed in the USA
240115LV00001B/80/A